MY DAUGHTER SUSAN SMITH

Linda H. Russell
with
Shirley Stephens

Printed in the United States of America

Authors Book Nook
P. O. Box 513
Brentwood, TN 37024-0513

www.authorsbooknook.com

To all my grandchildren with love—

Nick, Matt, Michael and Alex

CONTENTS

Prologue

She was never a violent person, never abused her children. She never committed an act of any kind that those close to her could point to later as an omen of the killing of her children. She loved them dearly. They were her life. But she sent three-year-old Michael and fourteen-month-old Alex to their deaths in John D. Long Lake on a dark October night more than five years ago.

To the State of South Carolina, she is inmate 221487. But she is my daughter Susan Smith. Her sentence: prison for the "balance of her natural lifetime"; no possibility of parole for thirty years. She is assigned to a psychiatric building at the Women's Correctional Institution in Columbia, South Carolina.

The children's birthdays are terrible reminders to Susan of the tragic event. August 5, 1996, would have been Alex's third birthday. All day long I wondered how Susan was doing, coping with that day virtually alone with her thoughts inside a prison.

At six-thirty in the evening, the phone rang. I grabbed it on the first ring, then quickly pressed "1" to accept the collect call.

"Mama," she sighed, "I still can't believe it's happened." Her voice cracked, "I miss them so much."

"I miss them, too," I said softly.

We've had this same exchange so many times. She still can't explain how the tragedy happened.

I've driven up and down the roads that Susan drove that dark night, trying to understand a depression so deep it could lead to killing. Mile after mile, she drove down the pitch-black road; and the longer she drove, the more isolated, the more lonely she became. Finally, she lost touch with reality. And the unthinkable happened.

For the last five years, I have watched Susan struggle with an overwhelming, uphill battle only she could fight. I have had nothing more to offer than my love and support. With her grief, guilt, despair, and illness to contend with, my one goal has been to instill in her the will never to give up hope. She has tried to keep me from knowing—to keep me from worrying—about how difficult her life is. The prison walls are not her struggle, as bad as such confinement is. Her real struggle lies in the unseen walls of mental illness. She has mutilated herself, cutting her arms and wrists with whatever object she could find. Several times she has been put on suicide watch for her own protection. She has developed an eating disorder, which is a mental disease in itself.

Towering over everything is the reality of Susan's terrible act. Dealing with it is an overwhelming task for family and friends. Everyone close to Susan knows she is not a cruel person. All of us are convinced something went terribly wrong that fateful night.

We all have faithfully stood by Susan. According to prison policy, she has a certain number of persons on her visitors' list. She rotates her visitors; but some—like Barbara, Walt, her best friend Donna, my mother, her brothers Michael and Scotty, and Scotty's wife, Wendy—have remained constant. She rotates the other visits among different family members and friends.

When I go to see Susan, several usually ride with me on the sixty-mile trip. Our visits take place in a large room that has about fifteen square tables with four straight chairs arranged around each one. The tables are numbered, and we are assigned a table after everyone is processed. We get something to eat out of the vending machines and just talk and catch up on everything. We talk about things that happen in the prison. We talk about things that are happening in our family and in Union.

We keep Susan involved with what's going on. Close friends send her invitations to their weddings. When Donna and Mitch were planning their wedding, we talked about that a lot. Susan was sad she couldn't be there, but she wanted to know everything—the colors they were using, who was in it, what songs Donna and Mitch picked out, where they were going on their honeymoon. For a wedding present, she cross-stitched a wedding-prayer design, and I had it framed for her. It was beautiful. We sent her pictures of the wedding festivities. She was delighted to receive them.

Susan always sends Christmas presents to everyone in her family and to close friends. The Christmas of '97, she cross-stitched designs on T-shirts for a number of people. She gave me a sweatshirt with colorful bunnies cross-stitched on it. It was a lot of cross-stitching! Shortly after that Christmas, they quit selling the shirts in the prison shop. Now she does her "shopping" in a Christian supply catalog and has the items sent to me to give to everyone. They are not expensive gifts, but it keeps her in touch and gives her something to do.

The only presents we can send to Susan are money, magazine subscriptions, and newspapers. When Barbara Garner asked what she wanted for the Christmas of '98, she said she wanted a *Good Housekeeping* magazine.

It came out in the trial that Susan's stepfather, Beverly Russell, sexually abused her when she was a teenager. For a time he visited her in prison. I never encouraged or discouraged the visits. I felt she should make the decision. One day she simply told me she had taken him off her list. She says she doesn't hate him. She just doesn't want him to visit. His name never comes up anymore.

I try to put myself in Susan's place. How would I deal with such grieving over my children? How would I feel, knowing I am responsible for the deaths of the two people I loved more than anyone else on this earth, but don't understand and can't explain why things happened? Would I give up and allow myself to slip away into a world of insanity? Or would I have the strength that Susan has found?

She has progressed a little, but only a little. The improvement has come with the help of some caring therapists, medication, friends and family who love her. She has a job working as a teacher's aid that she enjoys very much. I don't think she is as suicidal as she has been. But she is far from being well. She is not where I hope for her to be.

Susan is reminded of the tragedy in so many ways. She thinks of her children when she sees the children of other inmates come to visit. I have caught a glimpse of her, out of the corner of my eye, as she watches them. She can't keep her eyes off them. When they stumble or fall, she catches her breath. She told me one day that she was anxious for one of her friends to have a baby, so she could hold it. She didn't have to wait long, because Donna and Mitch celebrated the birth of their son the following spring. Susan picked out a gift for the baby from a catalog.

I think Susan has enough faith to know the Lord has already forgiven her, because she is truly sorry. But even though we can receive the Lord's forgiveness, forgiving ourselves is another matter. She will have to come to the point where she can forgive herself, but she is not there yet. Before she can forgive herself, she has to get well enough to realize how sick she was that night.

One day, out of the blue, Susan said she was afraid there might come a time when no one would visit her. Her statement surprised us all. I asked her why she would even think such a thing. She answered that some of the women never have visits. Their families just forget about them. I quickly assured her that, as long as there is breath in me, she will never be forgotten; and the rest of her family and friends feel the same.

Later, I expressed my concerns to Scotty. "If I should die," I questioned, "who will watch after Susan?"

"Mama," he assured me, "as long as I live, you don't have to worry about Susan. I'll visit her."

I visit Susan every time prison officials will let me, and I will as long as I am on this earth. I love her now just as I have always loved her. So do the rest of her family and friends. Her struggles are our struggles.

In the nearly five years since Susan was found guilty of murder, I am just now beginning to understand the silent devastation of mental illness. Obviously, I have to accept that Susan was responsible for the deaths of her children. But where does responsibility lie for what happened along the way that got her in that mental shape? This book is a quest for understanding—for myself and for others.

1

Our Worst Nightmare

October 25, 1994. Just after nine o'clock at night, my daughter Susan Smith told the police a black man jumped into her car, put her out on the highway, and took her children, Michael, three, and Alex, fourteen months. For nine days, she repeated the same story to the Union County sheriff and detectives, South Carolina law enforcement agents, and the FBI.

On the ninth day, relatives and friends gathered at our house, as they had on the previous eight days. The house was jammed with people. Most of my extended family were there. Susan's ex-husband, David Smith, and his mother, father, and stepmother were there. Barbara and Walt Garner, who were like grandparents to Susan's children, had been there since early in the morning. Their daughter Donna, Susan's best friend since childhood, was there.

Around two in the afternoon, a friend called to tell us a news conference was scheduled for 4:00 p.m. at the courthouse. The friend gave no details about the purpose of the conference, only that it was about the status of the investigation. Around three, an announcer broke in and said they had an unconfirmed report that Susan had made some type of confession. I shrugged it off as more of the wild media speculation our family had encountered constantly for the nine days. At four o'clock, an announcer said the conference was being delayed but gave no reason. We impatiently wondered why.

My son's wife, Wendy, had just returned to her job, after being off for a week. Shortly after five, she was picking up her two sons at Judy Cathcart's day care. Judy asked her what was going on.

"I don't know," Wendy replied, puzzled. "What are you talking about?"

"They're coming across the TV with something about a confession."

My Daughter Susan Smith

Wendy ran to the phone and called Scotty at our house. She asked my son what was going on.

"I don't know. I don't know," Scotty said, his voice trembling. "God, it's our worst nightmare! They're saying Susan has confessed. I can't believe it."

"I'll be there in a minute, Scotty," she told him. "I'll be right there."

Wendy nervously hung up the phone and turned to Judy. "Something's wrong. Would you please take care of my children? I'll be back as soon as I can."

I was sitting in the swing on the screened-in porch when the TV announcer gave the "breaking news" report. I heard Donna yell, "Oh, no! Oh, no, no, no!" I rushed inside.

The look of horror on Donna's face stunned me. "What's the matter?" I asked.

"They said Susan killed the kids," she sobbed, then fell into the closest chair with her head in her hands.

Walt and Barbara, standing near their daughter, were in a state of disbelief. Shaking his head back and forth, Walt insisted, "I don't believe it! I don't believe it! I won't believe it until I hear it from Howard Wells." Howard is Union County's sheriff.

Scotty dropped to his knees on the den floor and buried his head in his hands, crying, mumbling something like, "It can't be true." Wendy knelt down beside him, tears streaming down her face.

I stumbled back out to the porch and fell into the swing. A chorus of wails came from inside the house. I heard someone throw up in the bathroom.

It can't be true; it can't be true, I agonized silently, over and over and over. I was too numb even to cry.

A helicopter flew over the house and landed in the road. I cringed at the possibility that it was the press. They had hounded us mercilessly, day in and day out.

Someone called out that Howard Wells was coming up the driveway. I went inside and hurried toward the front door. My husband, Bev, was already there to meet the sheriff.

"Is it bad news?" Bev asked.

Howard didn't answer. He didn't have to. The sad look on his face told it all.

"Is everybody here?" he asked, stepping inside. He was visibly shaken. "Please get everybody together. I can't say this but once."

Everyone stood in the den, crying and leaning on one another. Howard solemnly stood near the TV. "Susan has confessed," he said softly. "I got to you all as fast as I could." His voice cracked, "It had already leaked. I'm sorry."

Howard assured us he came as soon as he could. He explained that Susan had told them where the car was. Then, when it was located, he sent divers down to verify that the children were inside. After his brief explanation, Howard motioned to David to go into the bedroom with him.

Scotty fell back on the sofa. Hedy, my sister-in-law, slumped into the rocking chair by the TV, sobbing. My brother Tim sat down in front of her, tears streaming down his face. Bev fell backward into the recliner. Barbara, Walt, and Donna huddled together, crying and leaning on one another.

Leigh and Paul, Tim and Hedy's children who were college students, drove up outside. They had gone to pick up my mother, as they did every evening. I hurried to meet them at the back door.

"Susan has confessed," I said, my voice cracking. "The children are dead."

Mama's mouth flew open. "It can't be! It can't be," she sobbed. Paul reeled back. Leigh instinctively held her arms out to catch him, a look of utter shock frozen on her face. Once inside, they joined their parents, hugging and crying.

When Howard came out of the bedroom, he sat on the den floor and leaned against the wall. David stood close by him, his head hung down, his eyes red. Howard's eyes were red, too. He is more than a sheriff to us. He is godfather to Scotty and Wendy's two children, Nick, 13, and Matt, 10. Mama and I stood behind the sofa, leaning on it for support.

"This was a terrible tragedy," Howard began, "but with understanding there will come forgiveness." He told us that he had to go to a news conference and said they could keep the press away, if we would all stay at my house. He left police officer Bobby Hicks, who is a family friend, and another officer there to help us.

I retreated to the porch swing, my head spinning. Bev stayed in the recliner, crying. I had no desire to have him comfort me. We had both gone through the nine days worrying about the children, but not together. We lived under the same roof, but we hadn't really been together for a long time.

"What in the world has happened?" I whispered. "I don't understand. God, please help me understand," I begged. I still couldn't cry. The pain was too deep. My precious grandchildren were dead, and I couldn't understand why.

After a few minutes, I thought about Barbara and Walt and how they loved Michael and Alex. I went inside to check on them and found them in the hallway. "Are you all right?" I asked.

"I don't believe it," Walt said, shaking his head. "I don't believe it."

"Well, Walt," I sighed. "I guess we'll have to believe it. Howard just told us." My words belied my feelings. I couldn't believe it, either. Sometimes, I still can't believe it.

As I turned to go back out to the porch swing, Leigh met me, tears streaming down her face. "Linda," she sobbed, falling into my arms, "I still love Susan."

"I know you do, Leigh," I said softly. "We all love Susan."

Sitting in the porch swing, I thought about the men who would retrieve the car and take the children out of their car seats. "Lord," I prayed, "be with them. They've got a hard thing to do."

I glanced inside the den. David was standing behind the sofa, crying. His dad and stepmother were beside him, also crying and trying to console him.

David looked toward the porch. Our eyes locked. *Is he expecting me to console him?* I wondered. "What do you want me to say?" I asked, throwing my hands up in despair and disgust. I couldn't say one comforting word to him. That was an awful moment.

I knew too much about David's relationship with my daughter to have any sympathy for him. I saw him put down Susan so many times. He cheated on her, even though he knew about her problems. He manipulated her. He threatened her. He did everything he could to make her life miserable. Console him? I couldn't bring myself to do that. The look of disgust on his face revealed he knew how I felt.

I dropped my head to my hand and whispered, "Dear Lord, the man has just lost his children. Is my heart so cold I can't feel an ounce of compassion for him?"

I looked up to see David suddenly jerk himself around and move toward the kitchen, out of my sight. At the same time, I heard a lot of shouting inside. I went to see what was going on and quickly realized David wanted to get out of our house as fast as possible. Two police officers were talking with him, trying to dissuade him; and his relatives were screaming at them.

I learned later that someone had suggested they disguise David, so he could elude the press. One of the officers put his jacket and hat on him. But the other officer stepped in and said, "No, you can't do that. It's against regulations." The officer then told David they couldn't protect him if he left.

"What do you mean you can't protect him?" David's stepmother screeched. "He is the *only* victim here!"

The only victim! I exclaimed silently. *Preposterous*! *There were only two victims and they were Michael and Alex.*

I don't know what David said to his family, but they all headed for the back door, determined to leave with or without police protection. The officers did their best to keep them from hurting themselves as they lunged en masse through the door to face the horde of reporters gathered in the driveway.

I put my hand on Bobby Hick's arm. When he turned to me, I asked how Susan was. He hugged me and said, "Oh, Linda, I wish you didn't have to know all this. We'll take good care of Susan."

"Thank you, Bobby," I said quietly, then turned around and went back out to the porch swing.

With David's family gone, my thoughts returned to the enormous task of trying to understand what had happened to Susan and what had caused her to do something like this. I kept asking God to help me understand.

****

My Daughter Susan Smith

At the 7:00 p.m. news conference, Sheriff Howard Wells stood on the courthouse steps and made the formal announcement of Susan's arrest to the large crowd gathered there, to the nation, and to the world:

"Susan Smith has been arrested and charged with two counts of murder in connection with her children Michael, 3, and Alexander, 14 months."

The sadness and despair that bore down on the group gathered at our house was beyond anything I could have imagined. My disbelief was entrenched. In various ways, we all kept saying, "The Susan we know couldn't have done this." We were sure something terrible must have happened to her.

Sitting alone in the dark, everything was too bizarre to fathom—my precious grandchildren sent to their deaths by my own daughter. The pain and the hurt was so deep, gripping my whole being. Half of my hurt was for Susan. I shut my eyes and prayed to God that it would all go away.

"Linda," someone said softly. I opened my eyes to see a woman bending down in front of me. "Linda," she repeated earnestly, "you're going to have to think about a lawyer for Susan." It was the friend of my cousin, Margaret Gregory. She had driven to Union from Columbia in the afternoon. Later, I learned she was a victim's advocate.

"A lawyer?" I questioned incredulously. "A lawyer? This is ridiculous! Susan doesn't need a lawyer! I can't imagine one of my children ever needing a lawyer for anything." She didn't argue. She just said I needed to think about it. She went back into the house, surely shaking her head in disbelief.

Looking back, I don't know how I could have been so dense. It seems now that my mind was frozen in time. From the beginning of the tragic ordeal, I didn't think about Susan's needing a lawyer, even when people began to suspect her. At the moment she was arrested, the thought didn't occur to me, either. I would not and could not believe Susan had done such a terrible thing. Why get a lawyer if she hadn't done anything?

Around nine, Solicitor Tommy Pope and a woman came to our house. Someone suggested I come into the den. Pope introduced the woman as a victim's advocate. Victim's advocate! That assumption flew all over me. How dare he bring a stranger into my home to "help us." We were a group of heartbroken people, but I certainly didn't consider myself, nor the rest of my family, as victims. I didn't need this woman. I needed my friends and family around me. She was an intruder, an outsider. I didn't want nor need nor understand how she could help. How could she possibly know or understand what we had gone through the past nine days? I excused myself, stepped into the kitchen, and told Bev to take care of them.

Tommy Pope was barely out the door when Howard Wells arrived. He had a letter for me from Susan. He said she wrote it a few hours after her confession. After his short visit, I went into my bedroom, shut the door, and began to read the letter.

Written on lined paper, the letter was folded like the notes kids pass in school. On the outside was this statement: "I love you!" A heart was drawn for the word *love*. Inside, written vertically along the edge of the paper was this statement: "I've never felt so unloved, so lonely, or so scared in my life."

The sad letter went like this:

"Dear Mom,

"Writing you this letter is going to be very painful. I don't even know where to start. I know sorry isn't enough, but I don't know what else to say. I have never regretted or been sorrier for anything more in my life. I was not "me" that night. I hope you know that because you know that I would never do anything to hurt Michael or Alex. I <u>love</u> and <u>miss</u> them so much, Mama. I would do anything in this world if I thought it would bring them back home.

"I'm sorry that I have hurt you so much, but believe me, I am living in a true hell right now. I know I deserve it, though. I never realized how awful a jail could be. It is awful Mama and I am so scared and lonely I don't know what to do. I know this may be asking too much, but I need you now more than ever. I know what I did was wrong and I have prayed harder than you could imagine that the Lord will forgive me and give me the strength to make it through each day, but I need you and Beverly and Moe and Scotty, too. I know you must be very angry and hurt and if I could, I would take all of that away from you. I hope that one day, you will find it in your [drawing of heart] to forgive me and to know that I wasn't "me" that night. Mama, I love you so much and would never do anything intentionally to hurt you or anyone else. I hope that you will believe me. I am in more pain than you could imagine. It hurt like hell to see you and everyone else hurt like you did and me knowing the truth.

"I broke down today and told Howard the truth because that's what Michael and Alex deserved. They deserved to be laid to rest by the ones who loved them the most. It hurts so much to know that I won't be able to attend their funeral. I know, and now you know, that Michael and Alex are with the Lord in Heaven and they are being taken care of. As a mom, that means more than words could ever say. I know I've let you down and I am so sorry!!! I need some help because I cannot handle life anymore. I know this hurts but its how I feel—if I could right now, I would take my own life. I don't deserve to live after what I did and I may not survive this, but I'm going to try. Howard and Pete Logan have faith and hope that every-thing is going to work out for me. All I know is that I am pray-ing every chance I get. I will follow God's road because I know it will lead me to the right direction.

"Mama, I don't want to close but its late and I've got to go to court tomorrow at 10:00. I don't know when or if I will be see-ing or talking to you. I'm not sure if you even want to see or talk to me. I hope you do but I don't blame you if you don't.

"I hope that you will include me in your prayers! Again, I am so sorry for everything! Take care of yourself as best you can and remember that I love you more than you'll ever know. Please help me Mama. I need you!

"Love always,
"Susan"

My eyes filled with tears as I read. By the time I got to the end, I could hardly see the words. When only family was still there, I gathered everyone into the den and read the letter to them. It was an incredibly sad time.

Our Worst Nightmare

I woke up before dawn the next morning, thinking about Susan and the children. I saw the children smile and heard their laughter and pictured Susan loving them. It all seemed so real.

When the first light of dawn came through my bedroom window, I went to the kitchen, made some coffee, and sat down in the breakfast nook. With the birds chirping outside, I wrote a reply to Susan, assuring her that we all still loved her very much and always would. I never sent the letter to her. I wanted to tell her in person.

2

I Want to Be with My Daddy

Margaret's friend didn't give up. She talked to Bev about getting a lawyer for Susan. He didn't say anything to me about it until the next morning, but he went into action that night and got in contact with our family lawyer, Robert Guess. Robert recommended David Bruck, an outstanding anti-death penalty lawyer. He had recently worked with him and was impressed with his skills. Bev gave him the go-ahead to contact him.

Sitting in David Bruck's office the day after the children's funeral, I asked him how Susan was and when I could see her. He said he had already scheduled a visit for the next day. I then asked for a copy of Susan's confession. I knew I had to read it.

I took a deep breath as Bruck handed it to me and said, "It is very, very sad." Here is her exact confession, taken from the transcript of the trial:

"When I left my home on Tuesday, Oct. 25, I was very emotionally distraught. I didn't want to live any more! I felt like things could never get any worse. When I left home, I was going to ride around a little while and then go to my mom's.

"As I rode and rode and rode, I felt even more anxiety coming upon me about not wanting to live. I felt I couldn't be a good mom anymore, but I didn't want my children to grow up without a mom. I felt I had to end our lives to protect us all from any grief or harm.

"I had never felt so lonely and so sad in my entire life. I was in love with someone very much, but he didn't love me and never would. I had a very difficult time accepting that. But I had hurt him very much, and I could see why he could never love me.

"When I was at John D. Long Lake, I had never felt so scared and unsure as I did then. I wanted to end my life so bad

20

and was in my car ready to go down that ramp into the water, and I did go part way, but I stopped. I went again and stopped. I then got out of the car and stood by the car a nervous wreck.

"Why was I feeling this way? Why was everything so bad in my life? I had no answers to these questions. I dropped to the lowest when I allowed my children to go down that ramp into the water without me. I took off running and screaming 'Oh, God! Oh, God! No, what have I done? Why did you let this happen?' I wanted to turn around so bad and go back but I knew it was too late. I was an absolute mental case! I couldn't believe what I had done.

"I love my children with all my [symbol for a heart]. That will never change. I have prayed to them for forgiveness and hope that they will find it in their [symbol for a heart] to forgive me. I never meant to hurt them!! I am sorry for what has happened, and I know that I need some help. I don't think I will ever be able to forgive myself for what I have done.

"My children, Michael and Alex, are with our Heavenly Father now, and I know that they will never be hurt again. As a mom, that means more than words could ever say.

"I knew from day one, that the truth would prevail, but I was so scared I didn't know what to do. It was very tough emotionally to sit and watch my family hurt like they did. It was time to bring a peace of mind to everyone, including myself. My children deserve to have the best, and now they will. I broke down on Thursday, November the 3, and told Sheriff Howard Wells the truth. It wasn't easy, but after the truth was out, I felt like the world was lifted off my shoulders.

"I know now that it is going to be a tough and long road ahead of me. At this very moment I don't feel that I will be able to handle what's coming, but I have prayed to God that he give me the strength to survive each day and to face those times and situations in my life that will be extremely painful. I have put my total faith in God and he will take care of me."

Susan signed that confession November 3, 1994 at 5:05 p.m. It was witnessed by an FBI agent and a State Law Enforcement Division agent.

My Daughter Susan Smith

I had seen Susan upset many times, but nothing came close to the despair she described in her confession. My daughter, who was the most wonderful mother, said she couldn't be a good mother anymore. That was beyond my understanding. She loved her children too much to think that.

Susan's confession is only part of the explanation for this terrible tragedy. I've had a lot of time to think back over her life since that awful day. A lot of things led up to her terrible act.

****

October 25, 1960, I was sixteen and two months pregnant. Harry Vaughan was seventeen. He was good looking and a charmer. I loved him very much.

Mama and Daddy liked Harry, but they thought we were too young to get married. They thought it would be better for me to go to a home for unwed mothers and give the baby up for adoption. That's how most people felt then. But I declined that offer. Instead, Harry and I went to the minister's house, along with his sister and her husband. We spent our wedding night in the upstairs bedroom of my new mother-in-law's home, where we planned to live.

Michael was born on May 18, 1961. With his dark hair and dark eyes, he looked a lot like Harry. He was a beautiful baby. Within four months, I was pregnant with Scotty. By then, the new had worn off. Harry wanted to hang out with his buddies to all hours. I didn't like that and let him know it. I wasn't pleased with our living arrangement, either; and Harry wasn't what you would call the most dependable worker. I never knew when he was going to come home and say he had quit his job.

Shortly before Scotty was born, we found a three-room basement apartment. Then, when Scotty was three weeks old, a better apartment became available in Union's public housing. I was proud of that apartment and cleaned and cleaned and cleaned. We had two cribs, an old bedroom set, a hand-me-down sofa, kitchen table, and TV. Daddy co-signed for us to buy a washer from Sears. It was when we lived in this apartment that I first saw Howard Wells, whom I would later know as Union

I Want to Be with My Daddy

County's sheriff. He was a friend of the little boy next door.

The promising bliss didn't last long. Harry's dislike for work reared its ugly head again. He quit his night watchman's job, because he didn't like working by himself all night. Then he quit a job with the Kohler Company, because he didn't like driving to Spartanburg by himself every day. This time, I took the babies and went to Mama's. I asked her if I could come home. "Linda," she said, "you know you can come home anytime you want, but these are Harry's children; and he has got to learn that he is going to have to work and support them."

I thought about things for a couple of hours, then went back home. I told Harry I was back, and I was going to sit there until the children didn't have anything to eat. Then I was going to have him put on the chain gang. He soon found a job, and I went to work at a local textile plant.

Things got better financially. We moved several times, each time to a little better place. Mama cashed in a small insurance policy she had on me and gave us $250. We used it for a down payment on a little white frame house.

I quit my job in the textile plant because I wanted to return to school. Harry went to work for the fire department. I found a job after school that gave me enough money to pay the sitter, with fifty cents a week to spare. I finished high school in June, and Michael started first grade that fall. Harry later went to night school and got his high school diploma. I went to work as a receptionist at a local sweater plant, then to a better job in production control at The Torrington Company.

I left home so early that I never really got to know my brothers, Newell and Tim, until they were adults. Hedy and Tim, Newell and his wife, Joan, and Harry and I became best friends. We were also close friends with Glenda and Wayne Lawson. The eight of us had many, many good times together and played thousands of hands of penny poker.

Harry and I had some good times together, and my family all loved him. He was very special to Mama. But, as I look back, our marriage was in trouble from the start. We argued about almost everything. Harry had always been jealous, but things went from bad to worse. He accused me of things he seemed to sit around and make up in his head. He became obsessed with the idea that I was unfaithful to him, but I never was. To avoid his accusations, I took one of the children with me everywhere I went.

We went to a lot of parties and dances; and, of course, there was always drinking going on. Harry's jealousy got worse whenever he drank. I finally told him I couldn't continue to defend myself against his imagination. He eased off a bit.

Eight years after Scotty was born, I was expecting Susan. She made her entrance into the world on Sunday, September 26, 1971. She was a beautiful, happy baby. At the time, my nephew Eddie was living with us. He was close to Scotty and Michael's age; so Susan had three older siblings to spoil her. And they did a good job of that, along with aggravating her a lot.

When Susan was only a few months old, I was offered a better job in the industrial engineering department at Wambel. Harry felt that I was moving forward and he was standing still. He was jealous of everything about me.

There was a part of Harry that few knew about. He gave the impression to friends and co-workers that he was a happy person, but he experienced prolonged bouts of depression. To make matters worse, he developed a drinking problem. He became so dependent on me I felt I had four children to care for.

By the time Susan was born, our marriage was moving to the point of being beyond repair. We were constantly getting each other back for things that happened the day or the week before. We had one blowup after another, often over trivial grievances. We held grudges and brought them up when it was convenient to whatever point one of us was making.

In the midst of all this, Michael, who by now had picked up the nickname *Moe*, began to have learning problems at school. Susan also was a handful with her temper tantrums. But we interpreted them as part of the terrible two's.

When Moe was evaluated, it was determined that his intelligence was normal, but he needed a special learning situation. He was referred to the York Episcopal Home for Children and stayed there for a year. After he came back home, our family had follow-up services for a year.

In preparation for the trial, Susan's lawyer enlisted Dr. Arlene Andrews to do an in-depth study of the mental history of both sides of Susan's family. Dr. Andrews, who is founding director of the Council on Child Abuse and Neglect in Columbia, South Carolina, was able to gain access to all of the records related to Susan, including Moe's records. In the files of the psychologists, she found that they described Harry's and my marriage situation as "psychological warfare." They also recorded in their notes that "there is something deeply personal and painful between them that prevents them from forgetting and forgiving."

On one occasion, a psychologist pointed out to Harry and me that we were making Susan unhappy. In front of the psychologist, we argued about who made her unhappiest the most. After the visit, the psychologist stated in her notes that Susan "is doing the exact same thing to her parents that they are doing to each other. The little girl is no problem in the day-care center, and the parents can't believe this. As soon as she comes home, she gets right into the game of making all unhappy. It was the same with Michael [Moe] when he was here. All the boys liked Michael, and he was no problem. It is at home when the trouble starts."

Looking back, I know the psychologist was right. At the time, though, Harry and I never connected Susan's problems to the problems between us. We just felt the terrible two's would pass, and she would grow out of it.

Susan demanded our undivided attention during this period. If I went to the bathroom and shut the door, she lay down on the floor and cried for me to come out. She didn't sleep much, either. We put her to bed at a reasonable hour, but she got out of bed and played with her toys. Harry and I took turns staying up with her. It wasn't unusual for her to be playing with toys in her bedroom at two in the morning. One night, when we finally got her to go to bed, she came to our room and tried to sleep with us. I knew we would never get her out of our bed, if I let her in. When I refused, she got her little blanket and put it on the floor beside me and whimpered. When she fell asleep, I put

125580

her back to bed. She didn't try to sleep with us again.

Solving that problem didn't stop Susan's terrible two's. Anytime she didn't get her way, she threw a temper tantrum. I attributed the problem to a number of things—the three boys picking on her, her desire for attention, the fact that everybody in our household was at least nine years older. I also reasoned that maybe Harry and I didn't know how to deal with a child anymore.

At my wit's end, I took Susan to her pediatrician. "She's driving me crazy," I told him. "Check her over from head to toe to see if anything is wrong with her." She did have a kidney infection that was treated quickly, but taking care of that made no difference in her behavior. On a later office visit, the pediatrician told me, "She's just a damn little spoiled brat. Take her home and beat the hell out of her." Of course, he didn't want me to literally give her a beating. He just thought a good spanking would help the situation. I took his advice and gave her a spanking when she needed it. It helped a little, but it didn't solve the problem completely.

When Susan was about three, our marriage situation was so bad that something had to give. I told Harry maybe we could make our marriage work if he would give up his beer and we could get back in church. He said he wasn't going to give up his beer. He moved out shortly after that conversation. Moe was thirteen and Scotty twelve.

Telling Scotty and Moe that Harry wasn't going to live with us anymore was very painful. We stopped at the Dairi-o for ice cream that day on our way home from my mother's house. When I told them the sad news, they both cried. In a letter Scotty wrote to Susan after she was arrested, he told her how he felt when he learned Harry and I were separating. "I remember crying and having no sense of understanding whatsoever," he said.

I didn't go into any long explanation when I told Susan about the separation. I just said her daddy wasn't going to live with us anymore. I didn't think she was old enough to understand the situation. But, as I heard during the trial, she was aware of a whole lot more than I thought. She told Arlene Andrews about an incident that happened before we separated the first time. Harry came into the kitchen and yelled at me. I yelled right back, and a big screaming match ensued. Susan remembers running to her room and sitting on the bed and crying. I never knew about that incident, or possibly others. She kept her fears and sadness to herself.

Unfortunately, I thought I was protecting Susan from the bad things that were happening in our family by not talking about them. As a result, she spent two years of Harry's and my separation not knowing what was going to happen to our family. She had no way to express her fears and feelings. Since she didn't bring up the subject, I figured she was handling everything okay.

Harry was always good with the kids. Scotty remembers that Susan's "little brown eyes and Daddy's lit up whenever he came to visit." They did miss their daddy, but they didn't miss the tension. As far as I could tell, they seemed to adjust to the separation.

Harry and I got back together in the fall of 1974 for about three months. We went to counseling to try to settle our differences and to help him deal with his depression and threats of suicide. Nothing worked. We separated again shortly after Christmas.

At the trial, Dr. Andrews talked about the effect of the separation on Susan. She noted that "three and a half is a very critical age in human development." She went on to say that it is the age when children are really learning to trust and that separation is real important to a three-year-old. "It can create anxiety in them, nervousness, and sort of a mistrust about who they can count on," she explained, "because that's just sort of a point at which normal human development, learning to trust and count on, is critical."

A friend testified at the trial about the effect the separation had on Susan at the age of six. She said, "I found Susan to be sad....I thought she was unhappy and scared at times." She told about observing Susan when she was at her daughter's birthday party. All the children were jumping around and laughing and having a great time. Susan was sitting at the table, staring into space "like she wasn't there, like this party wasn't going on." At the time, my friend thought it was because of Harry's and my separation and divorce and all that our family was going through. She explained that she was not saying Susan never laughed; she was just saying she saw a sadness that was unusual. To me, Susan was a happy child. If I saw any of the sadness, I figured it was something that would pass when our family situation was resolved.

I didn't want to get a divorce right away. I thought the break would be easier if I waited for Harry to find someone else. And frankly, I was afraid of what he would do to himself or to me. He had threatened suicide a number of times. He accused me of going out with other men when we were separated and followed me at times.

Six or seven months went by. Harry and I tried to relate peaceably for the children's sake. Then one day, without warning, he showed up with a shotgun I had bought for him as a Christmas present years before. He marched into the kitchen and stood the gun beside the door.

"What are you doing with that?" I asked.

"You and me are going for a ride," he said firmly and angrily. The desperately sad look in his eyes terrified me.

"What do you mean?" I asked, trying to control the terror.

"I mean we're going for a ride."

"You're crazy," I said, my heart racing madly. "I'm not going anywhere with you."

Michael, Scotty, and Susan heard the noise and came to the kitchen. The sight of Harry standing there with a gun and yelling about me going somewhere with him scared them to death. When Harry saw the kids, he quickly switched from being in a rage to talking with them. While he was distracted, I eased between him and the gun, grabbed it, and ran to my neighbor's house to call the police. I wasn't worried about the kids. I was sure Harry wouldn't harm them.

I went back to the house when the police arrived and took the children to the home of my friend Glenda, then went back to talk to the police officer and Harry. The officer reasoned with Harry for quite a while and finally calmed him down. After the officer left, Harry asked for the gun, promising he wouldn't do anything stupid. I refused to give it to him. I later loaned the gun to my brother Tim to use for hunting.

Harry wouldn't leave me alone. He walked into our house anytime he wanted, often hostile. He became more and more depressed and threatened suicide. I could see the depression in his eyes. I went to counseling with him to try to help him over the depression and threats of suicide.

When Harry and I separated, we had two cars, both paid for. One was a Plymouth Fury that we bought new. The other was a Volkswagen station wagon. I asked Harry for only $40.00 a week child support and let him have the Fury. I kept the wagon because it was cheaper to drive. He sold the Fury and went into debt for a big Oldsmobile.

Harry soon lost the Olds because he couldn't pay for it. He bought an old Chevy with torn upholstery. It was a piece of junk. Then he lost his job. He called me at work one day and asked if I would swap cars with him for the day. He needed to go out of town to apply for a job. I told him that would be okay. I expected him to bring my car home that evening, but he didn't show up.

I called Harry's apartment, but there was no answer. I didn't hear from him the next day at work and again couldn't get him on the phone. I went by his apartment after work and got his landlord to let me in. All his personal belongings were gone. I just knew he had gone to Florida.

Scotty was really hurt by what his daddy did. He said he just couldn't believe he would do us that way. Susan kept asking when her daddy was going to bring our car back. Several weeks later, he showed up at the house and gave me some money. He said he was back in Union and had moved into his old apartment. He wouldn't say where he had been. I told him I wanted my car back, but he refused to let me have it.

A week or so later, Harry called and asked Susan if she wanted to go get some ice cream. "Are you going to bring my mama's car home?" she asked, standing on a chair to reach the wall phone. I assumed he said no, because she put her little hand on her hip and said, "I don't want to go then!"

On my way to work the next day, I went by Harry's apartment. I knew he always left his keys in the car. I parked his car and took mine. He never said a word about that.

Along with stopping by my house unannounced, Harry began harassing me when he came by. If a date was there, he would threaten the man or make a nuisance of himself in other ways. I decided I couldn't wait any longer for him to find someone else. I had to get him officially out of my life. October 1977, I filed for divorce on grounds of being separated for at least a year. We had been separated three. Our divorce was final three months later.

Shortly after our divorce was final, Tim called to tell me Harry had asked for his gun. He didn't want to let him have it but felt that he had to; it was his, after all. I wondered how Harry knew Tim had the gun. Scotty told me his daddy called and said a friend wanted to borrow the gun, and he told him Tim had it.

I called Harry that night and asked why he got the gun. He admitted lying about the friend wanting to borrow it and said he just wanted it; it was his. The heaviness in his voice was alarming. He sounded so down, so depressed. "Please, Harry," I said, "I'm begging you not to do anything foolish. Don't forget, you have three children who love you." He said he couldn't promise anything.

I immediately called Harry's brother Junior and asked him if he could come over. I told him about Harry having the gun and that I was afraid he would kill himself. He said he would do what he could.

January 14, 1978, I went out on an evening date and returned home around 12:30. Moe was in his bedroom asleep. Scotty and his friend, John, were spending the night with Harry. Susan was spending the night with a friend in Spartanburg, thirty miles away.

I had just fallen asleep when the phone rang. Harry was at the other end of the line, cursing and accusing me of everything in the book. I had no idea what he was upset about. I told him we could talk when both of us were wider awake and hung up. In a matter of minutes, he was at my house, banging on the back door. I refused to let him in.

I called Scotty at Harry's apartment and told him Harry was trying to get in the back door. "Do you have any idea what your daddy's so upset about? Did you say anything to him about me going out on a date?"

"No, Mama," Scotty assured me, "We were just sitting here watching TV, and Daddy got up and said he would be back in a minute. He didn't seem mad or anything. Do you want me to come on home?"

"No, stay there. I'll be okay."

I frantically called Tim, told him Harry was banging on the back door, and asked him to call the police. I also asked him to come over to my house, because I was afraid Harry would kill me if he got inside.

I ran into my bedroom and got a pistol. I had just started down the hall when I heard the glass break in the back door. The thought raced through my mind, *What if he takes this thing away from me and kills me with it? What in the world will my children do?*

I ran back into my bedroom and stuck the gun under the covers. When I turned around, Harry was in the doorway. He threw me down on the bed and grabbed for my neck, yelling that he was going to kill me.

"Let's talk about this," I urged, desperately pushing him away.

"No! No!" he screeched. "It's no use."

He lunged at me, again grabbing for my neck. As I pushed him back, someone banged on the front door.

"Go to the back door!" I screamed. "The back door!"

Two policemen rushed into the bedroom, with Tim close behind. One officer grabbed Harry by the arm and pulled him off me.

"Damn you," Harry yelled, jerking away. "I'm not going with you. I'll go with Pete." He pointed to the other officer. He and Pete went way back.

As they walked out the door, the policemen paused to tell me I needed to get a warrant against Harry.

"Where do I get a warrant?" I asked. "I've never gotten a

warrant." He told me to call Maurice Gregory, the city judge.

Before Tim left to let Hedy know what was happening, I asked him to call Mr. Gregory and have him issue a warrant. I told Tim I would get dressed and pick him up to go with me. When I pulled up to his house, he motioned me inside. He said Mr. Gregory wanted me to wait until eight in the morning.

I picked up the phone and angrily dialed Gregory's number. "I want a warrant, and I want it right now," I demanded.

His smart reply was, "I guess if you have to have it now, I'll just have to get up and issue you one."

"That's fine!" I snapped. "Where do I go to get it?"

"You're going to have to come down here and get it. I'm sure not going to bring it to you."

"That's fine," I agreed curtly. "Where are you?"

He said he lived in an apartment in the rear of Brown, Bolton, Jolly Funeral Home. He told me to knock on the front door, and he would come and get me.

Gregory promptly answered the knock. A sliver of light from his living quarters reflected eerily on the stainless steel tables as he led us through a very dark room where they embalm corpses.

Seated in his office, Mr. Gregory asked me why I wanted the warrant. I told him exactly what had happened, that Harry had broken in my house and tried to kill me.

"You ought to charge him with breaking and entering," he advised.

"Look, Mr. Gregory," I replied. "He's the father of my children. I don't want him to be sentenced and serve time. I just want to keep him from hurting himself or me."

He wasn't pleased, but he gave me the warrant. I took it by the police department, assuming Harry was there. But that was not to be. He had talked the officers on duty into letting him go home. He told them he would willingly come down there when they got the warrant.

The policeman at the desk told me they would serve the warrant as soon as they could. Actually, I think it ended up being a restraining order because I wouldn't charge Harry with anything.

Since Harry wasn't in jail, I decided to stay at Tim and

Hedy's for the rest of the night. I wanted protection if he came back. When I called Moe to tell him where I was, Scotty answered the phone.

"What're you doing home?" I asked.

"John and I were running home to see about you, and Daddy picked us up. He took John to our house and me back to his apartment. When we got to his apartment, he told me to drive the car home. I told him I wasn't suppose to drive without him in the car, but he said it would be okay this one time." Scotty only had a driver's permit.

Scotty was really scared and upset about everything. He wanted to stay with his dad, but Harry went into his apartment and locked the door. Scotty banged on the door and begged Harry to let him in. He refused to even open the door and ordered Scotty to "go on home."

Scotty shouted through the door, "I love you, Daddy," then left. I assured him he had done all he could and told him I would be there in the morning.

I was lying on the sofa, still trying to calm down, when the phone rang. Tim answered it, then came into the den. "It was Moe," he said solemnly. "The police called and said Harry shot himself. They've taken him to the hospital."

"Oh, No!" I yelled, jumping up. "Is he okay?"

"I don't know," Tim replied nervously. "All Moe knew was that he had been taken to the hospital. I'll go get him and Scotty right now."

Hedy heard all the activity and came into the den. "I knew this was going to happen," I told her. "That's why I wanted the warrant so bad."

With Hedy standing beside me, I called the police and told the dispatcher who I was. He asked me to hold the line while he checked about Harry.

"I'm sorry to tell you this," the man began softly, "but Harry Vaughan just passed away."

My knees buckled. Hedy put her arm around my waist to keep me from falling to the floor. She then took the phone from my hand, placed it in the cradle, and helped me to the sofa.

When Tim and the boys came through the back door, Hedy

sent them to the den. Sitting between Moe and Scotty, I solemnly told them their father was dead. They broke into tears.

"I wish he would have let me stay," Scotty sobbed.

"You couldn't have done anything, Scotty," I assured him. "You didn't know he was going to kill himself."

Harry had placed the twelve-gauge shotgun between his legs and shot himself in the chest. Barely alive, he dialed zero and asked the operator to send help. He lived for forty-five minutes.

We called all the family. Tim went to pick up Mama. Everyone else quickly gathered at Tim and Hedy's house.

I waited until nine o'clock to call Iris about picking up Susan. No one answered. I sent Tim to my house, four doors away, to see if they were there. Susan was already on her way to his house.

"Why is everybody here?" Susan asked as she stepped inside the den. "And why is everybody crying?" I made some excuse that she accepted and told her we needed to go home. Mama, whom Susan calls MaMa, went with us.

On the short walk home, I kept asking myself, *How do you tell a six-year-old child that her father is dead*? I asked Mama to come into the bedroom with me while I told her. Susan and I sat on the side of the bed. Mama sat at the foot, looking very sad.

"Susan," I began softly, "do you remember when my grandmother died and went to heaven to live with Jesus?"

"I guess so," she said.

"Susan, your daddy died last night and went to heaven to live with Jesus just like my grandmother."

"What do you mean?" she asked, a puzzled expression filling her face.

"He's gone to heaven to live with Jesus, just like my grandmother."

"I don't believe it," she protested. "I'm going to call him."

"Susan," I pled softly. "He's not home. He's gone to heaven."

She jumped off the bed, ran into the kitchen, and climbed up in a chair to reach the wall phone. As I stood right behind her, she dialed her daddy's number and let the phone ring for a long

I Want to Be with My Daddy

time. Finally, she said, "He's not home," then solemnly put the phone in the cradle and turned to me.

"If he's really in heaven," she said decisively, "I want to be with him."

I tenderly lifted her down from the chair and took her in my arms, holding her close until she wanted me to let go. Only later did I learn that she went into her room to cry.

At the trial, Dr. Andrews stated that Susan was sort of left on her own to deal with Harry's death, partly because all the family was so devastated and partly because we were determined to protect her. She observed that a lot of the family members didn't even remember Susan being around at that time, because they were so upset. But my mother remembers that she was very sad, and she tried to comfort her.

Since Harry and I were divorced, I didn't know where I stood. I learned that, because we were divorced, Harry's family would be responsible for the arrangements. They used the same funeral home where I had asked the judge to issue the warrant.

Scotty, Moe, Susan, Mama, and I went to the funeral home early. I held Susan up to the casket. She watched her daddy to see if he would start breathing.

She asked all kinds of questions about what was going to happen. When I told her people would be coming, she said she didn't want to stay. When Tim and Hedy got there, I asked if they would take her home while I stayed with Moe and Scotty. The visitation time was tough, but people were very comforting.

The next day, I somberly got ready to go to the funeral. As I stood at the mirror in my bedroom, combing my hair, Scotty came in. "Mama," he said softly. "I just want you to know that I don't blame you for Daddy's death. It wouldn't have been right for you to be unhappy so he could be happy." He added thoughtfully, "I think Daddy has been dead inside for a long time. If you're dead inside, you're not really alive, anyway."

As I reached out to hug him, I thought, *What a mature statement has come from this fifteen-year-old son of mine.*

Harry was buried on Tuesday, January 17, 1978. He would have been thirty-five on March 15. The day after the funeral, I went to his sister's home, where all his family had gathered. I knew they wanted to know everything that had happened the night of his death. I told them everything I knew. I also told them I would pay for Harry's funeral expenses and any bills he had with the $10,000 insurance policy that was found at his apartment. I was surprised he had the policy. I thought it had lapsed long before.

I don't know how to say this without being misunderstood by Harry's family, and I wouldn't hurt them for the world. But I don't think I realized or would admit the intense fear I had been living under with Harry until one night when I arrived home rather late. I parked the car and started to get out, but I couldn't move. I just knew Harry was hiding in the bushes and was going to jump out on me.

I reasoned with myself. *Harry is dead. Nobody who is dead can be out there. When people die, they don't come back. Daddy died; my grandmother died; and they didn't come back! Harry can't be out there, because he is dead, just like them.*

Finally, I got up the courage to get out of the car and dashed for the house.

A month or so after Harry's suicide, I went to see the counselor at the school in York who had counseled with our family when Moe was there. I wanted to know why Harry would do such a thing when he had three children he loved very much. The doctor pointed to depression as Harry's primary problem. He made the comment that Harry had been depressed all his life. At the time, that conclusion seemed preposterous to me. I can believe it now, though. I think Susan's depression goes back to early childhood and is linked to a high incidence of depression on both sides of her family.

Susan was so young when we separated, I didn't think she knew her father. But she did feel very close to him. Along with a framed eight by ten picture of him that she slept with occasionally, she also treasured a recording of him talking in the background while Moe was teaching her to talk. She listened to the tape for a long time after his death.

During Susan's trial, I heard people say things like, "She was the apple of his eye," and "Susan would light up when she was near her father." Somehow, I never noticed that interchange.

Our family didn't talk much about Harry's death. We just went on with our lives as best we could. I thought Susan had put her father's death in the past, because she never brought up the subject. The fact that things weren't as they seemed came home forcefully to me when I heard Hedy testify at the trial. She told about an incident when Susan was at her home shortly after Harry's death. Susan and her cousin Leigh were in the bathroom, and Leigh called for her mother to come in there.

When Hedy opened the door, Leigh said, "Mother, Susan is crying. She said her father killed himself."

"He's gone to heaven," Susan sobbed, tears streaming down her face. Hedy took her in her arms and tried to console her.

I hadn't heard of this incident until the trial.

I never told Susan about all the events surrounding Harry's death. She didn't learn the details until the trial-preparation time when Dr. Andrews told her. I didn't deliberately withhold the information. She never asked, and I didn't want to bring up such a painful subject. And she seemed happy. But I underestimated the profound effect her daddy's death had on her. I didn't realize that all of these experiences had taken an incredible toll on her and would surface in bizarre ways.

3

Emotional Adolescence

The terrible two's were still going strong when Susan started kindergarten. But by the time she started first grade, she had made a complete turnaround. The temper tantrums were a thing of the past. She liked school, and she liked her teachers. She did neat work in school and made good grades. She played with her cousin Leigh and other children in the neighborhood every day. She and Donna stayed all night at each other's house almost every weekend. She and Leigh took dancing lessons. They both marched in the Christmas parade. She enjoyed her friends and she enjoyed life. From everything I could see, she was turning out to be a sweet little girl.

Susan was in the second grade when Bev and I started dating. The manager of a local bank, whom I had been dating, introduced us. When the bank manager and I broke up, Bev and I just kind of drifted together. At the time, he was in the process of getting a divorce that would be final in a couple of months.

From the moment Bev and I met, I was impressed with his good looks, outgoing personality, and gentle manner. He was tall, had dark hair and an impressive build. He commanded a strong, but kind, presence. He was a gentleman in every respect. Strangely, I didn't know who he was, given our small town. I was three grades ahead of him in school and somehow completely missed him. I had never been in the appliance store he owned in Union. I didn't even know he was the nephew of a former governor of South Carolina, something he told me with great pride.

Bev rented a little white frame house that was located a short distance from downtown Union. He laughed about the bathroom being on the back porch and water freezing in the commode. He wasn't in the greatest financial shape then. He drove an old car with a torn top that his grandmother left him. I even

38

loaned him bed covers to use when his children stayed overnight.

After Bev and I had dated for several months, we started talking about getting married. One hot, August day I needed to go to the courthouse on company business. On an impulse, I called Bev and asked if he wanted to meet me there and get our marriage license. He was waiting at the entrance when I arrived. Right away, we started making marriage plans, and I backed out. I backed out several times; then Bev backed out. It was my prerogative to change my mind, but it hurt my feelings when he backed out.

Just before Christmas 1979, Bev suggested, "Why don't we get married on the weekend?"

"Okay by me," I responded quickly. "But I don't want a big hoopla." That sounded good to Bev.

We didn't tell anyone we were getting married. Bev's father was in the hospital, and we didn't want him to feel left out. We also knew we would have to involve everyone if we told our families. We simply wanted a small, quiet wedding.

The morning of our wedding day, my friend Glenda dropped by. I told her we were going to the minister's house to get married and asked her to get her husband Wayne and wait for us at Tim and Hedy's house.

On the way to the minister's house, Bev asked if I was going to back out. "I don't know," I chuckled, "we're not there yet." After the ceremony, we went by the hospital and told Bev's relatives. From there, we went to Tim and Hedy's and visited a while.

Bev's youngest daughter Tami was already planning to spend the night with him. When we picked her up, Bev told her she could spend the night with Susan. She was happy about the marriage and happy about staying all night with Susan. We then went to our house to tell Moe, Scotty, and Susan. They weren't surprised we got married, but they were shocked that we didn't tell them ahead of time. "Mama," Scotty said, "I can't believe you did that without telling us."

At first, I was miserable and mad at myself for giving up my independence. It was a big adjustment after being single for

My Daughter Susan Smith

five years. I couldn't believe I had gotten myself chained down again. We even discussed getting an annulment. But Bev was good to us, all of us. He wasn't the least bit jealous and gave me all the freedom I wanted. Right away, he got us back in church. I respected his honesty, his deep faith, and the loving, dependable person he was. It wasn't long before I realized that I did, indeed, love him.

Bev's family was not very accepting of me. The older girls blamed me for their parents' breakup, even though I came along after it was a done deal. It was different with my children. They liked Bev from the moment they met him. Moe and Scotty respected him and accepted him without question. Susan, who was eight, liked him, too.

I think Bev's gentle manner played a large role in being accepted. Moe and Scotty could remember the turmoil we lived in with Harry. Not once in our marriage did Bev raise his voice to me or the children. I was the children's disciplinarian; he was their friend. Actually, as I look back, I realize he ran from conflict. He had a way of manipulating me to make things go his way without a big fuss. He overcame with kindness.

Shortly after Bev and I married, Susan started asking me if I really loved her. She asked in a way and with a frequency she had never done before. She even wrote a letter to me on my birthday expressing her concern. It went like this:

"Dear mother. I wrote this note to you because I love you. I'm writing this letter because I want to tell you happy birthday. I'm telling you happy birthday now because I forgot to tell you this morning. Tomorrow, if we don't go off, I will help you clean up because I want you to have a very happy birthday. Mother, I'm not writing this letter just because I love you. I'm writing this letter because you are nice, sweet, and pretty. That makes me feel happy. I hope you are happy too. Mother, I hope you are happy about this letter. I sure am happy about it. Mother, I hope this letter proves that I love you and that you love me. Mother, I'm trying to help you have a happy birthday, and I think you will have a happy birthday. Mother, you are the best mother I ever had in my whole life. I think you and Bev

Emotional Adolescence

are nice. I'm wishing you a happy birthday. I like you and I love you. Hope you like me and love me. I know you do. Happy birthday mother. Love Susan V. I love you very much mother." [She drew a heart at the end of the letter.]

One Valentine's Day, Susan made a card for Bev and me. On it she wrote, "I love you mom and dad. I hope that you love me. Love Susan."

I wasn't surprised by Susan's need to be sure I loved her. She liked to write notes like that. She even wrote a letter to Santa Claus asking him "Do you love me? Check the box." She drew boxes under the question with yes and no beside them for him to check. I guessed her note was part of her adjustment to my remarriage. After all, she had enjoyed my undivided attention for a long time. I tried to fix things by telling her over and over that I loved her.

At the trial, Dr. Andrews pointed out that there was nothing terrifically unusual about Susan's wondering if I loved her, considering the fact that she had experienced the loss of one parent and was adjusting to a stepparent. She noted that, when there is a remarriage, "sometimes children at that age also will feel like maybe they are losing mom, because they are losing her attention to the new stepparent. And in this case, too, there were three new stepsisters."

When we first got married, Bev moved into my home on Seigler Road. Eventually, he bought his ex-wife's share of their house in Mount Vernon Estates. We then put both our houses up for sale. We hoped to buy a home large enough to accommodate our two families. When my house sold in a week, we decided to move into Bev's house and look around for something bigger.

I was anxious about the move. The house on Seigler Road was the only home Susan had ever known. She didn't want to move away from her neighborhood friends. I knew she would miss walking to Stacy's house two doors away and her cousin Leigh's, also close by. Moe wasn't happy about leaving his friends, either. Scotty was away at college. I wondered how he would feel coming home to a house he had never seen.

I cried all morning the day we moved. Hedy came over and cried with me. Actually, I don't know which one of us cried the most. For a long time after we moved, she cried every time she passed our house, which was practically every day. It was on her way to everywhere.

I had worked at Bev's store some during the time we lived on Seigler Road. When I first started working there, the books were in a mess. I got all the records in order, established controls, and set up policies and procedures. Bev's accountant jokingly told him that I was the best investment he had ever made. Later, I trained a girl to do the bookkeeping and went back home. I had always worked because I had to, but my first want was to stay home and be a housewife and mother.

Later, I had to return to the store. Unemployment in Union was thirty percent, and times were rough for everyone. I loaned the proceeds from the sale of my house to the store to help reduce the debt. Moe also worked at the store with us. There were times when Bev and I felt like we lived there. We teased about putting a mobile home in back. I eventually got to go back home.

In June 1984, Scotty and Wendy married. They had met in the ninth grade when her parents moved to Union from Pennsylvania. I got to know her well before they married, because she baby-sat Susan. A pretty girl then and now, she is slender, with long, blonde hair and blue eyes and a bubbly personality to match her good looks. She and Scotty dated for six years before getting married. Their son Nick, my first grandchild, was born in October 1985. They asked Sheriff Howard Wells and his wife Wanda to be his godparents. Wendy and Wanda were co-workers then and had been good friends for some time.

Susan turned thirteen the year Scotty and Wendy married. That birthday marked a radical shift in her attitude and outlook. Overnight, she went from a sweet little girl to a sullen adolescent. Her feelings toward Bev and me changed dramatically. Her affectionate notes were a thing of the past. At times, it seemed she didn't like me anymore. And she resented Bev with teenage passion for not letting her watch MTV. She thought he was old-fashioned. She told him all her friends watched that

Emotional Adolescence

channel.

The change in Susan wasn't totally unexpected. I could remember being a teenager and the conflict that developed between me and my parents in the struggle for independence. I
thought I knew more than they did, and they seemed so old-
fashioned. I assumed it was the same with Susan—that what
was wrong with her was emotional adolescence, only a phase
she was going through. I figured she would get through the teen
years just like I did. Still, the intensity of her change frustrated
me.

On a Saturday morning during the winter of 1985, Scotty
and Wendy stopped by to visit, as they often did. Susan was
down in the basement with Bev's daughter Tami. While we sat
in the den talking, the phone rang. It was Sherry Jackson,
Susan's eighth-grade P.E. teacher. She asked to talk to Scotty.
They were friends from high-school days. Shortly after the call,
Scotty and Wendy left, saying they needed to pick up something and would be back.

When Scotty and Wendy returned, I suggested we sit around
the kitchen table and drink a cup of coffee. The minute we sat
down, Scotty solemnly handed me a note, saying, "You need to
read this."

Opening the note, I recognized Susan's pretty handwriting.
"It's a note Susan wrote to Sherry Jackson," Scotty explained
with a troubling look in his eye.

Horror and disbelief gripped me as I read Susan's words. She
told her teacher she had made up her mind to kill herself, and
no one was going to stop her. She said she had been taking aspirin every day, convinced it would build up in her body and
eventually kill her.

"I can't believe this," I told Wendy and Scotty, trying to
hold back the tears. "Susan has not said one word to me."

They were in a state of disbelief, too. Susan hadn't said anything to them, either. We agreed that we wouldn't tell her about
having the note, but all of us planned to watch her closely.

A short time later, the assistant principal came to our house
to discuss Susan's problems. He asked that Bev and I give approval for her to see the school counselor. We agreed to that,

although I didn't really think she needed counseling. At the same time, I thought the counseling couldn't hurt anything.

I could not get beyond thinking Susan was just going through a phase. Most people at one time or another think about suicide. What concerned me tremendously was the fact she was talking with other people about things that should have been kept within our family.

But even though we thought Susan was going through a teenage phase, Bev and I took her suicide threats very seriously. Susan didn't know it, but I watched her like a hawk. I had always taken her to school every morning and picked her up after school, and I continued to do that. I made sure I knew where she was every minute. Each night, after she went to bed, I counted the aspirins in the bottle. Bev took the bullets out of his guns that were on display in the den. We did everything we could think of to guard against suicide.

In preparation for the trial, Dr. Seymour Halleck, professor of psychiatry at the University of North Carolina, was enlisted by the defense to evaluate Susan. Based on many hours of interviews, he testified that Susan began to think obsessively about suicide at the age of thirteen. He said she thought of suicide over and over, in a way she couldn't seem to control, in a way she couldn't seem to stop. She said nothing at home about her suicidal thoughts, but she talked to counselors and teachers at school about wanting to be dead and wanting to be in heaven with her father. She told one teacher she had thought about suicide as early as ten years old.

One counselor told me Susan was having a hard time dealing with her father's death. She had been asking why it happened. Even before the counselor said anything, I picked up on her attitude toward me about this. It became clear that she blamed me for Harry's death. Moe had a photo of Harry that he kept on his dresser. When Susan was in a bad mood, she would get that photo and take it to her room. If I came in the room, she stared at the photo and gave me an accusing look. She also said things to indicate she thought her daddy might still be alive if we hadn't gotten a divorce.

Things got so unpleasant between Susan and me, I decided

to keep her home from school one day to talk about her father. While she was eating breakfast, I told her, "Ask me anything you want to know about your daddy, and I'll tell you."

"Just one thing," she fired right back. "Who wanted the divorce, you or my daddy?"

"I'm the one that filed for divorce," I replied.

"That's all I want to know," she snapped, then turned silent and hostile.

"Susan," I said firmly. "I didn't kill your daddy, and I'm not the one who left you. He was. I stayed and kept care of you kids. I'm the one who chose not to live with your daddy, but he was the one who chose not to live. I'm not going to allow you to put the blame on me."

She said nothing but stared at me with a disgusted look on her face. Shortly, she went to the den and turned on the TV. She spent the rest of the day watching TV and doing things in her room.

The following Sunday, Bev and I took separate cars to church. He and Susan went to Sunday School, and I went later to the worship service. Bev sang in the choir; I sat in my usual place. Susan wouldn't sit beside me, as she usually did. Instead, she sat behind me and exited the church without saying one word to me, then rode home with Bev.

I arrived home first and was preparing dinner when Bev and Susan came in the kitchen door. Bev greeted me, but Susan hurried by me with an angry look pasted on her face and headed for her bedroom. Her attitude went all over me. I had had enough! I followed her into her bedroom, shut the door, and told her to sit down on the bed, that I had something to say she needed to hear.

Standing in front of her, I snapped, "I'm tired of this, and you're not going to treat me like this any longer. If you're so miserable living with me, pack your clothes, and I'll take you to a halfway house."

Her mouth flew open, the shock written all over her face.

Without another word, I left the room, shutting the door behind me. I paused outside the door for a minute, not believing what I had just said. I would never have carried through on the threat, but I did want to scare some sense into her.

When Susan came out to eat, she was a different person, smiling and pleasant, even to me. I felt that I had indeed scared some sense into her. From that point on, things were better.

As David Bruck questioned Dr. Halleck at the trial, Bruck made the observation that counselors and psychologists and other people take different stances toward the kind of behavior Susan exhibited at the age of thirteen—telling people she wanted to be in heaven with her father, writing a suicide note, taking aspirin to kill herself.

Responding to that observation, Dr. Halleck made a strong statement about the way Susan's obsession with suicide should have been handled: "If Susan Smith had walked into my emergency room at the age of thirteen with this history, she either would have been immediately hospitalized, or a very intensive treatment program would have been arranged before she walked out of that emergency room." He went on to say that the treatment program would have included intensive psychotherapy, talking therapy, and probably medication. The medication would have been for depression, because he thought "this was the beginning of her depression, the first manifestation of it."

Hindsight is a wonderful thing. But I didn't have the benefit of that. What I saw was a child who was moving into the teen years with all the changes that take place mentally and physically. I thought she was going through the "thirteen-year blues." Living through it, the problems appeared to be connected with the adjustments of adolescence. I take only part of the blame for not recognizing it was more than that.

Susan went to Union High School the next year. She seemed alive and eager to get involved in school activities. She and Donna became Candy Stripers and also joined Jr. Civitan. They had a larger group of close friends that did lots of things together. She brought friends to our home anytime she wanted. She was a busy girl and seemed very happy.

4

Why, Bev? Why?

Debbie Green, Susan's ninth-grade English teacher, was someone students could talk to in confidence and without being laughed at. Early each school year, in a light-hearted way, she asked her students to tell her anything that might affect their school work. She had been doing this for most of her nineteen years of teaching. Word got around that she could be trusted, and students came to her with their problems.

Susan lingered after class one day to talk to Debbie. Holding her head down, she haltingly said, "I think you probably would need to know that I get depressed sometimes and that I have tried to kill myself before." During the conversation, she told Debbie she had thought about suicide for a long time.

Of that conversation, Debbie said at the trial, "That took me by surprise, because she was a beautiful child. It was totally unexpected."

When asked by David Bruck if she thought Susan was trying to gain her sympathy or to escape any work responsibility, Debbie said she didn't think so. She explained that Susan shared the information in a matter-of-fact way, as if it were something her teacher needed to know. She said Susan never took advantage of her kindness, emphasizing that she did beautiful work in her class and always got it in on time.

During that same conversation, Debbie asked Susan if she had been able to talk to someone about her depression and her feelings. She said she had not. The next day Debbie called the school counselor and told her what Susan had said. The counselor said she would take care of the legal end of getting her into counseling.

The counselor, Janie Sweet, called to tell me Susan had been recommended for counseling, and she needed my signed permission. I told her to go ahead and send the papers, and I would think about it. I didn't intend to return the papers, because nothing in Ms. Sweet's vague explanation convinced me that Susan needed counseling. The Susan I saw each day was a bubbly, affectionate, outgoing, pretty little girl, who was a typical teenager. I thought she had put the thirteen-year blues behind her. She made good grades. She had no weight problem. She had a group of good, clean friends, whom she felt free to bring by the house anytime she wanted. She wasn't into drugs or anything like that. Why would she need counseling?

True, I didn't think Susan needed counseling. I also had feelings about counseling that went much deeper. I didn't want her to be labeled as mentally unbalanced. No matter how much people talk about not being ashamed of getting treatment, there still is a stigma. It didn't seem fair to Susan to take that risk when I thought all that was wrong with her was being a teenager.

But Debbie Green kept on top of the situation. A week or so later, she checked with the counselor to see if she had been able to start counseling Susan. The counselor simply said, "No." Debbie called me and said she thought Susan could use counseling. She told me what Susan had said about suicide. I told her I didn't think Susan was dangerously suicidal; but if she felt she needed counseling, I didn't think it could hurt anything. It would be okay if Susan wanted to. But I wanted to have an agreement with the counselor that I could call her after every session. Debbie thought something could be worked out and gave me Janie Sweet's telephone number.

First thing Monday morning, I called Janie Sweet. I told her I would agree to counseling for Susan if I could call her after every session. She said that would be all right. With great trepidation, I returned the signed paperwork.

I called Janie Sweet after each weekly session and asked how things went. She would say, "It went fine; we had a good session," or "she talked about her feelings about her daddy today." Not once did she say it didn't go well.

I probed from time to time. "Think Susan is all right?" I would ask. "Yes, she's fine," was her typical answer. I got the distinct impression the sessions were between counselor and

Why, Bev? Why?

patient, that what they discussed was none of my business. It went on like that for about six months. Then, in one of my calls to her, Ms. Sweet said she would like for Susan to be evaluated at Hall Psychiatric Institute, which is at the state mental hospital in South Carolina. This evaluation was to be part of Susan's involvement in an experimental psychological study on depression in childhood.

When she said *experimental*, I heard nothing else. Not in a million years would I let anyone experiment with my daughter. I told her I would be willing to send her to a psychologist but not to an experimental study. She didn't suggest that as an option then. The alternative was for Susan to continue with Ms. Sweet.

It was partly my fault that I rejected Ms. Sweet's recommendation and partly hers. I still wonder why she didn't have me come to her office and carefully explain what was involved, why Susan needed to be in the study, and how it could help. Or, even better, she could have come to my home. It seems to me that something of this magnitude—my daughter being involved in an experimental study—should have been discussed in person, not with a casual telephone conversation, as all of ours were.

Susan had been in counseling about a year when Janie Sweet told me she was coming to the sessions to get out of study hall. She said their conversations had become only chit-chat. I asked her if she thought Susan was okay. She said she felt Susan had been going through delayed grieving for her father and that the counseling had helped.

After Susan finished the counseling with Ms. Sweet, things seemed to get better. She continued to be involved in Jr. Civitan. She and Donna logged one hundred hours at the local hospital as Candy Stripers and were working on the second hundred. From all outward appearances, Susan was happy. I relaxed a bit.

I went back to work at Bev's store to help out, because he was heavily involved in the Christian Coalition and was also involved in politics. A strong conservative, he put together a group of like-minded people and took over the Republican

Party. Actually, it wasn't much of a takeover. Besides our small group, there were only three people at the meeting.

As Bev spent more and more time in political activities, he began to let other areas of his life slide. He still attended church regularly and sang in the choir, but he gave up the position of lay leader, along with other duties. Where he once read the Bible faithfully and did a lot of biblical study, he now concentrated on political literature. Many times he had risen at 5:00 a. m. to prepare a Sunday School lesson. We usually prayed together in the morning. He no longer had time for those things. His life was controlled by politics. It seemed that the only places we went and everything we did involved politics. Our marriage was suffering. Our business was suffering.

In the midst of all Bev's political activity, the next bomb fell. Susan was almost sixteen. Debbie Green had taken a group of students to a Jr. Civitan retreat at Presbyterian College in May of 1987. One evening, all those attending the retreat gathered together in a dance area. Unknown to Debbie, Susan got into an argument with a girl over a boy named Rodney that both of them had been dating. They exchanged some cutting remarks, and Susan left the area in tears. It wasn't until the group returned to the dormitory at the agreed time of nine-thirty that Debbie realized Susan was missing. She went to look for her.

After considerable searching, Debbie spotted Susan sitting on the ground in a secluded area of the campus. As she came up behind Susan, she could hear her crying heavily. She softly called her name, and Susan turned around. Tears were streaming down her face.

Debbie asked her why she was there instead of at the dormitory. She said she had just been walking around. "I don't understand," Debbie said. "What do you mean just walking around?" She said she had been wandering around and that was where she ended up. Debbie eased her up and took her to a bench close by to talk.

She probed to find out what was bothering Susan. Susan said nothing in her life was going right. She talked about the fight over Rodney. She said her father had killed himself, that she felt deserted, that her father couldn't possibly have loved her, or he wouldn't have killed himself. She didn't think anyone loved her. She wanted to die.

Debbie had been around Susan enough to see her in different levels of depression. Many times she had seen her try to appear happy when she was very sad. She described what she saw on this occasion as the most severe state of depression she had seen in Susan.

She reasoned with Susan to make her feel better. She tried to build her up by pointing out her good qualities. She tried to convince her that people loved her. She tried to help her understand that her father's suicide didn't mean he didn't love her. For everything negative Susan said, she came back with something positive. After a while the reasoning worked, and Susan stopped crying. "I don't know how it worked," Debbie said on the witness stand. "I don't know if I had a guardian angel on my shoulder, but after a while all this reasoning seemed to work."

They sat there for a few minutes without saying anything. Susan broke the silence with a question, "Do you think it's appropriate for me to sit in my stepfather's lap and watch TV?"

Debbie didn't think she understood the question. "What?" she asked, trying to remain calm. Susan repeated the question. Debbie told her firmly that it was not appropriate for her to still be sitting in her stepfather's lap. Susan fell silent again.

This time Susan broke the silence by asking Debbie if it was appropriate for her stepfather to put his arm around her and sometimes touch her breast. Debbie was so shocked she didn't know what to say, but finally got it out. "I want to tell you this," she began, "if you ever feel inside that he has gone that one step too far, just that one step, you tell me, you tell your mother, you tell somebody." She could tell Susan had decided the behavior wasn't appropriate. She just needed to have her feelings verified by someone she trusted.

Susan returned to the subject of feeling nobody loved her. Debbie tried to reason with her, explaining that the feelings were false, that people did love her. After more than an hour of talking, Debbie felt Susan had calmed down sufficiently, and they went to the dormitory.

To this day, Debbie is convinced that Susan was looking for

a place or a method or a means to commit suicide. She feels sure Susan would have killed herself if she hadn't found her.

Debbie estimated for David Bruck that she had taught over two thousand kids when she taught Susan and worked with her in Jr. Civitan. Of Susan, she said: "I found Susan to be one of the most lovable children I have ever encountered. One of the most polite. Never questioned a thing. Was never, never argumentative about anything. She had all of this love to give, and yet inside she didn't love herself....that love was missing inside, because she didn't feel that she was getting it back. She was empty... She would hug people without even thinking about it. She would just naturally hug people....Didn't matter size, shape, color, form.... Susan was open to hugging a body. But yet she was so troubled. And she was so determined, it seemed.... I tried and I tried, and I did everything within the legal system to help Susan."

Debbie acknowledged to Bruck that she had taught other students who were suicidal and troubled. He asked how Susan compared to the rest. "She's the most troubled," Debbie replied.

At that point in time, Debbie didn't feel there were any other options for helping Susan. The counselor had released her after a year of counseling. I wouldn't allow her to be involved in the experimental study. She thought her hands were tied legally. Her only hope was that Susan would tell me about Bev.

And Susan did just that, pressured by the school counselor, who said she would tell me if she didn't. She broke the news to me on a Sunday evening. Bev was at church. Moe was watching TV in his bedroom. I was sitting on the sofa in the den, watching TV. She sat down at the opposite end and turned in my direction. "Mama," she said nervously. "I have something to tell you." Her eyes were wide open. She had the look of a child 'fessing up to a misdeed she knew would eventually be found out, and she wanted to get it over with.

"What is it?" I asked, silently anticipating what the misdeed could be. Had her grades dropped because of her volunteer work at the hospital? Did she get in a squabble with someone over a boy? What could possibly make her look so serious?

Haltingly, she said, "Bev has done some things to me."

"What has he done?" I asked.

She said he had touched her breasts.

My heartbeat raced. I was shocked beyond belief.

"When?" I asked, trying to keep my shock in control.

She said it was one time when Bev's daughter Tami and Donna stayed overnight. When my usual bedtime arrived that night, she had suggested that I go on to bed and let her sleep on the sofa. Donna and Tami would sleep in her bed. Bev said he was going to stay up for a while. After I left the den, Susan sat in Bev's lap. He became aroused and touched her breasts.

I looked at her in stunned disbelief. She seemed to have no understanding of where that could lead.

"Are you mad at me?" she asked.

"No, I'm not mad at you, Susan," I said. "But I don't understand why you let it go that far. Why didn't you stop it?" This wasn't a four-year-old. She was fifteen, and I felt she could have done something to make him stop. I was angry that she didn't get up and leave.

"I had to see if I could trust him," she explained.

Trust him? Her reasoning went over my head.

As we talked, Susan let me know she had told Debbie Green and a high-school counselor about Bev. I asked her why she didn't come to me, instead of going to them. She sheepishly said she didn't know why.

She wanted to know what I was going to do. Absolutely limp, I said, "I don't know."

Susan had been Bev's stepdaughter for almost eight years. In the beginning of her relationship to him, I think she copied his three daughters. They sat on his lap all the time growing up, even when they became teenagers. There was nothing wrong with that; it was simply father-daughter affection. Susan did the same in the pre-teen years. One time when we were at the home of Bev's aunt, Susan sat down in his lap and hugged him. She was ten at the time. That was okay. But when she became a teenager, I felt uneasy about it. He wasn't her natural father and, physically, she was turning into a mature looking young woman. I tried to tell Susan that what was all right for Bev's daughters wasn't all right for her. Bev said he was aware of

that, too, and always was careful that nothing would be miscon-
strued. Obviously, somewhere along the way, he lost his perspective.

While I waited for Bev, I sat on our bed, drinking a cup of
coffee. Seething inside, I stared into space, asking myself, *Why,
why, why*? I kept looking at the clock, the minutes ticking by so
slowly.

It was an incredibly long thirty minutes before I heard Bev
open the storm door at the back of the house. He came straight
to the bedroom, as he always did. I was on the edge of the bed,
facing the door. One look at me, and he knew something was
seriously wrong, but he said nothing as he took off his suit coat,
hung it in the closet, and turned to face me.

"Shut the door," I told him sharply. "We've got to talk." He
shut the door and sat down in the chair opposite me.

"About what?" he asked, a puzzled look filling his face..

When I said, "You and Susan," he looked like someone
whose worst fears had just been realized.

My voice cracking, I told him what Susan said.

After a long, deathly pause, he slowly and softly said he
never meant for anything to happen. He admitted it had happened as Susan said; but, before it went any farther, he pushed
her up and went to bed. He said he couldn't believe he had done
such a thing, that he felt like some kind of pervert. He was so
ashamed, so repentant, so sure it would never happen again.

I kept asking, "Why, Bev? Why?"

"I don't know a reason," he kept answering. "I don't know; it
just happened. I never meant for anything to happen."

My emotions went from extreme anger, to shock to disgust
to incredible sadness to a feeling of utter helplessness. I could
not believe something like this could happen in our family.
How could a kind, gentle, extremely religious man like Bev do
something like this? It was so bizarre.

We didn't yell or scream or even raise our voices. We just
talked. That wasn't unusual. Bev never raised his voice, and he
wouldn't listen if I did. I told him the school counselor knew all
about this and wanted me to call her Monday morning. I said I
was going to ask her to recommend a counselor. He was willing

to do whatever was necessary to resolve the problem. We both agreed that we could overcome with counseling.

I lay in bed awake for a long time that night with Bev beside me. *How could he have done such a thing*? I asked myself, over and over and over. Everything about him was so decent. It was Bev who got the kids and me back in church. He sang in the choir every Sunday. He never missed a service unless he was sick. He was a strong family man. He was active in the Christian Coalition. With all that, how could it happen?

I believed Bev then when he said he never meant for anything to happen, and I believe that now. I think what happened in the beginning was innocent on the part of both Bev and Susan. Neither one planned it. It just happened. I think it was Bev's responsibility to keep something like that from being repeated. He was the adult; he had the power.

But even as I felt Bev was responsible to control the situation, I couldn't understand why Susan went along with it, why she didn't defend herself. I told her she needed to learn how to protect herself. I said, "Susan, this world is full of men who will take advantage of you if you let them." Some have accused me of shifting blame away from Bev in emphasizing this self-protection to Susan, but I never intended to do that. I always agreed that Bev was to be held completely responsible.

Monday morning I called the school counselor. She suggested a psychologist in Spartanburg named David Heatherly. I made an appointment for three o'clock that afternoon. When Bev and I first went in, Dr. Heatherly asked us to explain how he could help us. Bev froze; he couldn't get one word out. I had to tell Dr. Heatherly why we were there.

Dr. Heatherly's area of specialization is marriage and family therapy—working with marriage situations, trying to keep families together. Bev, Susan, and I went to him together for a number of sessions. Susan went for private counseling after that, and Bev and I went to counseling together. The sessions did help us as a family, and we continued the counseling until Dr. Heatherly thought things were okay. After our last session, he told us to call if we needed him again.

At the trial, David Bruck asked Dr. Heatherly for his opinion about what had caused the abuse. He observed that when Susan lost her father, she stopped growing emotionally in terms of her sense of who she was. "The terrible loss left her very empty inside," he stated. He said when she first came to him for counseling, he saw a young woman "who appeared to be very bright, sort of cheery. But she also seemed to be willing to please everybody, rather confused about her identity in terms of who she was in contact with the family." He noted that she had some very childlike emotional and physical needs. She needed to have her hair stroked; she needed someone to think she was delightful; she needed someone to show her the kind of interest that she had never had from a father. "When Linda married Beverly," he said, "I think she had hoped that she now had a person that she could identify with and connect up to."

Dr. Heatherly went on to say that Susan was still a child when he counseled her and was very confused about whether Bev was her father or her lover. He said she didn't want to make any trouble for Bev and me. She wanted to keep the family together.

And about Bev? It was Dr. Heatherly's belief that "Beverly Russell in his own neediness crossed the line and did not see the true needs that Susan had and took those needs as being actually physical sexual needs." He placed responsibility for the sexual abuse squarely on Bev's shoulders and no one else.

I grieved as if someone close to me had died. My respect for Bev died. My trust in him evaporated. What I should do about Bev was constantly on my mind.

Bev and I talked a lot about our situation. He said we could overcome this. I wanted to overcome it. I wanted to give him the opportunity to restore my faith and trust in him. I had been through so many crises that I saw this as just another one to be dealt with. I viewed Bev as a good man who had made a big mistake. I couldn't see getting a divorce. I didn't want to throw away all those years of marriage and break up a household. Divorce wasn't something that would affect only the three of us. It would tear apart our whole family and the relationships that had been built between my children and Bev's and both our families.

Why, Bev? Why?

Bev's genuine repentance was a huge factor in my desire to save our marriage. He was kinder than ever. It sounds crazy for me to say after what happened; but I felt Bev was a good man, and I loved him. All the children loved him. Scotty told people that Bev provided stability for our family. There seemed to be more reasons to stay together than to divorce.

I think deep down, we both wanted to reclaim what we had before. Unfortunately, we never did resolve the issues. Instead, we kind of rocked along in our relationship and found a comfort zone, fooling ourselves into thinking things were okay.

Bev and I never told anybody about him and Susan, even other family members. We felt it was an unfortunate incident that had happened in our household and needed to be dealt with there.

5

The Illusion Shattered

While Susan was in counseling, her life was pretty much as it had always been. She had an after-school job. She did her volunteer work at the hospital. She and her friends went to one school activity after another and hung out together at the stadium. She and Tonya, the girl she squabbled with over Rodney, went back and forth with him as their steady date. He took Susan to the winter ball. Tonya went with him to the prom. On Valentine's Day, he had roses delivered to Susan at school. Rodney and Tonya are married now. They remain friends of Susan and keep in touch with her.

By January of 1988, everything seemed to be in order. Bev and I had finished our counseling with Dr. Heatherly in November of 1987. Susan had finished hers in late December. As far as I could see, it had helped. She seemed happy, and Bev and I were trying to rebuild our relationship.

On a Monday afternoon in early March, a call from Bev shattered the illusion. He told me Jenny Ward, supervisor of the Child Protective Services intake unit for Union County's Department of Social Services (DSS) was in his office.

"What's she doing there?" I asked impatiently.

"It's about me and Susan," he replied nervously.

A terrible sinking feeling gripped me in the pit of my stomach. Rage filled my whole body. "How far has it gone?" I asked. "Has it gone as far as it could?"

"Absolutely not," he assured me, as if that offense were so awful he would never be guilty of it. If it had gone that far, I would have said I hoped they put him in jail and threw away the key.

Before I could respond, Bev told me there was going to be a meeting with the sheriff, and he already had called our lawyer, Robert Guess. Robert had managed to get Sheriff Jolly to come

The Illusion Shattered

to his office, instead of meeting at the police department.

"You need to come right down here with Susan," Bev said, as if we had been waiting for his call. I told him I had to take a shower and would be there when I got ready. I intended to take my time, even if it meant he might be thrown in jail.

Bev's daughter Tami had come home with Susan after school. I told her to call her grandmother and tell her she was coming over there. I then told Susan, "We've got to go somewhere." After we dropped Tami off, I told Susan where we were going. She wasn't surprised, because she had already talked to Jenny Ward.

First thing Monday morning, Susan told one of her teachers that the sexual abuse had resumed, and she wanted it stopped. The teacher immediately went to Ann Campbell, the school counselor. Ms. Campbell said it was time to call DSS. Jenny Ward was at Union High within two hours. According to law, DSS had to respond to a sexual abuse case within that time period if the perpetrator was in the home.

Jenny Ward talked to the guidance counselor and several teachers, all of whom confirmed that the sexual abuse had occurred. She then talked to Susan. At the trial, Ms. Ward revealed details about this interview. Susan told her Bev had, on more than one occasion, touched her breasts on top of her clothes, that they had engaged in what she called French kissing, and that he had taken her hand and placed it on his genitalia while she pretended to be asleep.

As they talked, it became apparent that Susan was very concerned about the effect this information would have on her family. She was afraid our family might fall apart and didn't want that to happen. She felt responsible and guilty about everything that had happened. She thought she had betrayed both Bev and me. On the witness stand, Ms. Ward stated that Susan's response was typical for sexually abused children. They heap all the blame on themselves. She told Susan she had done nothing wrong, that adults are responsible for protecting children. She assured Susan she was there to protect her and to work to keep the family together.

Immediately after talking to Susan, Jenny Ward went to

Bev's appliance store to confront him. He didn't deny the charges. In fact, he told Ms. Ward he was glad she was there, that he felt a weight lifted off of his shoulders in talking to her about the problem. During the conversation, she discovered that Bev had been in counseling for this same type of behavior.

Ms. Ward explained to Bev that DSS employees were required to report this type of conduct to law enforcement, because it was of a criminal nature. She made the call to the sheriff's department from Bev's office.

Bev asked if he would need a lawyer. Ms. Ward said he would, since she would have to refer the matter to the family court for intervention. That's when he called our lawyer and then called me.

The investigation continued in our lawyer's conference room. Along with Susan and me, others present at the meeting were Jenny Ward, Sheriff Jolly, and David Taylor, a detective from the sheriff's office. Bev waited nearby in Robert Guess' office.

Jenny Ward began the meeting by asking Susan to tell exactly what had happened. My stomach drew up in knots as Susan tearfully related what had happened. She said Bev watched her when she was in the bathtub and came into her bedroom at night and had her fondle his genitals while she pretended to be asleep. I couldn't believe my ears. I knew nothing of this. Later, I would recall times at night when Bev was in Susan's area of the house. When I asked what he was doing, he always had an acceptable excuse for being there—like fixing a leak in the bathroom sink. I had no reason not to believe him.

After Susan finished, they asked me what I knew. I told them I only knew about the one incident that had happened more than a year before. "I thought it was all behind us," I said.

At the trial, Judy Clarke of Susan's defense team asked Ms. Ward if Susan was anxious to repeat the information about the sexual abuse. She emphasized that she wasn't. "Sexual abuse is a very difficult issue to talk about," she stated, then explained that it is so "because children feel they have betrayed so many people. They feel they've betrayed the perpetrator....She felt that she had betrayed her mother. And also that there was a pos-

The Illusion Shattered

sibility it would go public.

"Even as adults," Ms. Ward noted, "it's very difficult....to discuss their sex lives. It is more difficult for a child to discuss these issues, especially when they are filled with so much guilt....She was very scared. She was very anxious. She did not want anything to happen to her family. She only wanted the sexual abuse to stop."

After the meeting, Jenny Ward talked to Susan and me. She told us what Bev did was a criminal offense and that Susan would have to make a decision about filing charges against him. She informed us that David Taylor, the detective who met with us, would come to our home the next day to talk with Susan and me about pressing charges.

Jenny Ward also talked with Bev. She lined out his options. Either he would have to leave our home; or Susan would have to leave and stay in a safe place, perhaps with a relative or family friend. A third possibility was foster care. Bev quickly agreed to leave. He said he didn't want to disrupt Susan's life further. That afternoon he packed some clothes and went to his mother's home. He let her think we had separated. I told Moe Bev was staying at his mother's, that it was a temporary thing, and not to say anything to anyone. I don't think he knew then about Susan and Bev. I certainly wasn't going to tell him.

The possibility of filing charges against Bev overwhelmed me. All evening I thought about it. Susan and I talked about what would happen if he got indicted and what the public exposure would do to our family. I even woke up during the night, thinking about how Susan would look if this went public, what people would say, how a lawyer would rip her apart on the witness stand, that Bev could get a prison sentence. I thought about what a messy trial would do to our family and to Bev's mother, his aunts, and his three daughters, all living in Union. I could not put our families through that shame and humiliation. Bev had done a terrible thing, but I still had feelings for him. I loved him and hated him at the same time. By morning, I had decided that I wanted to take care of the situation through counseling, without criminal prosecution.

Even so, I told Susan the decision was up to her. I would

stand by her whatever she decided. There was no question with her. She did not want to press charges. She was absolutely terrified at the prospect of things going public and her family being torn apart.

When the detective met with us in the afternoon, he carefully explained what would be involved in pressing charges. Seated opposite Susan in our den, he looked her in the eye and asked if she wanted to press charges.

Susan turned to me and asked, "What do you want me to do?"

"I don't want to prosecute," I replied, "but it's up to you."

She turned back to the detective and said firmly, "No, I don't."

The detective pressed the point, saying, "Are you sure? That is your decision?"

Susan said firmly, "Yes."

He then asked me, "Linda, do you want to prosecute?"

I replied, "No, I don't for a lot of reasons."

I know my refusal to press charges could be construed as pressure on Susan, but the bottom line was she didn't want to prosecute, either. She would have made that decision, even if I had said I wanted to prosecute. I did what I thought was best for Susan. The alternative might have been just as bad, or worse.

After the meeting with the detective, I told Susan I should divorce Bev for what he did. She broke down and cried. "Please don't divorce him," she pleaded. "He's the only father I've ever known."

Her plea jarred me. The only father she had known? How could she possibly feel that way about him now? I was determined to divorce Bev. But, given Susan's reaction, I decided to wait until things settled down.

Naturally, Jenny Ward was extremely disappointed when told about Susan's decision. At the trial, Judy Clarke asked her why she felt so strongly that Bev should be prosecuted. She replied, "Because I have a child that has said to me, and law enforcement has heard this child say, 'My stepfather has sexually abused me by placing his hands on my breasts, by engaging in open mouth French kissing {which is a form of sexual exploitation} and by him placing my hand on his genitalia.' That is child sexual abuse. It is criminal in nature. The child said it. The perpetrator admitted it. That's a case.".

Judy Clarke led Jenny Ward through a series of questions designed to determine why Bev wasn't prosecuted. She began with these two: "Is it safe to say that Beverly Russell was a very prominent man in the county? Very wealthy?" and "Could you just tell us what you know about his connections in the county at the time?"

Ms. Ward answered, "I think most people would know everybody in Union County, at least know of them. And he had some place of business. Came from a very well respected family. Was very prominent in politics."

Ms. Ward passed over Judy Clarke's suggestion that Bev was "very wealthy," possibly because it wasn't accurate. Bev's family could be described as prominent because of political connections, his uncle being a former governor of South Carolina and a federal judge. But he wasn't wealthy then and isn't wealthy now.

Because Susan refused to press charges, DSS quickly took action to monitor the situation. Ms. Ward obtained a family court order regarding the sexual abuse that made it possible for the proceedings to be confidential. The family court order labeled the offense physical abuse or neglect, instead of sexual abuse, because there had been no physical penetration. And the order was sealed.

At the trial, Ms. Clarke asked if it was typical for such an order to be sealed. Ms. Ward said it was "the only order I have had sealed in twenty years. But I didn't care. The only thing I wanted was help for the family. I didn't want it to be a public information."

Under the family-court provision, Bev formally agreed to move out of our home. The three of us were required to have family and individual counseling. We chose to go to Dr. Heatherly again.

During Bev's and my counseling sessions with Dr. Heatherly, I tried to get an answer about why Susan hadn't defended herself. I knew something was wrong with Bev, but something was wrong with Susan, too. I needed to know what was wrong with her, so I could deal with the problem. I could divorce Bev and get him out of my life, but I couldn't divorce Susan.

I showed Dr. Heatherly the suicide note Susan wrote when she was thirteen. He read it hurriedly and handed it back to me. When I kept pushing him to tell me what was wrong with Susan, he snapped, "Linda, Susan is in love with Bev."

My mouth flew open. In love with Bev? *Oh, my God,* I thought. *What a mess. Now what am I going to do? Susan is begging me not to get a divorce, and she thinks she's in love with Bev.* It was crazy!

Since then I've learned that it is common for incest victims to think of their relationship to the perpetrator as an affair. It is a defensive strategy to make the behavior seem less offensive.

At the trial, Dr. Halleck gave his assessment of the situation. "What is striking," he said, "with regard to this whole event that happened with her stepfather is that she feels almost fully responsible. And indeed, in many ways her family did treat her as though she was responsible."

His assessment was not completely accurate, as far as I am concerned. I put on Bev the major responsibility for the sexual abuse, but I did place some responsibility on Susan. She was sixteen. She could have defended herself. That was the reason I tried to get Dr. Heatherly focused on her. Maybe he thought I was trying to defend Bev, but I wasn't. I needed to understand Susan. I wanted to know why she would go along with the abuse.

****

My birthday came up less than a month after Bev moved out. Susan wanted to give me a big birthday party. We both knew Bev had to be invited, because none of my side of the family knew he had moved out. But we had to get permission from DSS to invite him. Jenny Ward said it was okay if other people were around. With that okay, Susan called Bev and worked everything out. All the family came. Susan didn't say anything about the situation; Moe didn't say anything; and Bev and I cer-

The Illusion Shattered

tainly didn't. Everybody had a great time. I was just there.

After several months of counseling, DSS made an appointment to talk with us about Bev's moving back in. Jenny Ward talked with the three of us individually and together and checked for certain things. She wanted to see Susan's bedroom and our bedroom and how close they were. She told Susan she should lock her door at night and not go down the hall by our bedroom nor use the bathroom adjacent to it. Shortly after her visit, we got formal notification that DSS was satisfied it was time to get our family back together.

When Bev returned home, he told his mother we had resolved our problems. I kept struggling over whether or not to divorce him. Every time I said anything to Susan about going in that direction, she cried and begged me not to do that. I agonized over what was best for her. Was I going to run Bev off and have Susan think she was in love with him? If Bev were away for good, how would I ever know what was going on? Would Susan sneak around to be with him? How would I keep up with the two of them? I finally decided the best way I could protect her was for me to have both of them under the same roof. At least I would know where they were. I always had made sure I knew where Susan was, and that would continue with a special vigilance. I did intend to divorce Bev at some point but only when I felt Susan was all right. In the meantime, I would make do.

For nearly two years, I was like a prisoner, controlled by other people. My life revolved around Susan and Bev's schedules. I made sure I knew where one of them was at all times. I did my shopping when I knew Susan was in school. The two of them appeared to get things back in order. From everything I could see, Bev seemed to be very sorry for his big mistake and never intended to repeat that behavior. Our lives went on, and I didn't talk with anyone about the struggles I was constantly in.

Interestingly, Susan's DSS file was discovered missing before the trial began. In addition, the card that contained the name and address information on the family and the case control log, which is where a running sequence of reports related to the case were recorded, were both missing. When Judy Clarke asked Ms. Ward if it was normal that all of those things would be missing when a file is lost, she said it wasn't.

A big investigation was undertaken by SLED (State Law Enforcement Division) into the missing files. I personally think politics were involved. The same reason the family court order was originally sealed was the same reason the file turned up missing. Bev was a big-time Republican.

****

Bev and I tried to go on as usual. We really couldn't communicate, though. We avoided talking about anything important. My rage toward him constantly seethed just below the surface, although there were times when I could put it aside and almost love him again.

Susan didn't seem to notice the tension between Bev and me. She was pleasant and easy to get along with. She stayed very busy, working at an after-school job and being involved in all kinds of activities at school. She was getting good grades and making plans to go to college. She did all the normal things a girl her age did. She went to proms, winter balls, ball games, and hung out with the crowd at the stadium and other places. She was always home on time. I often got compliments from her customers at Winn-Dixie about what a sweet person she was. In her senior year, she was named friendliest girl in the senior class. Few people knew about her troubles. For most people, she seemed like a happy, outgoing, well-adjusted young woman. I wasn't completely relaxed about her, but it seemed she had pulled through the unfortunate situation.

Bev stayed busy, too. He started studying to get his broker's license. After many hours of intense study, he completed the requirements and was working for a business in Spartanburg. I managed the store, working every other day and keeping my housework caught up on the other days.

I drove Susan to school, picked her up afterwards, and took her to her job at Winn-Dixie. I began to get suspicious of her relationship to the store manager. She was seventeen; he was over forty and married. When I saw them talking at the store, the way they related was suspiciously friendly. It all came out in the open one Saturday morning. Susan got up early and said she was going shopping. It was too early to go shopping. "Wait and let me get dressed and go with you," I suggested. Trapped, she admitted she was going to meet the married man.

I tried to reason with her about getting involved with someone like that. I told her it was wrong to go with a married man; and besides that, he was too old for her. She wasn't persuaded. Nothing made sense to me. She said she didn't think people should have sex outside marriage, but here she was going with a married man. She defended the relationship by saying they were just friends; they weren't having sex. Her reasoning boggled the mind. Susan didn't know it, but I had been there. During the three years that Harry and I were separated, I got involved with a married man. I knew it was wrong and didn't intend for it to happen; I just gradually fell into the relationship. I am sorry it happened and have never repeated that mistake. I envisioned nothing but sadness for Susan if she continued this type of behavior.

Recently, I heard a psychologist on TV make the observation that daughters of fathers who commit suicide often tend to be promiscuous. And at the trial, Jenny Ward said that one of the results of sexual abuse is promiscuity. "You will have multiple relationships," she said, noting that they usually aren't lasting relationships because the person is seeking so much love and attention and approval. "Oftentimes," she noted, "you will have mental health issues; depression, psychosis, depending upon the severity of the abuse."

It is horrifying to realize that Susan had two strikes against her, and I didn't know it. I had no idea then what bearing these unfortunate circumstances had on her long-term behavior, but I saw the result right before my eyes. I was frustrated that I couldn't do anything about the situation. There seemed to be no way I could control her behavior.

Soon after our conversation, Susan said she wanted to go back to see Dr. Heatherly. I wondered how he was going to handle this new development. Would he wish he had listened to me when I was trying so hard to understand Susan? The counseling did little to change things. Susan continued her relationship with the manager, only this time she tried to hide it from Bev and me.

Early in 1988, Bev threw himself into politics. At the urging of friends in the Republican Party, he ran for the State House of Representatives. In October, shortly before the election in November, Matthew, my second grandchild, was born. Scotty called me around one in the morning to proudly tell me. About a half hour later, he called back. Something was wrong with the baby. Two-thirds of his blood was missing, and he was on the way to surgery. The doctors were afraid his liver had burst. I told Scotty I would be there as soon as possible. I woke Bev up and told him we needed to go to the hospital.

The Bev I married would have been praying with his eyes open during that ride. The Bev behind the wheel talked about putting up political signs along the new highway we traveled down. I didn't care about political signs. I cared about my grandchild who might already be dead. I prayed all the way to the hospital, "Please, God, let the baby be okay."

The doctor came into the waiting room shortly after we arrived at the hospital. The surgery was over. Matt's liver was enlarged but had not burst. He would be okay. Soon after that scare, I planted an azalea bush in my backyard. I call it my Matthew bush. Every time I look at it, I think of Matt and thank God that he is a happy, healthy, active eleven-year-old.

Susan graduated from high school in the spring of 1989. She had taken all college prep courses, was a member of the national Beta Club, and graduated with a "B" average. She had been accepted at Winthrop College and wanted to go there, but I didn't feel she was ready to leave home. I talked her into going to the USC campus in Union for a year. She did that; but after that year, she wanted to work a year before returning to college. I talked my head off, but she held firm. She wanted to buy a car. She went to work on the third shift of a local knitting mill and continued to work part time at Winn-Dixie. With $2500 from the estate of Harry's father, she saved enough to make a down payment on a burgundy Mazda; and she paid it off in a year.

The Illusion Shattered

I worried about Susan constantly, not for any one reason, but because of everything that had gone on in her life and because I hadn't gotten any adequate answers about what was wrong with her. Without any specific warning that something was severely wrong, she came into our bedroom one morning around two and woke me up. She was crying and scared. She wanted me to take her to the hospital, because she had taken two bottles of extra strength, over-the-counter pain medicine. The night before, she had gone to Foster Park and started taking pills as she walked around the lake. She wanted to die. At 2:00 a.m. she changed her mind.

Bev and I rushed her to the emergency room at the hospital in Union. As I stood in the emergency room beside her and looked down at her lying on the bed, I thought, *How does Susan get herself into these situations? What is so wrong that she would want to kill herself?*

Later, she told me why. She wanted to die because she had messed up again. She was still involved with the married man. To make matters worse, she had gone to bed with a former boyfriend who worked with the married man. Actually, she went to his apartment to talk about her involvement with the married man, because she was ashamed. She didn't intend for anything to happen, but one thing led to another. The next day, Susan told the married man what had happened and asked him to forgive her. He was too angry to talk about it. She was terrified she would lose both men. That's when she decided to kill herself.

The doctor recommended that Susan be transferred to Spartanburg Regional Hospital to have her stomach pumped. I rode in the ambulance with her, and Bev drove the car. The doctor in Spartanburg determined that she had taken more pills than originally thought, and he immediately put her in ICU. They were afraid of liver damage.

When the doctor talked to Bev and me, he said Susan needed to go to the psychiatric ward for evaluation when she was able. I told him I didn't want Susan going to a psychiatric ward, that I would rather get her an appointment with Dr. Heatherly. He rather sharply said that she needed help and, if it were his daughter, she would go to the psychiatric ward. I asked Susan what she wanted to do. She said she would go to the hospital as the doctor suggested.

We visited her every day, and she called us several times a day. For the most part, only family members and her closest friends visited her. When they were there, she laughed and talked like nothing was wrong. In spite of her cheerfulness, though, the notes from the night nurse painted a very different picture of her mood. One time she had an anxiety attack late at night. She told the nurse what she was really upset about was that she was in love with her stepfather, and he told her he had just used her.

While Susan was still in the hospital, I called her doctor and more or less demanded that he talk with me. I told him I wanted to know why Susan would try to commit suicide just because something went wrong in her life and what I could do to help. I also emphasized that I wanted them to help her while she was there. He was rather nonchalant about the situation but finally agreed to make an appointment. When I arrived for the appointment, a social worker greeted me. The doctor was occupied elsewhere. She talked in rather vague terms and basically gave me no help. I concluded from the conversation that the doctors were not going to discuss anything about Susan with me, because she was now eighteen, an adult in the eyes of the law.

The next thing I knew, Susan was coming home, with no recommendation of further treatment. It was not until the trial that I learned she had been diagnosed with overreaction to stress. She was never given any medication for depression. The therapist's notes indicate treatment was terminated because she said she wasn't depressed any more. I was shocked that they would release her, simply because she said she wasn't depressed anymore, given her medical history. We had spent a lot of money and heartache; and when it was over, I didn't know anymore than when she went in.

Susan resumed her work schedule and going out with friends. Bev and I rocked along in our marriage. To the outsider, little had changed. Bev smiled all the time and seemed happy. When I went to church with him, I had to sit there and watch him sing in the choir and afterward relate to all those people who thought he was a great guy. I remember reading in the church bulletin, "Please remain standing in reverence until the choir leaves." I couldn't stand in reverence and watch Bev leave, without thinking what a hypocrite he was. I would turn around and get my purse. I gradually quit going with him at all. One time he even quit going because I wouldn't go. That was amazing, because going to church for him was as regular as getting dressed in the morning. I told him, "Look, you go everywhere else without me. If you want to go to church without me, you can." He finally started back.

Sometime during 1989, I was sitting in the store office doing paperwork. A childhood friend came in. I hadn't seen him for at least twenty-five years, but I had heard he was a minister. He had a sense of urgency about needing to talk with me, if I weren't too busy. We chatted a few minutes about things in the past, then he said, "Linda, I don't know why, but the Lord has sent me to you."

"Why would he do that?" I asked.

He replied, "I learned a long time ago not to question when God laid it upon my heart to do something. I have tried for months to get you off my mind, and I finally gave in and here I am."

Silently I questioned, *Why has the Lord sent this man to me?*

He asked if I were a Christian and if I had been saved. I replied that I was a Christian and, yes, I had been saved. We talked for a few minutes longer, then he went on his way.

Left alone, my thoughts soared to the future. *Was this a warning that something was going to happen to me or someone close to me?*

I had long ago asked God's forgiveness for the foolish affair with the married man. That was behind me. I felt that I was a good person, so why had God sent the man my way? I wondered about his visit for a long time.

Not long after that, a male customer came in when I was alone in the store. I don't remember his name, what he looked like, what he was shopping for, or even if he bought anything. I only remember talking with him across the counter. He told me about a time he almost drowned. While playing underwater, he suddenly began to feel that he could stay there forever. He said everything was so pretty and peaceful and that he had the most pleasant feeling. Then something told him he needed to go up. Later, he went to his doctor because of a lingering headache. When he told the doctor about being in the water, the doctor said he had almost drowned. He looked at me and said, "I'm not afraid of drowning anymore." I had related this conversation to Susan and commented that it was an easy death. I wondered if this was the reason she chose water for her suicide attempt and the children's deaths.

I think the Lord sent these two men to prepare me for what was to come. Obviously God knows what I'm going through, and cares.

6

Susan and David

Susan was in high school and working part time at Winn-Dixie when she first met David Smith. He was a couple of years ahead of her in school. She was attracted to his good looks and outgoing personality. When they first met, he was engaged to a girl named Christy. After they started going steady, he continued to date Christy. Every time Susan insisted he choose between her and Christy, he asked her to be patient. He said Christy would kill herself if he broke up with her. I didn't think much about this going back and forth, passing it off as teenage things. Little did I realize David was playing games with Susan, even then.

Since Susan and David worked at the same place, they usually got together after work, and Susan drove her car home. I can remember only a few times that he came to our house to pick her up. So, we really didn't get to know him. And we didn't know how serious they were.

In early February 1991, we found out. That evening, Bev and I were in the den watching TV, stretched out comfortably in our recliners. Susan came in from work with David. They sat down on the sofa, looking very serious. She said they had something to discuss with us. I suspected the worst—that she was pregnant.

Making every effort to remain calm, I asked what they wanted to talk about. Susan froze. David blurted out, "Susan's pregnant." The confirmation hit like a thunder bolt.

I suppose I looked at them dumbfounded for a moment. Susan wanted to marry this boy I hardly knew. And she was so young, only nineteen. She was still doing young-girl things, like staying all night back and forth with Donna and Leigh.

Trying to conceal my shock, I calmly asked, "What are you going to do about it?"

My Daughter Susan Smith

"We're gonna get married," Susan said, forcing a half-smile. David stared past us blankly. Bev looked away, leaving me to deal with the situation.

From that point, Susan and I did most of the talking. I guess the only other thing David said was that they were going to get their marriage license on Valentine's Day. That didn't surprise me. Holidays have always been important to Susan.

"When do you plan to get married?" I asked.

Susan's reply still rings in my ears: "March 15, because that's my daddy's birthday."

Her daddy's birthday? She wanted to get married on the birthday of a father she barely remembered.

"That soon?" I questioned, trying to find a way to get them to move the date past March 15, so we could get to know this person she wanted to marry. And I envisioned her decision bringing back sad memories for both Harry's and my family. To be reminded of that tragedy at what should be a happy occasion would be painful indeed. It was immediately obvious that the date was not negotiable.

I asked where they planned to get married. Susan said she wanted a church wedding. I asked where they were going to live. They planned to live with David's great grandmother, Mrs. Malone. The more we talked, the more it became apparent she and David had talked a lot about what they were going to do.

In his book, David tells his reaction to what he describes as the first time he had spent "any real time with the Russells." He said he almost burst out laughing from nervousness and the strangeness of everything. He noted that there was no screaming and yelling, but he could tell he wasn't exactly "Linda's dream for her daughter."

I can't say I was excited about the match, but it was mainly because David had made no effort to get to know us. I knew about his family but didn't know any of them personally. I remembered they caused quite a stir when they moved to Union when David was a child. His parents were Union's first hippies. Their son Billy, who was in elementary school, had long red hair. The son of a friend of mine who was in school with Billy said everybody talked about his hair and the hippie family. I had seen David's father around town and knew he was a meter reader at one time and that he once bought or rented an appliance from Bev's store.

The next day Susan got a home pregnancy test. She said she knew she was barely pregnant and didn't want to go to the doctor. One time the test would be positive, then negative. Finally, at my suggestion, she quit fooling around with that thing and went to the doctor. She had a big smile on her face when she returned.

"I'm pregnant!" she announced excitedly, as she came in the den where I was anxiously waiting for the report. "Now we know for sure. And can you believe it, Mama? That nurse asked me if I wanted to have an abortion! I can't believe she would even ask such a thing. There is no way I would ever have an abortion. This is a baby, and I already love it."

Susan and I had many conversations about her getting married. In the beginning, I asked her if she really wanted to marry David. She replied, "Yes, this is what I want." I told her there were a lot worse things that could happen to her than having a baby and not being married. I urged her to be sure this was what she wanted to do, because it was a lifetime commitment. I assured her we would stand behind her whatever decision she made.

We talked about David's commitment to the marriage. I asked if he had completely broken off his relationship with Christy. She said he had, and he really wanted to have a lasting marriage and wanted to build a home for the baby. She was so sentimental, so sure they would live happily ever after.

Although I was shocked about the suddenness of Susan's decision, I saw my chance to get out of my comfort-zone marriage. As soon as she was married, I planned to check on what I could do to make a living.

In the meantime, we all concentrated on wedding plans. Susan, Bev, and I agreed on an amount to spend; whatever was left would be their wedding gift. I tried to talk Susan out of a church wedding. I told her something simple with family and a few friends would leave her and David more to get started on. She was adamant. She wanted a church wedding but would keep it simple, with only one attendant. Donna would be her maid of honor; David's father would stand up with him, in place of his brother Danny, who was in the hospital, gravely ill with Crohn's disease.

We went to a bridal shop in Spartanburg to look for a wedding dress. We found a satin candlelight gown that Susan loved and we all agreed looked beautiful on her. A friend of mine who went with us was going to direct the wedding.

David claimed in his book that I didn't think Susan should have a pure white wedding dress because she was pregnant. That is absolutely untrue. Susan made the choice herself, not me. She selected off-white, because the shade looked better on her. She thought the stark white made her look washed out.

Susan made arrangements with Ruth Wood, the florist at Winn-Dixie, to do the flowers. She asked her first cousin Debbie to play the organ. David's distant cousin Mia and a young man she sang duets with were to be the vocalists.

Bev fell in with the wedding plans in his enthusiastic, extroverted, winsome way. But I didn't want him to give Susan away. As far as I was concerned, he had forfeited any claim to that privilege. I wanted her to ask her brother Moe. But she wanted Bev, and I didn't want to cause a big argument over it.

At the time, I thought David attended Bogansville Methodist, which was near his great grandmother's home. Mrs. Malone was a longtime member there. I suggested to Susan that it would be good to get married in that church, if they were going to live in the community and attend church there. I thought it would be a good foundation for them to build their marriage on. They agreed; so the ceremony was held there instead of Buffalo Methodist, where Susan had always gone. As it turned out, David didn't attend much.

David's brother Danny died less than two weeks before the wedding. He was only twenty-two. Susan went to the funeral with David. Bev, Moe, Scotty, and I also attended the service in the chapel at the funeral home. The minister at the local Jehovah's Witness Kingdom Hall, where David's mother attended, was in charge. We also attended the interment at Bogansville Methodist Church and a memorial service that was held the fol-

Susan and David

lowing Sunday night at the church. That's where we met David's sister Becky, his parents, Dave and Barbara, and Mrs. Malone.

After the memorial service, we stopped by Mrs. Malone's house. As we were sitting in the den, David's father pointed to a picture of "The Last Supper" hanging on the wall, then turned to me and asked, "Linda, do you remember when I had long hair like that?"

I laughed and said, "That long hair was probably the only thing you had in common with those men in the picture." He laughingly agreed.

After that friendly exchange, he asked, "Don't you remember when I worked at Wambel and wore my hair in a pony tail?"

I politely said, "I guess so"; but I barely remembered he even worked there. We worked in different areas of the company.

David tells a false story in his book about his father's employment at Wambel. He claims that, when his father reported to the personnel office and announced that he had a job there, I responded, "No, you don't." From that point on, he says, he and I didn't get along. That event never happened. I never worked in the personnel office. I was in the industrial engineering department as systems analyst and then became secretary to the manager of the company. I don't remember liking or disliking David's father. In fact, I don't remember relating to him. It is true he stuck out in Union because of his long hair. David acknowledges that fact, affectionately calling him "a freak" and saying he had hair all the way down to the middle of his back.

Susan asked David if he wanted to postpone the wedding because of Danny's death. He said he didn't, that they should go ahead with their plans. When she asked him about a rehearsal party, he said he wasn't about to ask his father to pay for it, because he already had gone to the expense of renting a tuxedo. Susan was upset; but I suggested she let it go, that Bev and I would take everybody out to eat.

The wedding took place as scheduled on March 15, Harry Vaughan's birthday. I was able to put that fact out of my mind, because birthdays aren't that big a deal to me. It was Susan's wedding day, and I was excited about that. No one else said anything about the date, not even Harry's family. We all enthusiastically joined in the celebration. The wedding turned out to be simple, sweet, and pretty. I thought Susan was a beautiful bride in her long gown with a chapel train. She was so happy! Donna was beautiful in her long, peach satin dress. Scotty and Moe were ushers. Bev's daughter Tami was at the guest registry. Leigh served the punch that her mother Hedy made.

All the relatives and friends were so happy for Susan. Walt Garner lightheartedly, yet seriously, told David he better be good to Susan.

After a honeymoon in Gatlinburg, Tennessee, Susan and David moved into Mrs. Malone's house. Susan didn't like the living arrangement at all. She liked the old country home, and she thought Mrs. Malone was a sweet person; but Mrs. Malone's home wasn't hers. She wasn't free to change curtains, replace wallpaper, move furniture—all the things a woman wants to do to a house. And she was homesick. I told her she would get used to being there, and it would become more and more her home as our home became less and less home to her.

Shortly after Susan married, I told her it was time to clean out the teenage junk in her room. "You're married now," I said, "and it's time to throw away old love letters and other mementos." Those things, I thought, had no place in her marriage, and she agreed. Susan is such a pack rat. She threw away several thirty-gallon trash bags full of stuff.

With David, it was another matter. The entire time Susan lived at Mrs. Malone's, he never removed pictures of his former girlfriends. There they were, on top of the TV. Susan asked him to take them down, but he said they weren't his. They belonged to Moner, as he called his great grandmother. Susan certainly couldn't ask Mrs. Malone to remove the pictures from her own house; so they stayed where she could see them every day. She told me David also kept all his love letters from a former girlfriend. She asked him to destroy them, but he refused. He even continued to carry Christy's pictures in his wallet until after Michael was born. For a young lady, barely more than a girl, who desperately needed a man's love, this callous behavior was a terrible jolt.

David's mother left his father barely a month after Susan and David married. His father continued to live nearby in one of the little houses Moner owned. A few weeks later, David called Susan from work. He had been calling his father but got no answer. He wanted Susan to check on him. He knew his father was still having a hard time dealing with Danny's death and was depressed about his marriage breakup.

Susan found Dave on the bed, semi-conscious from an overdose of pills. She called 911 and then David and me, extremely upset. Here was a young woman, whose father committed suicide, who had tried to commit suicide herself, and now witnessed an attempt by her father-in-law. Later, she told me what a horrifying experience it was.

Dave ended up in the psychiatric ward at Spartanburg regional hospital where he met his future wife. He told Susan and David he would have shot himself, but he couldn't remember where he put his gun.

Things rocked along. Susan and David put Michael's nursery furniture on layaway and began preparing a room for the baby. They put up paneling in what previously was his grandmother's bedroom and decorated the walls with Mickey Mouse figures. Against my advice about putting money in someone else's house, they went into debt and put new carpet on the floor. They were so proud of that nursery.

Susan began telling me about pesky things David did. One day he wouldn't talk to her. She said he did that all the time. "He just sits, staring into space, and won't say a word," she lamented. Each time it happened, she begged him to tell her what was wrong, but he wouldn't say anything. I finally advised her to stop asking. "The more you ask, the more you reinforce his behavior," I told her. "The more you beg, the more he knows it bothers you, and the more he'll keep it up. The next time he acts like that, just ignore him. If he wants to talk, listen."

On another occasion when Susan stopped by, she was as blue as I had seen her. "I'm really hurt, Mama," she said, choking back the tears. "David said the only reason he married me was because I was pregnant."

My Daughter Susan Smith

I angrily pointed toward the bedroom and said, "Susan, go look in that mirror. You're beautiful. You could have done better than David Smith. Don't ever let him make you feel like he did you a favor by marrying you. If he ever throws that up to you again, look him straight in the eye and tell him that works both ways. Ask him why he thinks you married him." I never did tell Susan, but I learned from a friend that David told his co-workers at Winn-Dixie the same thing.

Even with all the little aggravations, Susan and David were both excited about the baby. On October 10, 1991, David took her to the hospital. She called just before they left. I was out of my mind with excitement and immediately started calling family members and friends.

When my children were born, I stayed first in the labor room, then the delivery room, and finally a hospital room. When Susan was admitted, she stayed in one room during labor, birth, and the hospital stay. Her visitors were allowed to stay in the room until just before delivery. Along with David's father and stepmother, most of Susan's family, the Garners, and Donna's fiancé, Mitch, were there waiting for the new member of the family.

I hadn't planned to stay in the room for the birth, but when everyone was leaving, I didn't want to go. I had this intense desire to make sure Susan was okay. I asked the doctor if I could sit in a chair in the corner of the room. He said that was fine with him if it was okay with Susan and David. They both said it was fine.

Just as Michael was about to be born, the nurse said, "Come over here. Don't you want to see?" I really didn't, but I went over and watched the delivery. Michael was a big, beautiful baby!

I had no inkling David objected to my being in the birth room, but his displeasure came out in a recent conversation with Susan. I remarked that, in a lot of respects, her trial came down to David getting revenge on me. "Susan," I asked, "what did I ever do to make David hate me so?"

She replied, "Mama, it was because you stayed in the birth room when Michael was born. David was so mad he threatened

Susan and David

not to let you see the baby." He didn't think I should have been in there if his dad wasn't, that I should have stayed in the waiting room, too. I don't even remember that his dad wanted to be in there. Even so, how can a person relate to reasoning like that?

I don't think there has ever been a mother who was any more proud of her baby or loved him more than Susan did Michael. He was a wonder to her. She said she was a little scared about her abilities in caring for a new baby. I told her a mother's instincts would take over. She would do just fine.

She called a few days after getting home from the hospital. David was at work. She sounded worn out. I offered to pick her up and bring her to our house to spend the day with me. That sounded great to her. When she got to my house, I told her I would take care of the baby and suggested that she take a long, relaxing bath and go to bed and sleep as long as she wanted. She needed that break, and I enjoyed having her and Michael at my house.

Members of our family and the Garners went often to Mrs. Malone's to see Susan and the new baby. Mrs. Malone was always very friendly and never seemed to mind all of us visiting. Due to her age, she seldom left her house. She enjoyed the company, and we all enjoyed visiting with her, especially my mother.

David found a way to busy himself elsewhere when we came to visit. He continued the pattern he set before they married and never made any effort to be part of the family. I always felt that he thought I would go away if he ignored me, but he didn't know how much I loved Susan and Michael.

I think one reason David kept his distance was because he was jealous of our close-knit family. He also may have been distant because his commitment to the marriage was tentative. At the trial, Dr. Andrews read a card Susan wrote to David that reflected the growing turmoil in their marriage at this early stage. Michael was less than three weeks old. She wrote the letter after a fight. The card itself read, "I have everything I need to be happy. I have you."

The note she wrote on the card went like this:

"Dear David,

"I have been so miserable since I left home today. I feel as
though we were just falling apart, that our marriage is falling
apart. I'm really scared, too. David, do you still love me? Sometimes I feel like you don't. For instance, we haven't really kissed
since I came home from the hospital. Every time I go to kiss
you, you act like you don't want me to. I feel like I have to beg
you sometimes just for a kiss. You really hurt my feelings when
you turn away when I go to kiss you. Also, I feel like I can't
talk to you anymore. I have noticed that whenever I want to talk
seriously about something, you say you are tired, and I never
know when you are kidding. But even if you are kidding, we
still don't talk. Things have really changed. I feel so distant
from you and I used to never did. David, I truly love you with
all my heart, and I have since the day we met. I don't want to
lose you, but I feel like I am. I feel like you are unhappy with
me, and that scares the hell out of me. When I married you, I
felt in my heart that we would be together a lifetime. That we
would grow old together and take care of each other until the
day we died. Now I'm beginning to believe that was just a
dream. I really do want things to be okay between us. I want
you to tell me if you feel the way that I think that you do. I
hope that I was wrong about some of the things that I said, but
only you know. David, let's please sit down and talk and really
let our feelings out, our true feelings. Well, I guess I'll go. I
love you, Susan. PS, I'm really sorry about today. I hate it so
much when we fight."

Dr. Andrews made some observations about the problems in
Susan and David's marriage. She said: "They had the kind of
problems that young couples typically have. They argued about
money, about some of their differences. But some of the text of
their arguments centered around Susan's dependence upon her
mother. There was a conflict developing between her mother
and her husband that became pretty tough after a while."

I knew David resented the fact that Susan talked to me a lot

Susan and David

and came by our house often. What was I going to do—tell her not to call or come by? The only reason I ever got involved in their marriage was because Susan called and asked me what she should do. When it came to anything said about David, she was always the one who brought up the subject. The advice I gave was meant to help her stand on her own two feet, to defend herself against David's cruelty. When she told me something about David, she would always say, "Now, Mama, don't say anything to David." I never did confront him about anything she said in confidence.

I wanted Susan to feel free to come by anytime she wanted. I knew she hated to be alone; she had always been like that. She often came by when David was at work, simply because she didn't want to be alone and because he seldom would come with her. At the trial, Dr. Halleck emphasized that Susan had a fear of being alone and that she got depressed when she was alone.

David was friends with a young, unmarried female who worked at Winn-Dixie. She was expecting a baby. The two of them talked on the telephone a lot. Susan told me David expected her to understand that they were just friends. He even saw nothing wrong with sitting in the bedroom and talking to her on the phone while Susan was in the den rocking their baby and keeping Mrs. Malone company. She wondered how David would feel if she were talking to a male friend while he was rocking the baby. I told her a married man didn't have any business talking with another female on the phone so much. Susan couldn't get David to stop, so she finally went to Winn-Dixie and told the girl she didn't appreciate her talking with her husband all the time and that she needed to find another friend to talk with. The girl evidently had good sense. She told David not to call her anymore.

Susan always looked forward to Christmas, but 1991 was even more special because of Michael. She loved to decorate a Christmas tree and had helped decorate ours since she was old enough to hang an ornament. We usually argued over how to decorate it. She liked velvet bows; I didn't. I preferred white lights and the balls all the same color. She liked a lot of different colors. One thing we agreed on was big Christmas trees. We always had a big, fresh cedar, because it smelled like Christmas.

Susan called to make sure we wouldn't go for a tree until she could come along. We went on a Sunday while David was working and picked out a huge tree. Michael slept in the portable crib while we decorated. We laughed about each of us having a tree. Now I could have mine the way I wanted it, and she could have hers the way she wanted it. The last tree we decorated together was in 1993, ten months before the tragedy. I haven't put up another one.

I knew Susan loved to buy Christmas gifts for everyone, but I knew she couldn't afford to do that this year, because she and David were having it hard financially. She didn't go back to work at Winn-Dixie because of the erratic hours. She was feeling down about their situation. I told her we were all adults. We would feel bad if they bought gifts when we knew they were struggling. In fact, I made her promise not to buy us anything. She didn't stick with her promise. She bought us one of the packaged jars of jelly that show up on store shelves every year at Christmas time. Later, she told me David spent over three hundred dollars on his father. He opened a charge account at Sears and bought him new tennis shoes, jeans, and I don't know what else. He said his father was alone and didn't have anyone to buy for him. Susan said, "Mama, I felt so bad about spending all that money on David's father, and all I could afford to get you was a ten-dollar package of jelly." I told her not to worry about it. I didn't tell her I thought his father should have been ashamed to take all that from them when they were having a hard time.

Shortly after Christmas, Susan and I were talking on the phone. I asked where Michael was. She said he was lying on the bed. I warned her about leaving him there because he could roll off. She laughed, "Mama, you worry all the time. Michael's not going to fall. I'm standing right here watching him." Momentarily, she screamed and dropped the phone. I could hear Michael crying, David shouting, and Susan crying, "Let me have him."

Susan and David

Susan came back to the phone crying hysterically, "Mama, Michael fell off the bed and David won't let me have him. He said it was my fault he fell." I said, "Susan, listen to me. Even if David won't let you have him, go look for bruises on his head. Then check to make sure no bones are broken. If he has a bad bruise on his head, don't let him go to sleep. Call the doctor." She said she would and hung up.

I waited a few minutes for her to call back. No call. I couldn't stand to wait, so I drove the twenty miles out there. When I arrived, Susan had already left to take Michael to the doctor. Mrs. Malone said, "I felt so sorry for Susan. She was crying and trying to get David to let her have the baby. He kept turning his back and wouldn't even let her see him. I told him to give her the baby. She wouldn't let that happen any more than you would."

I noticed David in the kitchen and asked him why he didn't go with Susan to the doctor. He said he had to go to work.

I stayed there until Susan returned. Thankfully, Michael wasn't hurt. Susan said, "Well, Mama, that's another time I should have listened to you and didn't. But I'll never leave him on the bed alone again."

It was getting harder and harder for Susan to cope with all the stress in her marriage. She told me David came in from work late one night in February, and they began to argue. She threatened to move back home. David shouted, "If you're going, you're going now." He then grabbed her under the arms, jerked her out of bed, and dragged her down the hall and across the den. He opened the front door, pulled her onto the porch, and angrily laid her down. He went back inside and locked the door behind him. Clad only in her gown in the freezing cold, she kept banging on the door and begging until David finally let her in.

On the witness stand, David said the two things he and Susan argued about most were money and sex. They had a hard time paying their bills, and Susan wasn't as interested in sex after Michael was born as she was before. That made him very unhappy. Susan told me many times about David sexually abusing her. To maintain what dignity she has left, I'm not going to give any details about that. I told her she didn't have to live like that. She could come home anytime she wanted. She said she was determined to make the marriage work. She wanted Michael to grow up in a home with two parents.

On March 16, 1992, one day after their first anniversary, David and Susan had a big fight. She called that morning, sounding stretched to the limit. "Mama," she said, "I can't stand to live like this any longer. Can I come home?"

"Susan," I assured her, "I've already said you could come home anytime you wanted. I don't see how you've stood it this long." I offered to help my daughter get her things moved, but she said she would just throw her and Michael's clothes in the car and come on. David said at the trial that he begged her not to take Michael when she left. I don't think Susan said anything to Mrs. Malone and David's grandmother Sarah, who was visiting from California. They were in the kitchen at the time and probably didn't realize what was happening. Mrs. Malone told me later, "I just couldn't believe Susan left like that." David says in his book that Susan was good to Moner. So, Susan meant nothing by not telling her good-bye; she was just too upset to say anything.

When Susan arrived at my house, she sat down in a recliner with Michael in her lap and sighed, "Mama, I feel like I've just been let out of prison."

Before Susan came back home, I had started calling around to see what I could do to train for a job that would support me. I put those plans on hold when she moved back in to concentrate on helping her get on with her life.

We borrowed the crib Wendy had used with Nick and Matt and put it in Susan's old bedroom. David wouldn't let her have the crib they bought for Michael. I felt sorry for her. She didn't have a penny to her name. We bought the necessities for Michael, and I gave her spending money. She asked David for fifty dollars a week.

Susan immediately started looking for a job and landed one at Conso. It was a much better job than the one she had before Michael was born. I kept Michael while she worked, and he was an absolute delight. I went with Susan to take him for his

Susan and David

regular checkups. On the way one time, we heard him say his first word. Out of the blue, he said, "bottle." We both were so excited.

From the minute Susan came back home, David turned on the charm. He sent flowers and cards, wrote sweet letters, and took her out on dates. A few times he even spent the night.

But David also went with other women. By May, two months after Susan left him, he was going with a girl named Jeanne, who worked with him at Winn-Dixie and was still in high school. He had a double standard, though. He became very angry if Susan went with anyone else. One night he followed her to a well-lighted church parking lot near our home where she was meeting a friend she had dated before she married. Once she got in the friend's car, David was on the driver's side punching at the young man. Susan jumped out of the car, ran to hers, and came on home. David quit attacking the man and followed her.

She ran into the house screaming, "David's coming! David's coming!" She then hurriedly told Bev and me what had happened

The words were barely out of her mouth when David lunged in the back door, ranting, raving, and waving his arms like someone out of his mind. He proceeded to pace back and forth across the room, red-faced, gesturing wildly with his arms. He screamed over and over about his wife talking with another man. I'll never forget the viciousness in his voice as he growled, "My wife, my wife, hasn't got any business...You know what she did. She was talking to a guy in a car." I sat in amazement, fully expecting him to foam at the mouth any minute.

After all the yelling, David stomped over to the rocking chair where Susan was sitting and gestured threateningly at her as she dodged his flying arms. He then bent down over her and screamed in her face. She looked liked a scared mouse. Realizing she wasn't going to defend herself, even with us there, I jumped up from the sofa, went over to David, and pushed him away. "Get out of her face," I demanded, "and leave her alone. If you had treated her halfway decent, she'd still be with you, instead of being back home."

"You didn't have any business being there when Michael was born," he snarled.

"That's over and done and can't be undone," I snarled right back. "Rest assured, if there's ever another baby, I won't be in there."

With that exchange, Bev had had enough. "You better leave if you can't act any better than that," he told David calmly. As if hit by a stun gun, David began to cool off, then apologized and said he needed to leave. Susan walked outside with him, talked for a few minutes, then came back in and went to her bedroom. A few minutes later, she rushed out of her room with a startled look on her face. "I think David's outside my window," she said nervously.

"Why?" Bev asked. "Did you see him?"

"I heard a sound from out there," she explained. "I know it's him."

Bev hurried out the front door and around to the bedroom window. Sure enough, David was crouched there. He had parked his car up the street and sneaked back. Bev told him again that he better leave. We figured he was trying to catch Susan talking on the telephone.

Not long after that episode, David and Susan started talking about going back together. Things were bad between them, but evidently not so bad they couldn't get back together. Susan talked to a boy on the phone during that time. David found out about it and got mad. He asked Susan what her mother had to say about that. She said, "She fussed at me and told me I shouldn't do that when we were talking about getting back together."

I asked Susan if she was sure she wanted to live with David again. She said she had thought about it a lot and felt she owed it to Michael to try to make the marriage work. She thought it would be better for him if they could stay together and provide a home. And she said she loved David. That was beyond my understanding. I couldn't understand then and I still can't understand how she could go back with him after everything he had done.

Susan did stand her ground on one issue. She refused to

move back in with David's great grandmother. So they worked out an agreement with her to live in one of the little houses she owned. According to their oral agreement, Susan and David would fix up the house and pay Mrs. Malone $100 a month for the duration of her life. That was the amount she received in rent from her other two houses. The house would become theirs at her death.

They worked hard on the house. I told them they needed to make a legal arrangement with Mrs. Malone. They thought that was a good idea. When they went to a lawyer, they discovered that Mrs. Malone had deeded all her possessions to Sarah, with the provision that she would have use of everything until her death. Mrs. Malone went to see the lawyer, but there was no way to cancel that arrangement.

David told his grandmother what they wanted to do. Sarah would have no part of it. He and Susan were sick. Neither of them wanted to rent, even though I told Susan it would be better to rent a while and see if they could make their marriage work. They started looking for a house and found one they liked but needed money for a down payment. Mrs. Malone gave them $3,500 for improvements they made to her house; and we gave them $5,000, with the understanding that the money was to be repaid if they sold the house.

They were able to furnish the house with help from both sides of the family and things they bought themselves. David brought the bedroom set they had been using at Mrs. Malone's. They bought a used sofa and love seat, a used kitchen table, and a used washer and dryer. Bev let them have a refrigerator that someone had traded in. The previous owners had left the range. I gave them some end tables. David brought the small TV component and VCR that his father picked up from display at Wal-Mart for $50. I gave them some bar stools and miscellaneous kitchen utensils and a set of pots and pans. I had stored all their wedding gifts while they were living with Mrs. Malone. They finally were going to get to use them. They hung new curtains, painted the kitchen cabinets and Michael's room, and put up a Mickey Mouse border. Michael loved his room and would take everybody in to show them the Mickey Mouse figures.

My Daughter Susan Smith

The house looked very cute. Susan was excited about providing a home for Michael. By the end of November, she was expecting Alex. David berated her for getting pregnant. He didn't want any more children, but it seemed he had settled down and wanted to make the marriage work. I rarely saw him, though. He disappeared anytime I went over there. I shook it off, because I was going there to see Susan and Michael.

January 1993, only three months after they went back together, Susan told me she wanted to go to a Christian marriage seminar that was being held in Greenville during the weekend. She and David had sent in a registration fee several weeks earlier, but they needed to borrow some money to stay overnight. That was my first hint they were having problems again.

I didn't know it at the time, but David was still seeing Jeanne when he and Susan got back together. His sister Becky was the one who told her. Susan called Jeanne, and she denied it. She did give her some troubling news, though—that everybody was talking about David and Tiffany Moss. Jeanne and Becky had followed David one night and saw him go into Tiffany's house. Susan found out from David's sister that he had a girlfriend and found out from the girlfriend that he had another girlfriend. How incredible! He, of course, denied everything.

In his book, David tells about meeting Tiffany when she went to work at Winn-Dixie as a cashier. He says it was only two weeks after he had ended his relationship with his sister's friend. He admits that as soon as he saw Tiffany, he knew there would be something between them.

He said that, on Tiffany's first day at Winn-Dixie, he set her up with some training videos and left her in the upstairs lounge to watch them. He went to check on her in an hour or so, and they exchanged friendly conversation. During the summer, he and Tiffany got to know each other better. One day he asked her if she had a boyfriend. He described the conversation as just friendly flirting in one sense but acknowledged in another sense that they both knew it was something more.

Tiffany would remind him that he was married and tell him to get away from her. He thought she was just teasing, yet half-serious at the same time.

Susan and David

David finally concluded something had to give. The date was June 28, 1993. He didn't remember the exact date; he relied on Tiffany for that recollection. Alex's delivery date was a little more than a month away. David was driving past Winn-Dixie that evening and saw Tiffany pull out of the parking lot and drive in the direction of her home. He stayed behind her for a few blocks, then pulled up beside her. They played cat-and-mouse all the way through downtown Union, as he described it. Near Foster Park, he pulled in front of her and to the side of the road. She stopped behind him. They got out of their cars, walked to each other, and exchanged their first kiss, then stood there talking for an hour. After that, they drove out to the country and parked, just talking, nothing else. He confesses the relationship eventually developed into more than talking.

In telling this, David admitted that there's really no excuse for a husband to be dishonest and unfaithful at anytime but especially hurtful to step out on a woman who is pregnant. He said he took the trust Susan put in him and "threw it away." He explained that he did it because he was out of his mind with loneliness and Tiffany was friendly and warm and Susan was disapproving and cold. Are these the words of a man who truly thinks it's wrong to commit adultery?

Susan had to be at work each morning at eight. When David worked the second shift at Winn-Dixie, he stayed out until the wee hours of the morning. If she asked where he was, he would tell her he was just riding around. Later, he told her he joined a body-building club and was going there after work. She learned through a friend that he didn't go there.

One night in July of '93, Tiffany rode by Susan and David's house after midnight. She was talking with David on her car phone and stopped in their driveway. Susan looked out the window when she heard a car drive up and saw Tiffany's car. She went outside and asked Tiffany what her problem was. David soon joined them. I guess that must have been quite a sight—a pregnant wife, a husband, and the "other woman," all having a nice little chat in the middle of the night. While they were standing there, David told Tiffany to remember what he told her and to "just be patient."

My Daughter Susan Smith

David's nickname for Tiffany was "Psycho." Whenever Susan tried to talk with him about her, he would laugh and say, "Oh, you mean Psycho. She's crazy." That, of course, was his way of playing games. While he was saying things like that, he scheduled Psycho to work when he did.

In spite of the serious problems in their marriage, Susan and David made plans together for the baby. They picked out a name well before the due date, Alexander Tyler; and the nursery was ready. They borrowed money from David's father and bought a new white crib. We gave Susan a little family baby shower and bought a white changing table. Walt painted the room baby blue, and Susan and Donna put up a teddy-bear wall border. Susan found a padded cotton wall hanging with teddy bears on it that matched the border. She and David bought a used chest of drawers, painted it white, and put down new carpet. The curtains were white eyelet. The crib bumper pad was light blue with white eyelet. Barbara and Donna provided a little blue nursery lamp with a teddy bear on it, and Susan bought a teddy-bear mobile for the crib that matched the lamp perfectly. The room looked so sweet and had a soothing, peaceful feel.

Susan was scheduled to go into the hospital at 6:00 a.m., August 5. Barbara, Walt, and Donna kept Michael the night before. When David didn't come home after work, she started calling friends to see if they had seen him. He didn't get home until 4:00 a.m. He admits in his book that he had a date with Tiffany. He left her to go to the birth of his son. Wasn't that thoughtful: to put his wife giving birth before a date with his girlfriend? Susan told me later that she lay on the nursery floor and cried herself to sleep because she was so hurt that David would do her that way.

I went to the hospital but had no intention of staying in the room during Alex's birth. As it turned out, Susan had to have a c-section. When Donna, Mitch, and I walked into her room after the birth, David was standing at the door. He looked straight at me and said, "I don't care if I don't ever get it anymore. This is the last baby." I couldn't believe my ears. What a time and what a way to make such a statement. Donna, standing beside me, was shocked, too. She, Mitch, and I just looked at each other without saying a word. Our eyes communicated our disgust.

We made a video of Susan holding Alex in the hospital. She said, "I am so proud of what I just brought into the world." Friends and relatives crowded in to visit her. David acted like he would rather be anywhere in the world than where he was.

Shortly after Alex was born, David announced that he was going on an overnight fishing trip with his buddies. "What buddies?" Susan asked. He wouldn't tell her their names or where he was going; and when he left, he had no fishing equipment with him.

Susan told me she knew David didn't go fishing. "I keep trying to get him to tell me the truth," she said, "but he won't."

Again, I suggested, "The more you ask him, Susan, the more opportunities you give him to deny it. Don't mention it to him again. Drop it." She took my advice and quit probing.

David's reaction to Susan's new approach was to leave two movie tickets on the bedroom dresser. She felt she had to ask about something so obvious. He admitted he took Tiffany to a movie in Greenville. Two weeks after that conversation and only three weeks after Alex was born, David moved back in with Mrs. Malone.

Because of the c-section recovery time, Susan needed help around the clock. We all pitched in. I spent nights with her. Wendy picked up Michael each morning and took him to day care at Judy's. I cleaned the house, washed clothes, and made sure Susan had something to eat. I came home in the afternoon for a short time to prepare a meal for Bev and Moe, and to bathe. Donna picked up Michael from Judy's and kept him until I got back to Susan's. Mama pitched in when we needed her. We did this until Susan could get on her feet. She returned to work at Conso when Alex was about six weeks old.

My mother had always been more patient with David than I was. But when he left Susan so soon after Alex's birth, that did it for her. From then on, she didn't have a dime's worth of use for him.

It seemed that David didn't want to give up the benefits of a marriage and family, only the responsibilities. He came and went as he pleased at Susan's house. She didn't like for him to come by unannounced, but she wanted to keep a good relationship with him because of the children. He dropped by often to see them for a few minutes, then went on his merry way. He told Susan he had "quality" time with Michael and Alex. All the while, he was still going with Tiffany.

Christmas Eve of '93 arrived, Alex's first Christmas. Susan brought Michael and Alex to the annual gathering at Mama's house. I could tell she was sad about being alone on Christmas Eve. I tried to get her to spend the night with us and let Santa come to our house. "No," she told me firmly, "David will want to come by on Christmas morning, and he wouldn't come to your house."

I said, "Susan, When David walked out on you and the children, he walked away from such things as spending Christmas with his children."

"I know, Mama, but I know that he'll want to see them."

Leigh went home with Susan from Mama's house. David dropped by soon after they arrived, and Susan asked him to put Michael's tool table together. He said he was too tired, that he would do it in the morning. Susan told him she wanted it put together that night so Michael could see it on Christmas morning. Leigh told me later that David looked at her in his pitiful little way and said, "Susan just doesn't understand how tired I am. I have to go home and get some sleep." Leigh and Susan put the tool table together.

Susan called David at 7:00 a.m. Mrs. Malone's sitter told her he didn't get home until 6:30 a.m. and was already gone again. The man who had been so tired and sleepy he couldn't put a tool table together for his son's Christmas hadn't been home all night. He arrived at Susan's just in time to see Michael get up.

Barbara, Walt, Donna, and Mitch arrived at Susan's at 8:00 a.m. Donna said Walt could hardly wait to get there to see Michael. He kept hurrying her, saying he was going to leave without her if she didn't step on it. She told him, "Daddy, it's not even eight yet." He replied, "I know, but I want to see Michael."

Susan and David

Bev, Moe, and I arrived at Susan's house shortly after the Garners. We were making the rounds of Bev's and my grandchildren to see their presents. We always did that on Christmas morning. David's father and stepmother arrived soon after us. Susan planned to prepare breakfast for them and David.

Susan borrowed my camcorder to record their Christmas morning. I have the video she made. Alex is lying on the sofa, with Susan softly saying to him, "Merry first Christmas, you precious little thing."

David left after breakfast. Susan packed her car, put the children in their car seats, and came to our house for Christmas dinner. David had completed his fatherly duties and was on his merry way again.

In his book, David identified a critical point in their drifting apart as Susan's decision to take a job at Conso, instead of taking up "her old lifestyle" and going back to work at Winn-Dixie. He claimed that decision started a chain of events that eliminated the chance that they would get back together. He thought her old life with him looked less attractive because of her new circle of friends and the possibilities that a prosperous life offered.

I can't imagine anyone buying that line. He was pursuing his girlfriends before Susan left him and began working at Conso. Long before she went to work at Conso, he was rude, unfeeling, and abusive to her.

The truth is this, in my opinion: If David had been even a reasonable husband—never mind a good one—Susan's tragedy never would have happened. She was a faithful wife; she tried to make a home for him and the children. She became promiscuous after he treated her so badly, which led to the liaisons that destroyed her life. She is in prison for doing a terrible thing, but the one who drove her to that tragic state of mind is walking free. David even admits in his book that Susan's tragic action could have been a product of all his "catting around and foolishness and lying."

****

While all of this was happening in Susan and David's marriage, I was still trying to resolve my own marital difficulties. When they went back together in November of 1992, I once more started making plans to divorce Bev. I simply couldn't forget what he had done, and he couldn't talk about it. To other people, things seemed okay, but nothing had improved. Instead of finding ways to resolve our problems, we just picked at each other. In fact, things got so bad between us, Bev moved to his aunt's house, saying he couldn't live like that anymore. About a week after he left, I went to church in Buffalo, assuming he would be at his old church. But there he was. After the service, he came running up to me. I said, "I'm going to Mama's. Want to go with me?" He was delighted for the invitation. After dinner, we came to my house and reconciled that day.

Things didn't stay better, though. Nothing was resolved. I never really dropped my plans to divorce Bev. But before I could do anything, I began to have serious trouble with my teeth and had to have extensive dental work done, including root canals and implants. It took months to take care of all that. And before that was behind me, Susan and David split again. Then in March of 1994, Moe was diagnosed with epilepsy. From March to November, he had to be monitored constantly. I was with him practically twenty-four hours a day until the doctor got his medicine right.

With all these problems hovering over me, I felt compelled to put off divorcing Bev. And I guess, deep down, I just couldn't let go. In spite of everything he had done, there was still some love there. He never mistreated me physically, but he had a hold on me that I couldn't seem to shake loose.

7

The Trigger Event

Susan dated David from time to time, even with the circumstances of his leaving. He came by for sex on a regular basis and demanded that she be there when he decided to come by. Never mind he wasn't there to share the responsibilities. Never mind he had a girlfriend. She kept hoping he would end the affair with Tiffany. All of us tried to tell her he was only using her.

David always wanted to own Susan. From the beginning of their marriage, he tried to force her to choose between him and her family and friends. He even got mad at her for signing her name Susan V. Smith. He told her when they married, she was no longer a Vaughan. I am convinced that, if David had succeeded in making Susan break all ties with us and her friends, he would have made life miserable for her, with no accountability to anyone. Love was not his driving passion toward her. It was control.

It was during one of her separations from David that Susan met Tom Findlay, son of the owner of Conso Products. He's not the average woman's idea of tall, dark, and handsome; but many considered him to be Union's best catch. Of average height, he has medium brown hair but very little of it. Susan was attracted to him because he was every bit a gentleman.

Tom and Susan introduced themselves to each other in the parking lot of Conso one day after work. At the trial, he remembered the time of their meeting as November or December of '93. He said he understood Susan and David had been separated for several months at that time. For a while, they just talked on the phone, then started dating in January.

On the witness stand, Tom told about a telephone encounter he had with David in March of '94. That evening, David was at Susan's house when she came home, hiding in Michael's bedroom. In David's book, he says he had bought flowers and champagne and planned to surprise her. After she got the children settled, she picked up the phone. David thought she was calling my house to let me know she was home, but he soon realized she was talking to Tom Findlay. At the trial, David said, "It hurt and, of course, made me jealous....actually I was kind of shocked."

David admitted in court that he came out of the shadows, grabbed the phone, and cursed Tom. Tom filled in the details during his testimony. He said he heard Susan yell, "Oh, my God, David." Then David took the phone and threatened him, saying, "You better stop talking to my wife, you son-of-a-bitch. You better watch your back. I'm going to get you."

While being questioned by David Bruck, Tom said he took David's threats very seriously. After that encounter, he slept with a gun under his pillow. He explained it was because he lived in an isolated setting. The house he rented from his parents was situated on thirteen acres with few neighbors.

When the solicitor asked David if he threatened other men Susan saw, he said he did. And why? He claimed it was because he wanted the marriage to work. He didn't mention the fact that he did this even while Tiffany was his steady date.

Susan and David were separated from August of '93 to June of '94. Within a month of getting back together, they were having serious problems again. David stayed out to all hours and was doing the same old things. Before they got back together, Susan had planned to go to the beach in late July with the Garners and Mitch. Since things weren't all that great in her marriage, she dreaded asking David to go along but knew she had to. She tried to be upbeat when she told me she had invited him. She said they would decide at the beach whether they would stay together.

According to everyone's account, David was an absolute jerk at Myrtle Beach. Barbara told me he wouldn't get up and have breakfast with them. Susan prepared his breakfast and took it to him on a tray so he could eat in bed. The two of them agreed there was no hope for the marriage before they came home. Tiffany was so anxious to know what happened she had the nerve to call Mitch to find out what went on with Susan and David at the beach.

Susan called me after they returned. "Mama," she said, "I just don't think things will work out." The next time she came by, she told me David was moving out. "Oh, Mama," she sighed, "David's been so good the past week; he's been like a different person. He came home after work every day. He's helped me with the housework and the children. We actually had fun. I asked him why he couldn't be like this all the time. I told him if he were, we could have a good marriage and a good home for Michael and Alex. Do you know what he said, Mama? He said he just wanted our last week together to be happy memories. Can you believe that, Mama?"

I wasn't a bit surprised.

By this time, Mrs. Malone was in a nursing home and her house was sitting unoccupied and furnished. I suppose David thought he could move in as he always had. But his grandmother Sarah had other ideas. She had the locks changed; so he had to get an apartment.

When David moved out, he took the bedroom set, TV, and entertainment center. He wanted to take the washer and dryer, but Susan insisted she needed them for the children. He even tried to get her to move out and let him have the house.

Since Michael had always slept with his parents, it was also his bed that David took. Susan and Michael had to sleep on the floor on an egg-crate mattress pad. Michael cried for his bed. I offered to lend them the bedroom set from her old room. She said I needed it. "Where would we sleep when we stay overnight?" she chuckled. A co-worker loaned her a bed and mattress she had in storage. She called the day she got it, saying, "Mama, you don't know how good it feels to sleep in a bed again."

The next items David helped himself to were the VCR and microwave. Susan was mystified about the VCR, because he had another one a girlfriend had given him. She called me all upset. "You're not going to believe what David just did," she said. "I can't believe it! I can't believe it! Michael's crying. He wants to watch *Robin Hood*." It was his favorite video.

"Well, Mama's got a VCR she doesn't use," I told her, "but it won't rewind. I'll buy you a rewinder."

Susan had taken the portable TV from her bedroom when she married and was using it in the bedroom at her house. When David took the TV, she moved the portable into the den and hooked up the VCR. Michael was truly a smart child. He recognized the video he wanted to watch, and Susan had taught him how to operate the VCR by himself. Since he didn't want to go to bed until Susan did, she used the video to get him to go to bed earlier. Every night he loaded a tape in the VCR, lay down on a pallet in front of the TV, and watched one of the Disney classics David's parents had given him, until he went to sleep.

After work the next day, Susan went by to get Mama's VCR. David came by with the VCR while she was trying to hook it up. He had remembered how much Michael liked the videos.

A week or so later, Susan called me around seven in the evening, crying. "David's been over here," she told me. "He pulled clothes out of the closet and threw them on the floor. Then he pulled the phone out of the wall and got me in a stranglehold. I was crying, and the kids were crying. Michael was screaming, 'Don't hurt my mama.'"

I nervously asked one question after another in rapid-fire order. "Is he gone? Are you okay? You're not hurt, are you?"

"I just want you to come over here," she said.

"Okay. I'm on my way."

Absolutely incensed about the situation, I stopped by Scotty's house and told him someone had to talk to David to make him understand he's got to answer to somebody. Scotty said he would. Then I started looking for David. I rode through Winn-Dixie's parking lot to see if his car was there. I would have gone by his apartment, but I didn't know where he lived. I never did find him and don't know what I would have said, anyway. I do know I would have liked to beat the dickens out of him with a baseball bat.

Susan was calmed down by the time I got to her house, but

Michael wasn't. He kept asking her, "Did Daddy hurt you?" And for a while after that episode, Michael would put his arm up to his neck and say to Susan, "Daddy hurt you. He do you like that."

"Daddy didn't really hurt me," she kept assuring him.

Many times after David moved out, I got up in the middle of the night to go to Susan's house because one of the children was sick, and she was scared. She worried that something would happen to her, like falling or passing out or anything that would cause the children to be there with no one to take care of them.

I think more out of loneliness than anything else, she began taking night classes at the local USC branch on Mondays and Wednesdays. Barbara and Walt kept the children on Mondays and David kept them on Wednesdays. Often, he would wait to the last minute to tell Susan he couldn't keep them.

David kept Michael and Alex overnight at his apartment only once. When I called Susan the next morning, she told me he had the children, saying, "Mama, I sure don't like waking up to a quiet house. I miss hearing Alex playing in the crib, and I miss having Michael curled up in a little ball beside me. It's too lonesome without them around." When she picked up the children from David's apartment, he told her he was never going to do that again, because Michael called for his mama all night, and he didn't get any sleep. Susan said she tried to explain that the apartment was strange to them, and they would have to get used to being there. She wondered if it ever dawned on him that, many nights, she got very little sleep.

I asked Susan once why she begged David to keep the children. I told her that among all of her family and Barbara, Walt, and Donna, we could keep them anytime she wanted. She looked at me sadly and said, "Mama, I know you and David don't like each other, but David is their daddy and I want them to know him." It finally sank in. Susan didn't want the same thing to happen to Michael and Alex that had happened to her. She wanted her children to know their father. She wanted them to have memories to look back on as they grew.

When she realized her marriage was really over, Susan began a downward spiral. I found it hard to understand that she truly loved David, but she did. She was deeply disappointed that the marriage didn't work. Emotionally, it was a stalemate. Mentally, she knew she had to get the marriage behind her and go on with her life.

She started divorce proceedings in late September. Her lawyer informed her that South Carolina allows only four grounds for divorce: habitual drunkenness, desertion of one year, physical abuse, and adultery. Separation for one year qualifies under South Carolina law as grounds for divorce due to desertion. But Susan and David had been together for six weeks during the previous year. They decided to ignore that period but needed a witness. Susan asked if I would testify to that.

"No way I'll testify to that," I told her. I didn't trust David.

Susan called back a couple of days later and said David had decided he wasn't going to agree with the one-year separation, anyway. He said she would just have to wait another year. "I can't stand this for another year, Mama," she sighed. "I just can't stand it."

I had watched Susan's anguish become more and more intense. I didn't think she could go on living the same way for another year. And what if David talked her into taking him back for a few days? Her turmoil might never end.

"Susan," I reminded her, "you and everyone in Union knows David has been going with Tiffany. Get him for adultery and name Tiffany."

"I hate to do that," she protested.

I told her she deserved better out of life than allowing David to keep her miserable for another year. "If he won't agree to the year's separation," I said, "then I don't see that you have but two choices. Wait for another year or file on grounds of adultery. You won't have any trouble finding someone to testify to that. Get out of the mess you're in and get free to find somebody who will be good to you and the children. It's up to you, though. If you want to wait another year, wait."

She called me a few days later. "Mama, I got him," she told me excitedly, "and I'm going to see my lawyer during lunch today. I got to thinking about what you said; so I borrowed $150 from Donna and hired Couter Knox. It was enough to pay him for one day's work. I thought Tuesday night was good because David was off work. Couter followed Tiffany to David's apartment. She didn't leave until four in the morning."

"Good for you!" I exclaimed. "That's great." I was amazed she had done all that on her own. "Now if you're going to file this," I advised, "put things in there that will make sure David can't drop in on you anytime he wants. He should have to call and make arrangements."

Right away, Susan took Couter's report to her lawyer and got things going. Of course, David was livid when the papers were served on him. He called Susan and read her the riot act. Most of all, he was mad at her for naming Tiffany.

Susan dropped by shortly after her lawyer filed the divorce papers. She stood at the kitchen counter to talk, while I washed the dishes. We did the usual chit-chat; then things suddenly got quiet. I glanced over at her to see why. With her head down, she had her finger pressed so firmly on the counter that the outer edge of her fingernail had turned white. She obviously was deep in thought. I waited for her to say something.

"I wonder who David will marry?" she said, as if thinking out loud. She then tapped her finger on the counter. "If I just knew it would be Tiffany, I wouldn't worry so much. Because I know she would be good to Michael and Alex."

"Susan," I teased, "the divorce isn't final, and you're thinking about him getting married." She looked up but said nothing.

I realize I misread Susan's statements that day. I thought she was merely jumping ahead to the future. I know now she was thinking about killing herself.

I told Susan David was out for revenge, warning her over and over not to see anyone until the divorce was final. The magic date, December 27, was less than three months away. "Less than three months!" I emphasized. "Just hold on that long, and you'll be free of him." I yearned for her to know the joyous freedom of life without David snipping at her heels all the time.

My Daughter Susan Smith

It was unrealistic to think Susan could exist for three months with no more social life than shopping, going to a movie with Donna, or occasionally eating out with friends. Actually, her social life really started to move once she filed for divorce. I didn't know it, but she resumed dating Tom Findlay, once he found out she had filed for divorce.

One Saturday, Susan called and asked if I would baby-sit. She wanted to go to a birthday cookout at the Findlay's. It was for Tom's father, Cary Findlay.

"Is everybody from Conso going?" I asked. "Is Donna going?"

She said a bunch from Conso were going, but Donna wasn't. That didn't sound good to me. I wondered why a select few would be invited. I told her I didn't think she should go to the party, and I couldn't keep the children. She cut the conversation short.

Later that evening I dropped by Hedy and Tim's. I was surprised to see that Michael and Alex were there. Hedy was having a big time with them, and I joined right in. Around ten that night, a lady who worked with Susan came to Hedy's door, saying she wanted to pick up the children. She said Susan was going to spend the night with her. I asked where Susan was. She said she was in the car. I went right past her to the car and opened the back door. The scene was shocking. Susan was stretched out on the seat, intoxicated and sick. I helped her into my car, then got the children.

The next morning Susan was so ashamed. She said she had a few drinks on an empty stomach and the alcohol slipped up on her. She told me, "Mama, I am sorry and I promise nothing like this will ever happen again." Hedy told me later that Susan called her and apologized and made the same promise to her. Susan wasn't a drinker. All this was something new for her. It was very troubling to see what was happening to her, and I couldn't do a thing about it. I just had to watch it happen.

At the trial, Dr. Halleck commented on this new pattern in Susan's life. He said she began to drink more after the separation and got intoxicated on a number of occasions, which was uncharacteristic of her. He stated: "Susan became much more seriously depressed after David left for the final time. She sees herself as a single mother without much money. She is subject to David coming in and out of the house at random, at will, even though there was an official separation. David often comes and insists on having sex, which she complies with, but in no way being a consenting partner. She does not enjoy it. She is worried about her sexual activity, which is at this time beginning to increase. So she is involved with Cary Findlay. She's also once again becoming involved with Bev Russell at this point." He also mentioned that she was involved with Tom Findlay and noted that this sexual involvement with four men was indicative of her downward spiral.

Susan told Dr. Halleck that she thought about suicide just about every day during the sixty or ninety days before the death of Michael and Alex. In the past, those thoughts had never been that frequent, nor for such a prolonged period of time.

A now-famous hot-tub party took place ten days before the tragedy—on October 15, 1994. Susan called me in the afternoon that day and asked if I would keep the children. She said a few people from Conso were getting together in the evening at Hickory Nuts. I told her that would be fine. Instead of bringing them over early in the evening, she brought them late, so she could help me get them ready for bed. She said she wouldn't be gone long. She would be back no later than 12:30.

The people who got together that night were a married couple, Tom Findlay, Susan, and another young woman. Well into the evening of laughing and joking, someone suggested they go to Tom's house. Once there, they all got into his hot tub.

I went to bed but checked the clock periodically. I couldn't go to sleep. When two o'clock came, I decided to look for Susan. I woke Bev up and told him to listen for the children. I was walking out the door when she showed up.

Once inside, I noticed she didn't have the usual big bow holding her hair back. Then I noticed her hair was damp. "Where in the world have you been?" I asked.

"A bunch of us went over to a friend's house and got in the

hot tub," she explained, then gave names of the married couple and two other singles.

"What in the world did you have on?"

She said she had on a friend's bathing suit.

"You didn't have any business doing something like that," I chided her. "You said you were going to Hickory Nuts. What if I had needed you? I wouldn't have known where you were."

"I'm sorry, Mama," she said apologetically. "I should have come on home when I said I would."

I was too tired to press things any further. The next day, though, I asked her if it didn't seem sort of odd that there was one single man and two women?

"Yeah," she replied. "She probably thought I was the fifth wheel, and I thought she was."

I found out later that things didn't go well for Susan at the party. In all the frivolity of the moment, she kissed the married man and Tom ended up having sex with the other single woman. Later, he let Susan know he didn't approve of her behavior. She was wrong, of course, but Tom's reaction was a crass example of the double standard that has plagued this whole case.

Susan knew she had messed up good. On Sunday afternoon, she went down to Wal-Mart and bought a thank-you card. When she arrived at work early Monday morning, she placed the card on Tom's desk. The card itself read, "Thank you for being gentle, sensitive, caring, understanding, very best friend." Susan underlined the descriptive words for emphasis. Along with the card was her letter of apology.

"Dear Tom:

"Just a note to say thank you for everything. I could never express in words how much you mean to me. I will always treasure our friendship and all of the many wonderful memories we have had.

"I want you to know that I have never felt with anyone the way I feel when I'm with you. I have never felt so needed. You are a very special person and that is part of why making love to you is so wonderful.

"I know how you feel about our relationship and I respect that. I'm appreciative of your honesty with me. I do want us to be friends forever and I'll never let anything happen that would change that.

"I do hope that we will be able to date some and be together again some day, but if we never made love again, my feelings for you would not change because having you as my friend is worth more than sex could ever be worth.

"Once again, I'm sorry for that Saturday night and would take it back in a heartbeat if I could. I really wanted to be with you and hated that I wasn't.

"Thank you for being there for me through all the rough times. You are a true friend. I want you to know that I will always love and care for you for the rest of my life. You are the best friend anyone could ever have.

"Well, I hope I said everything right. The bottom line is I'm glad we are friends and if that is all we can be, then we will just have to do a hell of a job being that. Who knows what the future holds for our relationship. I'm just going to live one day at a time.

"<u>One more thing before I go, please don't ever hesitate to call me if you ever need anything.</u> I will always be here for you.

"Friends forever,

"Susan"

On the evening of October 17, Tom sat down at his computer and wrote what has been labeled his "Dear Jane" reply.

"Dear Susan,

"I hope you don't mind, but I think clearer when I am typing, so this letter is being written on my computer.

My Daughter Susan Smith

"This is a difficult letter for me to write because I know how much you think of me. And I want you to know that I am flattered that you have such a high opinion of me. Susan, I value our friendship very much. You are one of the few people on this earth that I feel I can tell anything. You are intelligent, beautiful, sensitive, understanding, and possess many other wonderful qualities that I and many other men appreciate. You will, without a doubt, make some lucky man a great wife. But unfortunately, it won't be me.

"Even though you think we have much in common, we are vastly different. We have been raised in two totally different environments, and therefore, think totally different. That's not to say that I was raised better than you or vice versa, it just means that we come from two different backgrounds.

"When I started dating Laura, I knew our backgrounds were going to be a problem. Right before I graduated from Auburn University in 1990, I broke up with a girl Allison that I had been dating for over two years. I loved Allison very much and we were very compatible. Unfortunately, we wanted different things out of life. She wanted to get married and have children before the age of twenty-eight, and I did not. This conflict spurred our breakup, but we have remained friends through the years. After Allison, I was very hurt. I decided not to fall for anyone again until I was ready to make a long commitment.

"For my first two years in Union, I dated very little. In fact, I can count the number of dates I had on one hand. But then Laura came along. We met at Conso, and I fell for her like a ton of bricks. Things were great at first and remained good for a long time, but I knew deep in my heart that she was not the one for me. People tell me that when you find the person that you will want to spend the rest of your life with you will know it. Well, even though I fell in love with Laura, I had my doubts about a long and lasting commitment, but I never said anything, and I eventually hurt her very, very deeply. I won't do that again.

"Susan, I can really fall for you. You have so many endearing qualities about you, and I think that you are a terrific person. But like I have told you before, there are some things about you that aren't suited for me, and yes, I am speaking about your children. I'm sure that your kids are good kids, but it really wouldn't matter how good they may be. The fact is, I just don't want children. These feelings may change one day, but I doubt it. With all of the crazy, mixed-up things that take place in this world today, I just don't have the desire to bring another life into it. And I don't want to be responsible for anyone else's children, either. But I am very thankful that there are people like you who are not so selfish as I am, and you don't mind bearing the responsibility of children. If everyone thought the way I do, our species would eventually become extinct.

"But our differences go far beyond the children issue. We are just two totally different people, and eventually, those differences would cause us to break up. Because I know myself so well, I am sure of this. But don't be discouraged. There is someone out there for you. In fact, it's probably someone that you may not know at this time or that you may know, but would never expect. Either way, before you settle down with anyone again, there is something you need to do. Susan, because you got pregnant and married at such an early age, you missed out on much of your youth. I mean, one minute you were a kid, and the next minute you were having kids. Because I come from a place where everyone had the desire and money to go to college, having the responsibility of children at such a young age is beyond my comprehension. Anyhow, my advice to you is to wait and be very choosy about your next relationship. I can see this may be difficult for you because you are a bit boy crazy, but as the proverb states good things come to those who wait. I am not saying you shouldn't go out and have a good time. In fact, I think you should do just that. Have a good time and capture some of that youth that you missed out on. But just don't get seriously involved with anyone until you have done the things in life that you want to do, first. Then the rest of [life] will fall in place.

"Susan, I am not mad at you about what happened this weekend. Actually, I'm very thankful. As I told you, I was starting to let my heart warm up to the idea of us going out as more than just friends. But seeing you kiss another man put things back into perspective. I remembered how I hurt Laura, and I won't let that happen again and therefore, I can't let myself get close to you. We will always be friends, but our relationship will never go beyond that of friendship. And as for your relationship with B. Brown, of course you have to make your own decisions in life, but remember you have to live with the consequences also. Everyone is held accountable for their actions, and I would hate for people to perceive you as an unreputable person. If you want to catch a nice guy like me one day, you have to act like a nice girl. And you know, nice girls don't sleep with married men. Besides, I want you to feel good about yourself, and I am afraid that if you sleep with B. Brown or any other married man for that matter, you will lose your self respect. I know I did when we were messing around earlier this year. So please, think about your actions before you do anything you will regret. I care for you, but also care for Susan Brown, and I would hate to see anyone get hurt. Susan may say that she wouldn't care if her husband had an affair, but you and I know that is not true.

"Anyhow, as I have already told you, you are a very special person. And don't let anyone tell you or make you feel any different. I see so much potential in you, but only you can make it happen. Don't settle for mediocre in life, go for it all and only settle for the best. I do. I haven't told you this, but I am extremely proud of you for going to school. I am a firm believer in higher education, and once you obtain a degree from college, there is no stopping you. And don't let these idiot boys from Union make you feel like you are not capable or slow you down. After you graduate, you will be able to go anywhere you want in this world. And if you ever wanted to get a job in Charlotte, my father is the right person to know. He and Koni know everyone who is anyone in the business world in Charlotte. And if I can ever help you with anything, don't hesitate to ask.

"Well, this letter must come to an end. It is 11:50 p.m. and I am getting very sleepy. But I wanted to write you this letter because you are the one who is always making the effort for me, and I wanted to return the friendship. I've appreciated it when you have dropped me nice little notes, or cards, or the present at Christmas, and it is about time that I start putting a little effort into our friendship. Which reminds me, I thought long and hard about getting you something for your birthday, but I decided not to because I wasn't sure what you might think. Now I am sorry I didn't get you anything, so you can expect something from me at Christmas. But do not buy me anything for Christmas. All I want from you is a nice, sweet card. I'll cherish that more than any store bought present.

"Again, you will always have my friendship. And your friendship is one that I will always look upon with sincere affection.

"Tom

"P.S. It's late, so please don't count off for spelling or grammar."

Tom's letter was on Susan's desk the next morning, October 18. She was in tears by the time she finished. She read it a second time, then folded it carefully, put it in her pocketbook, and dialed Tom's extension.

"This is the sweetest letter I have ever received," she told him, her voice choking with emotion. "I really appreciate it." He asked her to go to a movie that evening.

Thursday, Tom went out of town on a business trip. Susan made plans to eat with Susan Brown. She wanted her to know she had no designs on her husband, that the hot-tub incident was just a frivolous moment.

David agreed to come by and keep the kids. He was in unusually good spirits when he arrived. Susan figured he was just trying to stay on good terms because of Michael and Alex. He even stayed a while after she returned and watched TV with her. She really couldn't understand why, but she didn't say anything.

Susan didn't know it, but David began to strategize about

getting revenge the moment he was served the divorce papers. He admits in his book that he enlisted friends to keep tabs on her and to report to him. He was determined to find a way to accuse her of adultery. He now was closing in on his target.

Alex was already in bed when Susan got home, and Michael was lying on a pallet, watching a Disney video. Susan lay down on the floor beside him to help him go to sleep. He went to sleep pretty fast, and so did she.

When David realized Susan was asleep, he grabbed her pocketbook and took it into the bathroom. He hurriedly searched through the contents, looking for evidence. His eyes were drawn to the neatly folded, white piece of computer paper.

He opened it up to see the greeting: "Dear Susan," then flipped to the end. His heartbeat skyrocketed when he saw "Tom." He carefully read every word.

The discovery was beyond his wildest dreams. As far as he was concerned, he had the evidence he needed to make an adultery charge stick. He was too excited to wake Susan up to say good-bye. He had to catch Tiffany before she left work.

A quick glance at the letter and Tiffany was equally out of her mind with excitement. David said they needed a copy of the letter but that everything was closed.

Tiffany gleefully offered to get copies made at the church where her mother worked. After she finished her shift, she went home to get the key to the church out of her mother's pocketbook. At midnight, alone in the church, she made the copies and took them to David at his apartment.

Early Friday morning David called Susan and offered to come by to take the kids to day care. He sounded unusually pleasant, but she wasn't the least bit suspicious. He had a certain ritual. He would drop by, play with the children, take them to day care, and then come back for sex with Susan. He cut the grass as a favor for sex.

While Susan was in the shower, David put the letter back in her pocketbook. He then took the kids to day care. She was dressed and drinking a glass of orange juice when he got back. She told him to help himself to something to drink. He did that and sat down at the table with a big smile on his face.

"Susan," he said light-heartedly, "I promised to help you clean the carpet in your car. Want to do that now?" She replied, "Sure."

When they finished cleaning the inside of the car, they went back inside to get something to drink. Susan could tell David wanted to talk. She waited for him to start the conversation.

He got right to the point: Why was she charging him with adultery when she was guilty, too?

She asked what he meant by that. He said he knew she was having an affair with someone at Conso. Without thinking, she admitted she had been involved with Cary Findlay but that was since they separated and filed for divorce.

David's look of surprise made her wish she hadn't told him. He said he had someone else in mind. It was Tom Findlay. Susan asked how he knew about her and Tom? He then arrogantly confessed that he had a copy of the letter Tom sent to her. She asked how he got the letter. He bragged that he went through her pocketbook while she was asleep.

"You have no right to go through my things!" she screamed. He screamed right back, saying she had no right to accuse him of adultery when she was guilty, too.

She angrily reminded him that they were separated when she started going with Tom. He fired back that the letter sounded like it had been going on a lot longer than that, that she must have been going with him before they were officially separated. He said he could prove that.

"I can't believe this," Susan cried, the tears streaming down her face. "You had no right to go through my pocketbook. You had no right."

David pressed his advantage. He told Susan he had more evidence against her. He had a tap on her phone. He had friends following her. He claimed he knew every step she had taken lately.

In rapid-fire fashion, he laid out the evidence before her. He asked how many times she had been to bed with Cary Findlay. She yelled that was none of his business. He named Bev and said he was going to tell the world about their relationship. He reminded her about telling IRS they were separated all of 1993 when they weren't. He would tell them she filed a false return. He knew about the hot-tub incident at Findlay's house. How would she like for him to tell everybody about that? How would she feel if he told Koni Findlay about her affair with her husband? It seemed he knew about every embarrassing event in her life. She was horrified, sobbing.

His voice rising, David moved in with his summation. It went something like this: "A lot of people are going to fall with you. Cary Findlay will lose his business. You and Tom will lose your jobs. Bev will lose his tax business, because he did your tax return. You'll be sorry big time for accusing me of adultery."

"You have no right; you have no right," she screamed through tears.

The telephone ringing interrupted the screaming.

"Susan," I said. "I need a table."

"A table?" she questioned nervously.

"Is the table you used for the Mary Kay party still on the carport?"

"Mama," she said with a quaver in her voice, "let me call you back. David's here, and we're in the middle of a fuss."

"Okay," I replied.

Around nine that morning, I had decided to have a yard sale. I planned to set up a table at the elementary school across from Mama's house, and she was going to come over there and help me. I put all the stuff in my car to take to Buffalo, but I needed a little table. I knew Susan had one that David had borrowed from Winn-Dixie.

I sat down to drink another cup of coffee while I waited for Susan to call back. After half an hour, I decided to go on by her house. I figured enough time had passed for her and David to have their fuss, and he would be on his way to work. When I got there, Mitch and Donna were standing at the kitchen door. I greeted them and asked where Susan was. Donna pointed to the bedroom and said she and Mitch needed to go.

The Trigger Event

I found Susan sitting on the floor, propped up against the wall and leaning forward with a look of utter despair on her face.

"What's wrong?" I asked.

"Mama," she sighed, "it's been one hell of a day."

"He didn't hit you, did he?"

"No, he didn't hit me."

"Are you sure you're all right?"

"Yes, I'm okay. But I've got a bunch of things to do. I have to wash some clothes and go to Wal-Mart to get a present. Michael's going to a birthday party for one of the kids at day care. I took the day off to get things done. And David's got me all upset. I haven't gotten a thing done."

"So, what's new?" I remarked.

"Yeah, so what's new?" she questioned with resignation.

She gathered up the dirty clothes, and we walked to the carport to the washer and dryer. She threw the clothes in the washer, then slowly turned around to face me.

"Mama," she said, leaning back against the washer, "I might as well tell you. I've been seeing Tom Findlay."

"Susan," I chided. "I warned you not to go with anyone until your divorce is final. Does David know?"

"Yeah. I just told him. That's what the fuss was about. I figured he knew everything, anyway. He and his friends have been following me, and he's even got my phone tapped."

"Did he tell you that?"

"Sure did."

"Susan, that's a federal offense. He can't do that."

"You don't know David. He does what he wants to. He's got it tapped. I'm sure of that."

Susan and David had so many fights, I wasn't overly alarmed about this one. She was always able to recoup. When I talked to her later in the day, it looked like she had put the fuss behind her. She and Donna went shopping and to various places around town, linking up with friends.

On Saturday, Susan took Michael to the birthday party. After the party, she and Donna went to a wedding. When she came by my house to borrow a dress, she seemed to be in good spirits.

Susan came by with Michael and Alex Sunday evening, too, laughing and smiling. The kids were also happy and playful. Bev and I detected nothing amiss with her. But the joyous spirit masked the heavy weight of David's threats. After she got home, she called Tom Findlay, extremely upset.

"He's going to tell everything about us," she told Tom. He protested, saying something like, "But you were separated all the times we've gone together."

She told him about the phone tap. Tom assured her David couldn't tap the phone, that it was a federal offense.

They talked for almost an hour, going back and forth between serious concerns and lighter subjects. She told him David was going to reveal her relationship to Bev. She said David knew all kinds of things and she didn't know what she was going to do. Tom kept telling her David couldn't do what he threatened. She kept insisting he could, but she was calmed down a bit when they said good-bye. He was someone she could talk to.

The calming effect of Susan's conversation with Tom was short-lived. Maybe one reason was because she hadn't told him everything about her screaming match with David. She left out one important detail—her sexual relationship with his father. She desperately hoped she could get up the nerve to tell him before David let him or his mother know.

David's threats hovered over her like a dark, ominous cloud. She believed every word he said. No matter what anyone said, she remained totally convinced he could deliver on his threats. She saw her world falling apart before her eyes.

At the trial, I learned that Susan told Donna about her sexual affairs after her fight with David. It was the first time she had told anybody other than David, but she was so distressed she had to tell someone. Dr. Andrews said the reason Susan hadn't told Donna before was because she didn't want to hurt her. She knew her behavior was a violation of Donna's strong moral code.

For David, the Friday blow-up was just another fuss in

which he got the upper hand. For Susan, it was an upheaval that lingered into the next week. Dr. Andrews talked with Susan for many hours about the Friday encounter and carefully studied every detail of the event. As a result, she labeled it the trigger event in Susan's downward spiral.

****

When the FBI searched Susan's house before she confessed, they missed a love note that was stuck in a Bible. "I miss you!" the note went. "I'm thinking about you constantly. I love you!" It was signed "Aunt Tee," probably what Tiffany called herself to Michael and Alex.

After Susan was arrested and before the trial, David counter-sued for divorce on grounds of adultery. He used Susan's three-month relationship with Tom Findlay when they were separated to prove his case. It didn't matter that he was involved with Tiffany before Susan met Tom. It didn't matter how many times he had committed adultery when they were living together as husband and wife. It was like hitting someone when they're down. Susan had no heart nor opportunity to contest his claim. The divorce was granted on those grounds.

The dissolution of Susan's marriage and taking steps toward divorce began her downward spiral, to be sure; but it was David's unholy quest for revenge that pushed her to the edge and cost him his children.

8

Auburn Sweatshirt

Monday morning at work, Susan talked briefly with Tom about David's threats. At the trial, he said he could tell she was concerned but didn't appear to be overly upset. Other people from Conso who testified noticed nothing unusual about her, either. As far as anyone could tell, Monday was a typical day for Susan.

But David's threats weighed heavily on her. She had called Southern Bell early Saturday morning to request that they check for a wire tap. A technician thoroughly checked the connections on Monday, inside and out. He found no evidence of a tap. That assurance didn't allay her fears, though.

Before she left work Monday, Susan asked Donna to pick up her children at Judy's. Barbara and Walt were going to keep them while she went to her classes at USC, Union. Michael and Alex loved to stay with Barbara and Walt.

Of average build and height, Walt is in his early fifties. His hair has turned snow white already. He has a calm, gentle, patient manner about him, never raises his voice. He was mush in the children's hands. Still, the children paid attention when he corrected them. "You don't have to tell Michael but once," Walt would say. In contrast to Walt's calm manner, Barbara has a bubbly personality. She often giggles when she talks.

The Garners saw Susan's children almost as much as I did. They went to the children's birthday parties, dropped by Susan's house on Christmas morning, used any excuse to be with them. Often when Walt came home from work, he asked Barbara, "Are the kids coming over tonight? I wouldn't mind if they did." It was Walt's way of suggesting that Barbara call Susan to see if she needed them to keep the kids. Barbara would joke, "Walt, you can't see them every night."

Walt's shop behind the house was a favorite place for Michael. That was where he "helped" Walt work on the '51 Chevy he was rebuilding. He would climb up on the bumper and quiz Walt about everything under the hood. Walt taught Michael the names of all the car parts. It was great fun for him to impress his mama when Walt pointed to the parts, and he recited the names.

Sometimes, Michael played games with Walt. He would point to a car part and say, "What's that, Walt?" when he knew what it was. Walt played along, scratching his head and saying, "Well, I don't know. I've done forgot. What is it?" Michael would laugh and tell him what it was. He was a happy kid.

Tools fascinated Michael. He was proud of his toy collection of tools that were "just like Walt's." He kept his tools in the trunk of a "Fred Flintstone" toy car that had belonged to his cousin Matt. Michael constantly asked Walt what he was doing with a particular tool as he worked on the car. One time he pushed a stool over to Walt's tool chest, climbed up on it, and pulled out the top drawer. As he stood there looking at all the tools, his eyes got big. "Walt's got everything!" he exclaimed, talking to himself. "He's got lots and lots of tools."

Michael's tools are still in Walt's shop in the trunk of the toy car. When Matt first gave him the car, Walt carved his name on it in big letters. Recently, Walt took the car out to show one of my friends. When he opened the trunk, he spotted two small socket wrenches Michael had borrowed from him. He chuckled and put them with his tools. I wondered if, at that moment, he could visualize Michael playing with those tools.

Walt and Barbara have an apple tree in their back yard. During the growing season, Michael picked apples to eat when he was over there. One fall when the apples had run out, Michael asked Walt if he could go get an apple. Walt told him the apples were all gone, but Michael didn't believe him. So Barbara took him to the tree to show him. Michael walked around the tree several times and looked and looked, trying to find an apple. Finally, he threw up his hands and said, "I eat 'em all up."

One day when Michael was in the shop helping Walt, he was eating a pear. He got the juice on his hands and put them on the car. The imprint of his little hands were still on that car when

My Daughter Susan Smith

Walt testified at the trial. He hasn't wiped them off yet.

When Michael wasn't watching Walt work on the car, he would play with his toys. On one occasion, he built a fence for some cows. He gathered all the cows up and put them in the fenced-in area and shut the gate.

After a while, Walt said, "I'll bet those cows are hungry. We better feed them. Don't you think you better let them out to eat."

"No," Michael said decisively. "I don't want to. I'll have to catch them again."

Walt chuckled. He had no comeback for that.

Michael loved for Walt to read stories to him. He often sat in his lap and listened to one story after another. He knew most of them by heart. Sometimes, Walt pretended to read some wild thing from the book. Michael would turn his head up to Walt with a puzzled look on his face and then look at the book. He knew when Walt wasn't saying the right words.

Many times Alex climbed into Walt's lap with Michael, but he usually didn't stay still very long. He was good for about five minutes, then he would scoot out to play with his toys. That Monday night before the tragedy, Michael climbed into Walt's lap and asked him to read a story. Alex was right behind him. Walt read one story to the boys. Alex stayed put. Walt read another story, and Alex still sat there.

"I can't believe he's sitting still that long," Barbara chuckled. "We've got to get a picture of this." She rushed to get the camera and took several shots.

The kids stayed in Walt's lap for fifteen or twenty minutes; then both boys got down and resumed playing with their toys. That was the last time Walt held the children in his lap. He treasures the memory.

Susan had two classes on Monday, British literature and aerobics. She went to her literature class; then, instead of going to aerobics, she went to Hickory Nuts to watch *Melrose Place* with friends from Conso. She felt guilty about asking Donna to pick up the kids when she didn't go where she said she would; but Donna would understand, she reasoned. They were best friends.

Auburn Sweatshirt

The usual crowd from Conso was there when Susan arrived, including Tom Findlay. She enthusiastically joined in the conversation. According to Tom, she seemed okay. "I mean," he said at the trial, "she was part of the group. We talked and joked and cut up." No one else noticed anything amiss. She left first, but no one thought anything about that, either. She said she had to pick up her kids.

As much as the boys adored Walt, Barbara, and Donna, Susan captured their attention completely when she came to pick them up. They always descended on her joyfully. It was no different that night. They were excited to see their mama.

The next day, Tuesday, a group of marketing people at Conso took a co-worker to lunch. He was a colleague from their English company, and it was his last day in the U.S. Susan was included in the group, sitting next to Tom.

Eating lunch with people at Conso was a frequent occurrence for Susan. In fact, soon after she went to work at Conso, she asked Susan Brown, the marketing manager, to include her in the group that regularly gathered together. She wanted to get to know Tom better. Susan Brown gladly included her.

Susan seemed happy enough during lunch. At least, that's how everybody remembers the occasion. She was quieter than usual, but no one thought anything about that. Entertaining an out-of-town guest changes the way people relate.

Back at work, though, things changed dramatically. Susan called Tom Findlay around 2:30 and asked him to meet her at the picnic table out front. Once they were seated, she told Tom she had something to tell him and didn't want anyone else to hear it.

At the trial, Tom told about seeing the tears form in Susan's eyes and asking her what had happened since lunch to upset her. She said David was still making threats. He had information that could hurt both of them. Tom asked what that information was.

She said it was something she didn't tell him Sunday night but should have. "You're going to hate me," she said. "Please don't hate me if I tell you." He assured her he wouldn't hate her.

She turned her head away to break eye contact. "I've been

involved with your father," she said, her voice trembling. "I've had a sexual relationship with him."

Tom was speechless, in a state of disbelief. After a few moments, he managed to mumble something like, "This is too weird."

Susan placed her elbows on the picnic table and dropped her head onto her opened hands. "I'm so sorry," she sobbed. "I'm so sorry. I didn't mean for it to happen. Please don't hate me."

"Susan," Tom said softly. "This doesn't mean our friendship is over. This information won't change that."

She raised her head and slowly turned to him, a look of incredulity flooding her face.

"But," he continued, "the intimacy part of our relationship will have to stop forever."

"I'm so sorry; I'm so sorry," she cried as tears rolled down her cheeks.

A call to Tom interrupted the conversation. Susan Brown had stepped outside to ask him a question. When she realized Susan was crying, she cut the conversation short and went back inside.

They sat out there talking for twenty or thirty minutes. Over and over, Susan said her life was in a mess, that everything was falling apart. David's threats were going to hurt people she loved. She didn't know how she could possibly handle everything.

Tom tried to console her. He told her not to worry, that David couldn't follow through on all his threats. He insisted David was bluffing, trying to scare her into giving him what he wanted in the divorce settlement.

Tom's reasoning worked. Susan stopped crying. He then said they needed to get back to work.

Susan went straight to her desk and sat down. The tears started flowing again. She desperately tried to pull herself together. When she once more got the tears stopped, she went to her supervisor's desk nearby.

"Sandra," she said nervously. "I need to go home."

"What's wrong?" Sandra asked, noticing the mascara streaks on Susan's face.

123

Auburn Sweatshirt

"Everything," Susan replied. "Everything."

"Don't you want to talk about it?" Sandra offered.

"I can't right now."

"Well, you know where I am," she said softly. "When you're ready to talk to me, give me a call; but for now, go on home."

Sandra thought she knew what was wrong. A week before, Susan became upset at work and told her she had a problem. When Sandra asked what it was, she said she was in love with someone who didn't love her. Sandra asked who it was. "Tom Findlay," Susan replied. Extremely surprised, Sandra could only say she was sorry. She didn't pursue the subject further.

Susan wanted to talk to Tom again before she left work. She walked back to her desk, picked up an Auburn sweatshirt she had been wearing to keep warm, and placed it across her arm. It belonged to Tom. Susan Brown had borrowed it from him to wear in her cold office and later offered it to Susan when she complained about being cold.

Susan stepped into the doorway of the studio where Tom was working. "I need to talk to you again," she requested, her voice cracking.

"Come on in," Tom said, walking to the door. He motioned to a chair near his desk and shut the door behind her. Susan slumped into the chair.

"I just don't know if I can handle all this that's happening," she said, her lips quivering. "I don't know if I can keep going. My life's in a big mess."

"Susan," he pleaded, "I forgive you for what has happened with my father. Please forgive yourself. We can still be friends."

"I know; I know," she replied, still fighting the tears. "I know you'll always be my friend." She stood up, took the sweatshirt off her arm, and handed it to Tom. "I'm going to give this to you, because I may not see you again."

On the witness stand, Tom said the first thought that went through his mind was, *Oh, my God! She's going to commit suicide.* But he tried to be calm. "You take it," he told her. "Take it home and wash it and bring it back to me. Okay?"

"Okay," she agreed and turned to leave.

My Daughter Susan Smith

"Susan," he called to her, almost in a whisper. She turned around to face him, a questioning look on her face.

"Tomorrow's another day. Things will be better then. You know we'll always be friends, don't you? Anytime you need somebody to talk to, I'll always be there for you."

"Thanks," she said, forcing a smile. "Your friendship means everything to me." She then asked him to hug her, but he declined.

After leaving the studio, Susan rushed by Susan Brown's desk as she went to see Donna down the hall. "I'm leaving now," Susan told Donna. "Why don't you walk with me to my car? I've got to tell you something."

"Okay. Sure," Donna agreed. She could tell something was terribly wrong.

While they walked slowly to the car, Susan told Donna about her conversation with Tom. She told her how bad she felt when he said they could never be anything more than friends.

Donna tried to convince Susan things would get better. They had had conversations like that many times, and it always helped. Their long friendship helped them to know what to say to each other. Donna offered to pick up the kids, but Susan said she didn't need to, that she would be fine. When they said good-bye, Donna thought she was okay. She figured they would talk later.

Susan glanced at her watch as she slid under the steering wheel. It was almost five. She didn't get away from work early after all. As she turned out of the Conso parking lot toward Judy's day care, a car pulled out from the Paradise Home Center across the street and onto the highway, staying several car lengths behind. When Susan made the turn to go to Judy's, the driver turned into the parking lot of Andy's Restaurant. The day care was clearly visible from that location.

After Susan picked up Michael and Alex, the driver continued in cautious pursuit. Susan didn't notice the car nor the driver.

The route from day care to her home took Susan by Hickory Nuts Restaurant. Approaching the restaurant, she saw Susan Brown in front of her, preparing to turn into the restaurant parking lot. She signaled to her, and Susan Brown signaled back, pointing to the parking lot. She pulled into the lot and left enough space for Susan to park beside her. As they rolled down their car windows to talk, the car on Susan's tail pulled into a parking space several rows down.

"Would you go to Conso with me?" Susan asked. "I've got to talk to Tom."

Glancing at her watch, Susan Brown answered, "Yes, I can. It's not five-thirty yet. Benjy and I are meeting friends for supper. I'm a little early. Sure, I've got time."

The sense of urgency in Susan's voice didn't surprise Susan Brown. She didn't know any details of her conversation with Tom, but she did know Susan was upset. She got into Susan's car and greeted Michael and Alex. They smiled bashfully.

Susan got right to the point. "I need to talk to Tom," she explained, "because I did something to upset him today."

"Really?"

"I played a joke on him, and I need to tell him that. It can't wait 'til tomorrow."

Susan paused, then said, "Well, I'll just tell you what happened...."

"Susan," Susan Brown interrupted. "I don't want to get involved in your conversations or personal matters with Tom."

"Oh? Okay."

When they got to Conso, Susan Brown started to take Alex out of his car seat, but He wouldn't let her lift up the bar. He wanted his mama. So my daughter took Alex and Susan Brown took Michael.

Sandra Williams was just leaving work when Susan drove up. She wondered why she was there but turned her head away, annoyed that she left work early, only to return.

The two Susans went directly to the marketing department and found the door locked. Susan knocked several times before Tom answered. "I'm sorry I upset you," she blurted out, stepping forward to hold the door open. "It was a joke. I was just playing a bad joke on you."

Tom froze when he saw Susan Brown.

"Susan knows about the story," she hurriedly explained.

"She knows it was a joke."

"I really don't know anything," Susan Brown contradicted, then took Michael by the hand and walked down the sidewalk. She wanted to distance herself from the conversation.

Susan kept insisting to Tom that she didn't mean what she said. She just wanted to see how he felt about her.

Finally, he blurted out sharply, "Fine, fine. I believe you, but I don't have time to deal with this now. I've got work to do. We can talk about this later."

Stunned by his blunt response, she replied, "Okay. I'll talk to you later." Visibly shaken, she turned away, then signaled to Susan Brown that she was ready to leave.

The two women quietly placed the children in their car seats. Susan kissed Alex as she buckled him in. She solemnly drove out of the parking lot onto the highway.

"Susan," she said softly, as they moved on down the highway, "I feel like I just lost the best friend I've ever had." Tears welled up in her eyes.

"Don't worry, Susan," Susan Brown assured her; "Tom's not one to hold grudges. He won't hold it against you. Things will be better tomorrow. You two will still be friends."

"I hope so, but that's hard to believe. I did something stupid. Really stupid," she added.

Susan Brown didn't ask for details.

Back at Hickory Nuts parking lot, Susan thanked her friend for going with her. "I can't tell you how much I appreciate it," she said. "I feel better now. Thanks for your encouragement."

The somber expression on Susan's face and the plaintive sound in her voice belied her words. The tears had stopped, but she looked so sad, so down.

"Why don't I grab a movie and come back to your house, and we can watch it together," Susan Brown offered.

"No, Susan," she insisted, "you don't need to do that. You've got people waiting for you. I'll be okay."

"No," Susan Brown insisted back. "I'll get a movie and we'll eat together. Benjy's going to shoot pool later with a friend, anyway, and I don't shoot pool. It won't hurt if I'm not there."

"No. I insist. They're waiting for you. Go ahead. I really will be okay."

"Well, if you need me, give me a call. Okay?"

"Okay, I will."

****

When Susan pulled into her driveway, her tail went right on by, turned around, and drove by again. Susan was too preoccupied with her problems to notice the car or the driver. She wouldn't have recognized the car, but she knew the driver well. It was Tiffany. She had borrowed her mother's car for that night's investigative assignment.

Tiffany was stalking Susan because David thought he needed more evidence than Tom's letter to countersue on the adultery charge or to get Susan to back down. David tells in his book that she gladly volunteered to get that evidence. She now thought she had all the evidence she needed, that the case was airtight, because she had witnessed the meeting between Susan and Tom. Out of her mind with excitement, she drove to a friend's house to call David. She told him about catching Susan with Tom. She also gave him the license-plate number of the car Susan followed into Hickory Nuts parking lot.

Tiffany asked David what he wanted her to do, since Susan was home. Should she wait outside Susan's house to see if she went anywhere? David told her he didn't think Susan was going anywhere, that she probably was in for the night. Certainly, he complimented Tiffany on her investigative efforts.

David tells in his book that, after talking to Tiffany, he called a friend in the police department and asked him to check the license-plate number. The buddy called him right back with the information. David knew who it was. That information made him think something more was going on than a meeting with Tom Findlay. He would call Susan to find out.

9

Driving into the Night

Susan called me after work that day of October 25. I was in the shower getting ready to go to the last flag football game of the season. Nick was playing. Like any proud grandmother who owns a camcorder, I had it loaded to catch the action.

Michael (Moe) told me Susan had called. He said she was at work, that she was leaving and would call me when she got home. It was almost six o'clock. I wondered why she was still at work; she got off at five.

I called Susan's house. She had just arrived home and said she needed to get Alex out of the car.

"Are you okay?" I asked.

"Mama, this has been one more hell of a day. If you're going to be home, I'm coming down there."

"I don't have anything cooked. You know I never cook on Tuesday. Bev goes to the Rotary."

"Yeah, I know. I'll fix the kids some pizza here."

"I'm getting ready to go to Nick's ball game," I explained.

"What time will you get back?"

"It starts at seven and lasts an hour. I'll be back by eight-thirty for sure."

"I'll just bring the kids to the football game."

"Don't do that. It's too cold. Why don't I come by there? That way you won't have to drag them out."

"Mama, you know how I am about being by myself. And David will call and ask what's wrong with me. I don't want to talk to him." I wondered why David would be calling for that reason but didn't ask. She could tell me later.

I learned later why David thought something was wrong with her. Friends probably had already reported to him that Susan left work early with tears in her eyes. But they likely didn't know why. He would want to know why. He would want to experience the satisfaction of knowing he was wearing her down.

"Will Moe be there to let me in?" she asked.

"Yes, he'll be here. He still can't drive."

"I'll go ahead and feed the kids here and pack a bag and give them a bath at your house."

"Okay, that's fine. I'll see you after the game. I love you."

"I love you, too, Mama."

While the kids ate pizza, Susan called Susan Brown at Hickory Nuts. The owner of the restaurant brought a cordless phone to the table where she was sitting with the crowd from Conso.

"Is Tom there?" Susan asked.

"Yes," Susan Brown replied. "At arms length," she added.

"Really," Susan chuckled. "Has he said anything about me? Has he acted mad at me?"

"No," she replied.

"I know you can't say much with Tom there. But will you call me when you get home?" Her friend said she would.

After the brief conversation, Susan packed a diaper bag and went to put it in the car. The phone rang. She ran through the doorway and grabbed for the receiver, gasping for breath. The minute she said hello, Michael and Alex jumped down from the table and started fighting over a toy. Alex screamed.

"What's wrong?" David asked.

"They're just fighting over a toy," she explained.

"I mean what's wrong with you?"

"Nothing's wrong," she insisted.

"Who's the guy you were talking to at Hickory Nuts?"

"I wasn't talking to any guy," she explained impatiently. "I was talking to Susan Brown. That's it; nobody else."

David's policeman friend had told him the car in the Hickory Nuts parking lot was registered in the name of Susan Brown's husband. Certainly disappointed that his wife was driving the car, he reverted to his original strategy.

"What's wrong?" he asked again. "Something's wrong. I can tell something's wrong by the sound of your voice."

"No, nothing. I'm okay," she insisted; but her voice broke.

David kept pressing. "Come on, Susan. I know you, and I know when something's wrong. Talk to me about it."

"Well, yeah," she said, "something is wrong. But I can't talk to you about it."

David was playing his usual games. He wanted to know how his threats had played out during the day. Knowing how naive Susan is, I'm sure she didn't detect the morbidity in his pressure.

After hanging up the phone, Susan sat down in the floor of the den and gathered chubby little Alex into her arms. With a little teasing, it didn't take long to get him to smile. While she soothed him, Michael jumped on her back, put his arms around her neck, and slid into her lap beside Alex. "I love you, Mama," he said, all smiles, his dark brown eyes shining.

"I love you, too, Baby!" she exclaimed, hugging and kissing him. That was the first time Michael had said he loved her before she told him first.

Even as she hugged her boys, Susan was emotionally exhausted, holding back tears and trying to contain her emotions for their sake. They were all over her, loving her. Maybe they sensed something was wrong and were trying to cheer her up.

After a few minutes, Susan picked up Alex, took Michael's hand, and went to the car. "We're going to see Grandma," she told them as she buckled their car seats. They were excited.

Susan backed the car out of the driveway and headed toward Highway 176. Tears spilled onto her cheeks. She grabbed some tissues from her pocketbook and wiped one eye and then the other. At the highway stop sign, she sat there for a few moments, trying to calm down.

"Are we going to Grandma's?" Michael asked.

"Yes, Baby, we're going to Grandma's in a little bit," she told him, making a special effort to keep her voice steady.

She turned right onto Highway 176, moving in the direction of Mount Vernon Estates, where I live. Shortly, she passed by Hickory Nuts Restaurant. She spotted Tom Findlay's car parked there. Knowing Susan, I can imagine what she was thinking as she drove by. Surely, she wondered who all from Conso were there, laughing and joking, as they usually did. She likely wondered what Tom was saying about her.

Susan's thoughts and actions that night are a matter of public record. As she drove, the event that happened in the afternoon, the thing that had upset her, dominated her thoughts. Dr. Halleck testified about the agony she was going through. She told him she was concerned about the mess she had made of her life. She was worried about David's threat to tell Cary Findlay's wife about her relationship with him. And she was worried about his threat to expose her relationship to Bev, about his threat to report her to IRS. She cried constantly, asking herself over and over why her life had gotten into such a mess, how everything could have gone so wrong. She was sure Tom hated her. She was sure David was going to ruin her. She was sure I wouldn't love her anymore.

She passed by Winn-Dixie where she and David met. This landmark brought back memories of their life together, of the failure of a marriage she thought would last until death do us part. Soon she would be a single mother. The thought of being alone terrified her. She started biting her fingernails.

The light turned red as she pulled up to Highway 49, which becomes Main Street through downtown Union. A short distance down that street is the white-columned courthouse where Sheriff Howard Wells has his offices.

"Are we going to Grandma's?" Michael asked again. "I want to go to Grandma's."

Michael's question pulled her back to the present. "Don't worry, Baby. We'll be at Grandma's soon."

She continued on south, moving closer to my house. She kept wiping her eyes and gnawing at her fingernails. She approached the intersection where Highways 176 and 215 intersect. A right turn goes toward Whitmire and my house, four miles away. The highway straight ahead goes to Carlisle, twelve miles away.

She went straight ahead, onto Highway 215. As she drove out of town, she reached down and turned off the radio. That was unusual for her. She always kept the car radio on.

With the street lights of Union behind her, an overcast October night plunged the car into thick darkness. "Nothing is going right in my life," she whispered. "My marriage is over. David will tell the whole world about Bev and Cary and the hot-tub party. Tom says we can only be friends, because I flirted with a married man and got involved with his dad. Why did I do those things? What am I going to do?" Mile by mile, she felt more and more isolated. The feelings of desperation consumed her.

She called toward the back seat, her voice quivering, "Kids, we can't live like this anymore. We can't live like this anymore."

There was no response. Michael and Alex were asleep.

Only a couple of cars interrupted the darkness as she moved down 215. Sections of the narrow highway are lined with trees and earth berms, increasing the intensity of the darkness.

I have asked Susan many times where she was going, why she didn't come to my house. She said that once she got in the car, she decided to ride around a while, until she could get herself together. Then she was going to go back home, call me, and say she had changed her mind about coming to my house. She had no travel plan. She only wanted to find a way to stop crying. She didn't want me to see her like that.

At Carlisle, Highway 215 dead ends into the Carlisle-Chester Highway. A service station and small market are across from the stop sign. Susan sat there for a moment, resting, crying, biting her fingernails. She glanced back at Michael and Alex. They were still asleep.

She turned left toward the Broad River. The darkness grew thicker and thicker. Two miles farther, she came to Broad River Bridge. She stopped the car, put the gear in neutral, and pulled on the emergency brake. With the car motor running, the headlights on, and the hazard lights blinking, she opened the car door and got out. She wasn't worried about the car being in the driving lane. She hadn't passed a car since she left Carlisle.

She walked to the bridge railing and leaned forward on it, her arms extended toward the water. A faint glimmer from the cloud-shrouded moonlight bounced off the river.

"What am I going to do? What am I going to do? I can't go on like this," she sobbed. She tried hopelessly to stop the flow of tears. She wanted to jump into the river with Michael and Alex and wondered how she could manage that.

"Mama, Mama," Michael cried. She rushed to open the rear door. "Don't worry, Baby," she said tenderly, kissing him on the cheek and hugging him. "Everything's okay."

Her heart beat furiously as she slid under the steering wheel into the front seat. Her hands trembled on the steering wheel.

At the trial, Dr. Halleck testified that Susan planned to commit suicide at Broad River Bridge and wanted to take the children with her. She had grown up without knowing her father. She didn't want her children to grow up without a mother. She was concerned, too, about the conflict between David and me and how that would affect the children if she weren't here. She knew they would be okay in heaven. Dr. Halleck noted that these kinds of thoughts are irrational.

"When are we going to get to Grandma's?" Michael asked sleepily.

"In a little bit, Michael," she said softly. "In a little bit."

She looked over at Alex. He was sound asleep. She eased the door shut to keeping from waking him.

Back at the 215 junction, Susan turned toward Union. The road splits a few miles down the highway. The left fork goes to Union; straight ahead goes to Monarch Mills, a community just east of Union, where Donna's fiancé, Mitch, lived. She took the fork to Union. Once inside the Union city limits, she turned down one street, then another, driving aimlessly.

David Caldwell, a state investigator, testified at the trial that Susan said she asked Michael if he wanted to go see Mitch. Michael excitedly said he did. She ended up in Monarch Mills but doesn't know what route she took to get there. She just knows she stopped at a red traffic signal where Highway 215 intersects with Highway 49.

She saw a black man standing on the street corner beside her car. He wore a knit hat and was dressed in blue jeans and a plaid jacket. She didn't remember ever seeing him before. Except for him, the street was deserted.

When the light turned green, she went straight ahead on Highway 49, still with no particular destination in mind. She forgot about going to Mitch's house. By then, she had chewed her fingernails to the quick. Her feelings of loneliness and isolation and desperation grew stronger and stronger.

Once outside Monarch Mills, the street lights ended. Driving down the narrow highway, she descended into blinding darkness. A couple of times she almost ran off the road because she was crying so hard. Six miles or so from town, her car lights caught the white lettering of the large sign: "John D. Long Lake." She impulsively turned left onto the gravel road that went to the lake. She remembers hoping the gate was locked.

But the gate was open, and she drove slowly toward the parking area beside the lake, stopping at the top of the seventy-five-foot boat ramp. She turned off her headlights, put the gear in neutral, and pulled the emergency brake in place. She sat still for a short time, surrounded by the dark silence of the night. Michael and Alex were fast asleep; the only sound was the hum of the car engine.

"Kids, we can't go on like this," she sobbed to the sleeping children. "We can't go on like this."

The trembling returned, starting with her hands, then moving over her entire body. She nervously opened the car door, stepped into the darkness, and eased the door shut. She wept audibly.

Looking in the direction of the lake, she saw a vast, dark, threatening expanse. She leaned against the side of the car for a few minutes to steady herself. She then opened the car door and slid under the steering wheel. Her hands shook violently, but she managed to release the emergency brake. The car slowly eased forward.

Frantically, she slammed on the brake, her leg trembling and her foot shaking on the pedal. She tried to calm down, to steady her foot. She eased her foot off the brake. The car rolled forward. She stabbed at the brake again, jerking to a stop.

She opened the door and got out without setting the emergency brake. With her back to the car, she sobbed, "Why do I feel this way? Why is everything so bad in my life? What am I going to do? What am I going to do?" She felt completely and absolutely alone, and the feelings terrified her. She had to get out of there. She started running up the ramp, away from the car.

She could hear the car moving when she reached the top of the ramp. She covered her ears with her hands as it gathered speed and rolled toward the lake.

Strangely, her mind suddenly shut out every sound. She heard nothing more, not even the splashing of the car as it moved away from the shore into the lake, not even the gurgle as it sank into the dark, muddy waters.

She stumbled and fell, catching herself with her hands. "Oh,

God! Oh, God!" she screamed, scrambling to her feet. "What have I done? Why did you let this happen?" She wanted to go back, but she knew it was too late.

What am I going to tell my mama? she thought. *What am I going to tell her? She'll hate me. David will hate me. Everyone will hate me.*

She ran on toward the highway, crying and screaming, "Someone, please help me! Someone please help me!" Approaching the highway, she saw a house on the opposite side, illuminated with flood lights. She ran toward the house, crying and screaming, "Someone, please help me! Someone please help me."

The image of the black man standing on the street corner flashed through her mind. She began to concoct her story.

****

Tiffany stayed at her friend's house for about forty-five minutes, playing with her children. On the way home, she drove by Susan's house to check one more time. She gasped at the scene. The house was dark and the Mazda gone. Frantic, she drove to Winn-Dixie to report to David.

David suggested several places to look. Tiffany searched for Susan for a solid hour. She drove through downtown Union, went by my house, took a run through Wal-Mart and Hickory Nuts parking lots, then back to Susan's house, and finally returned to Winn-Dixie, terribly disappointed that Susan had slipped through her net.

10

Coffee and Doughnuts

While I was at the ball game that fateful night, I thought about Susan the whole time, wondering if she was all right. I tried to reason that a hard day for her wasn't unusual; her job was often stressful. Her need to be with people wasn't unusual, either. She always needed to be with people. What kept echoing in my mind was the unusual urgency in her voice.

Games at the little-league level are limited to an hour. Nick made a touchdown just before time ran out. Naturally, he was very excited. I bragged on him and assured him I had caught it on tape. I then made a quick exit.

"Got to hurry," I told Wendy and the boys. "Susan's supposed to be at the house."

"Can we go see Michael and Alex?" Nick begged excitedly. Matt chimed in his agreement.

"Come on over," I urged Wendy. "We'll watch Nick's touchdown." Other than grandmother's pride, I had taped the game so Scotty could see it. He was in Charlotte on a business trip.

"Well, okay," she agreed, then turned to Nick and Matt. "But just for a little bit. You kids need to get in bed."

"Where's Susan?" I called to Michael, as I came in the den. "Her car's not out front."

"Haven't heard a word from her," he called to me from his bedroom, then came into the den. "You're not the only one wondering where she is," he continued, sitting down on the sofa. "David called, too. Said he wanted to talk to her about baby-sitting the kids tomorrow night."

"That doesn't make any sense. Why would he have to know that tonight? Wonder what he's pestering her about?"

"No telling. Donna called right after him. She wondered if we knew where Susan was."

My heart skipped a beat. Donna always knew where Susan

Coffee and Doughnuts

was. "Did she say why she was concerned about Susan?"

"No. She just wondered where she was. You know how those two are. They talk on the phone all the time. I guess she couldn't get her at her house and thought she'd be here."

"That's strange," I told him. "She said she'd be here. Maybe she decided to wait until after the game to come over. I'll put the tape in the VCR. Wendy and the kids will be here in a minute to watch Nick's touchdown."

"Where's Susan?" Wendy asked as she came through the back door. "I didn't see her car out front."

"I don't know," I replied. "She said she'd be here. Maybe she'll get here pretty soon. Let's go ahead and look at the tape and make sure I got the touchdown."

Wendy asked if Susan was having any trouble with David. I told her I didn't think so, at least nothing more than the usual aggravation.

I stopped the tape after Nick's touchdown. I knew Wendy wanted to get the boys on home, and they did leave soon after that, thinking Susan had changed her mind about coming over. The minute they were out the door, I dialed Susan's number and let it ring several times.

I hung up the phone and called to Michael, "I'm going over to Susan's. It's not like her to say she'll be somewhere and not show up." It was a little after nine. Susan would never be that late.

****

Shirley and Rick McCloud's house, located on Highway 49, is approximately seventy yards from the entrance to John D. Long Lake. About the same time I was driving across town to check on Susan, Shirley was stretched out on the sofa checking the TV listings. Her husband Rick was sitting in a chair across from her, also contemplating what program they would watch at nine o'clock. Rick Jr. was in his bedroom.

Suddenly, they heard a strange wailing sound outside. In her testimony at the trial, Shirley recalled that it sounded like an animal in distress. They rushed to the front window and looked out but couldn't see anything.

The door bell rang; then someone banged repeatedly on the locked storm door. Shirley cautiously opened the inside door. Standing before her was a young woman, dressed neatly in blue jeans and an "Auburn" sweatshirt. Her long, brown hair was pulled back, held in place with a big white bow.

The young woman moved her hands frantically across the glass, trembling and crying hysterically. "He's got my kids and my car," she cried, jerking at the handle of the door. "I can't believe it. Please help me! please help me!."

In a split second, a number of possibilities flashed through Shirley's mind: *Is she a decoy? Has her boyfriend kicked her out of the car? Has her car broken down?*

She opened the storm door wide enough to put her head out and quickly scan the porch. She then pulled the woman in and hurriedly shut the door and locked it.

The woman was younger than Shirley first thought, definitely in her early twenties. Thinking she was on the verge of collapsing, Shirley took hold of her hand to steady her, then put her arm around her shoulders. Rick got on the opposite side and helped take her to the love seat in the living room.

With Rick standing behind the woman, Shirley bent down and placed a hand firmly on each side of her face to calm her. "Please," she urged, "tell me again what you just said."

"A black man has my kids and my car," she sobbed.

Rick yelled to his son in the bedroom, "Rick, call 911."

Rick Jr. dialed the number while glancing from the bedroom door to see who was there.

"The dispatcher wants to know if she needs an ambulance," he called to his dad.

"No. No, she doesn't," Rick called back.

The young man relayed information from his father to the dispatcher about what had happened, what kind of car the young woman had, and a description of the carjacker. The dispatcher asked one specific question after another about the carjacker: Did he have on a jacket, a cap? Was he tall, short, slender, heavy? Each time, Rick turned to the young woman for the answer. For each question, she said she really didn't know but

Coffee and Doughnuts

then tried to give an answer.

After completing the 911 call, Rick and his son went to see if the car was nearby. He turned down the gravel road that goes to John D. Long Lake, drove to the parking area near the shore-line, and made a circle past the boat ramp. They saw nothing unusual.

While the men were gone, Shirley sat down on the sofa be-side the young woman. "Tell me what your name is," she re-quested gently.

"Susan Smith," she sobbed. Shirley didn't know the name.

"Now, tell me what happened."

She told Shirley that a black man jumped into her car at the red light at Highway 49 in Monarch. "He put a gun to my side," she sobbed, "and told me to drive straight ahead and not look at him. After a little while, I asked him, 'Why are you doing this?' He told me to shut up, or he would shoot me. So I kept driving. I didn't know what else to do."

Susan began to tremble uncontrollably. Shirley held her close until the tremors stopped. Then she continued, saying, "All of a sudden, he made me stop the car in the middle of the road, just down there." She pointed in the direction of the lake.

"Where down there?" Shirley asked.

"Right past the sign," she replied.

"The lake sign?" Shirley questioned.

"Yes, yes," she sobbed, "right there past the lake sign. He made me stop in the middle of the road, right in the middle of the road. There weren't any cars coming either way; nobody was there. And he told me to get out. I asked him why was he doing this? Why was he doing this? And he told me to shut up and get out of the car, or he was going to shoot me."

As she paused to catch her breath. Shirley patiently waited.

"I begged the man to please, please, let me take my kids. He told me to just get out of the car and pushed me out of the driver's side onto the road. He shut the door and started driving off. I grabbed onto the car door, pleading with him to please give my kids to me. He said, 'No; just shut up. Don't worry, lady, I'm not going to hurt your kids.'

"I fell down in the middle of the road, screaming for Michael and Alex. I really don't know how long I was there. All I know is the car was out of sight when I got up. I turned around and saw the bright light in your front yard and ran to it."

Susan began to tremble again. Shirley put her arms around her and held her close until the tremors stopped.

"I've got to call my mama," Susan told her. "Oh, what am I going to tell her?" she sighed nervously. "What am I going to tell her? I should have locked the car doors."

"Who is your mother?" Shirley asked.

"Linda Russell. I need to call her. I'm supposed to be over there now."

"Tell me your name again."

"Susan Smith."

Shirley picked up the phone from the table beside the love seat. She asked for the number. Susan stared blankly at her for a few seconds, then haltingly told her.

After dialing the number, Shirley asked Susan if she would like to talk to her mother. She said she would and reached for the phone. Michael was on the other end of the line. "Oh, Moe," Susan sobbed, "something terrible has happened." She dropped the receiver into her lap.

Shirley picked up the receiver. "This is Shirley McCloud," she said. "I live on Highway 49 just before you get to John D. Long Lake. I have a Susan Smith here. She is saying someone has taken her children and her car. Is her mother home?"

"What!" Michael exclaimed. "No, her mother's not here."

"Can you go get your mother?"

"I can't drive right now," he explained.

"Is there any way you can get somebody to get her mother?" Shirley asked.

"Yes; sure. I can call my uncle."

Susan asked for the phone. "Moe," she said, "You've got to get Mama as soon as possible. A black man's got Michael and Alex."

"What!" he exclaimed. "Don't worry, Susan. I'll get her. Are you okay?" She said she was, that the man didn't touch her and said he wouldn't hurt the kids.

After hanging up the phone, Susan nervously told Shirley, "I

Coffee and Doughnuts

need to call my stepfather."

"Who is your stepfather?" she asked.

"Beverly Russell."

"Where is he at?"

"Spartanburg."

Susan tried to make the call but was too nervous. Shirley briefly told Bev what had happened, that her mother wasn't home, and that Susan's brother was going to contact his uncle.

Susan called David herself and, through sobs, told him what had happened. After the call, she went to the bathroom to throw away her disposable contacts. She had been crying so much she couldn't wear them anymore. When she came out, her voice was still shaky, but she had calmed down somewhat. Shirley no longer felt she needed to sit right beside her. She suggested Susan get comfortable on the larger sofa in the living room and handed her a washcloth.

Susan looked around the room as she wiped her face. "Do you have any children?" she asked.

"Yes, I do," Shirley replied. "That big husky boy sitting out there on the deck is my son." Rick Jr. and his father were waiting outside for the police to arrive.

"Oh," she responded, looking in the direction of the deck. "McClouds? I know some McClouds."

As they were exchanging information about McClouds they knew, two police officers came rushing in. The deputies knelt down in front of Susan and asked her what kind of car she had, the license-tag number, color, and what the carjacker looked like. When pressed for details about the carjacker, Susan said he had on a plaid jacket, blue jeans, and a stocking cap. They quickly exited after getting the information.

Union County Sheriff Howard Wells arrived next, at approximately 9:16. He had picked up the call on his police transmitter while driving home from work. When he first drove up to the residence, he held a brief conversation with two deputies in a marked unit parked in the front yard. He sent them to be on the lookout for the car and went inside. Shirley related the information Susan had given her and took him to the living room. "She's really upset," she told the sheriff. "She just can't stop crying."

When Wells entered the room, Susan was seated on the sofa with her hands cradling her face. She looked up when he sat down beside her. He could see that her face was puffy and red from crying. "Do you recognize me?" he asked. She said she did. She recognized the face, dark brown hair, mustache, and sturdy build. But it was more than merely knowing what he looked like. She knew he was godfather to Scotty and Wendy's children. She had seen him at Nick and Matt's birthday parties. Yes, she knew who he was. And everything she knew about him was good.

Seeing someone she knew had a calming effect on Susan. Dressed in his two-piece suit, the sheriff didn't look like a policeman, and his approach was reserved, not confrontational. In a deliberately calming tone of voice, he explained that he needed to get as many details and information as possible so they could start a search for her car and her children. The quicker they got the information, he emphasized, the quicker they could begin the search. Could she answer some questions? She said she could.

"Could you describe the carjacker?" he asked.

Her voice cracking, she said he was a black man and had on a toboggan-type cap, plaid jacket, mostly red over white and blue, and blue jeans. She thought he was in his late twenties or early thirties, but she couldn't be sure. When pressed for other details, she said she couldn't give height and weight estimates because he was seated the whole time she was with him.

"Did he have a gun?" Wells asked.

She told him he had a small, dark handgun.

When asked about the children, she said Michael, three, had on white jogging pants, a blue-green shirt and a light blue jacket. Alex, fourteen months, had on a red and white striped outfit and a blue and red jacket. She explained that neither one had on shoes because she planned to give them a bath at my house.

She described the car: a 1990 Mazda Protege, burgundy. She couldn't remember the tag number but stated that it had a USC parking sticker on the left rear bumper and that the front bumper had a gash in it.

Wells didn't rush Susan. That wasn't his style. He let her an-swer the questions at her own pace. When he had secured the information he felt was essential to begin the search, he went outside. Two more police units had just arrived. He informed the officers of the search technique to be used. They passed the information on to other units stationed in the general area.

Using the McCloud telephone, Wells alerted the dispatcher of BOLO (Be on the Lookout for) information, talked with the supervisor of the local highway patrol and asked for assistance from all of their people. He made a call to SLED (State Law Enforcement Division) headquarters in Columbia. Chief Robert Stewart said he would put a helicopter at his disposal and help in any way.

Police in an unmarked unit searched the parking lot of John D. Long Lake and projected lights into the water and around the shoreline. They found nothing unusual.

****

Around 9:15 I drove through the intersection where High-way 176 meets 49. A few minutes later, I pulled into Susan's driveway. To my surprise, Tim and Hedy were parked in front. Tim jumped out of his car and came to the driver's side of my car. I quickly pushed the control button to open the window.

"What's up?" he asked, nonchalantly leaning down to the window.

"Nothing, I hope. Susan was supposed to be over at the house and didn't show up. I just came over here to check on things. You know me. I can't sit still until I know what's going on."

He looked surprised. "You mean you don't know?"

"Know what?"

"A black man jumped in the car with Susan."

"Oh, no!" I exclaimed. "I can't believe it. I've told her so many times to lock her doors."

"Calm down now, Linda," Tim urged. "Susan's all right. The man put her out and he's got the kids; but he told her he wouldn't harm them. Moe said Susan's down at the McCloud's, near John D. Long Lake."

"What's she doing way out there?" I asked.

"I don't know. They called your house, and Moe called us and said you were on your way over here."

"We need to call him right now to find out exactly where Susan is," I said. "Let's use Susan's phone."

I tried a key on Susan's front door that looked like the right one, but it didn't work. I nervously tried one key after another. Finally, I remembered Susan had the locks changed when David kept coming in her house unannounced.

Tim suggested we go to his house. As usual, Tim took a calm approach to the situation. Even though he is four years younger than I am, I have leaned on him many, many times.

"All I know," Michael explained when I called, "is that Susan is at the McClouds. She said something about the man taking the kids and promising not to hurt them. She was crying so hard I could hardly understand her."

"Do you know where the McClouds live?" I asked.

"The woman didn't give me an address. She just said her house is across from John D. Long Lake."

"Get dressed. I'll have Wendy come by and pick you up. We all need to be with Susan."

"I'll be ready."

We went through the phone book and picked out a McCloud. They didn't know anything about a Susan Smith. Tim called 911 and asked about her. The dispatcher wanted to know if Susan's mother was there. I got on the phone, and she gave me the number.

The minute I told Shirley McCloud who I was, she put Susan on the line. Before I could say anything, Susan said, "Mama, just hurry up and come on. Somebody's got Michael and Alex."

"How'd it happen?" I asked.

"Just come on, Mama. I'll tell you when you get here. Mrs. McCloud can tell you how to get here." Shirley McCloud then took the receiver and gave me the directions.

I called Wendy, told her what had happened, and asked her to pick up Michael. Then I called Barbara and Walt. They were there in no time, followed by Donna and Mitch. Bev pulled up right after them. I jumped into his car, and we led the way to the McCloud's.

At first, Bev and I talked about how it might have happened. "She should have locked her doors," I told him. "She should have locked her doors." Then we both fell silent.

Minute by minute, mile by mile, my chest got tighter and tighter. Suddenly, I was gripped by the horrifying realization that Michael and Alex were in the hands of a man who might kill them, and I would never see them again. Everything dovetailed into one big emotional upheaval. My heart beat faster and faster; it felt like my chest would burst from sheer pain. I tried to relax but nothing helped. By the time we reached the McCloud's, my chest was so tight I could hardly breathe.

Shirley McCloud met us at the front door. After I told her who I was, she said, "She was hysterical when she first got here, but she's settled down some now. I am so sorry."

As we all walked into the den, I saw Susan and David sitting on the sofa. Her eyes appeared to be frozen wide open, like she had just been frightened out of her senses. The expression jarred me. I had never seen her like that before. Howard Wells was in a chair beside them, looking extremely grave. Donna and Mitch stood nearby with blank stares on their faces.

I sat down beside Susan and hugged her tight. "Are you all right?" I asked with a nervous tremor in my voice. She nodded yes, then turned to face me. Her eyes were heavy with sadness.

"Susan," I said. "I've warned you and warned you about locking your car doors."

"I know, Mama. I'm so sorry."

"What did the man look like? Had you ever seen him before?" I asked. Nervously, I threw one question after another at her.

"Just average looking," she told me. "No, I've never seen him before." She tried to answer every question.

I asked Howard Wells what was being done to find the children. "We've got all the roads blocked off," he assured me. "We're getting a lot of people involved."

It looked like Howard wanted to talk with Susan some more, so we all hugged her and assured her the police would find the children soon. Barbara Garner wanted to stay. She sat down beside Susan, and David stayed on the other side. The rest of us went out to the front yard.

"I hope Howard gets through talking with Susan and David soon, so we can get out of this woman's house," I told everyone. I felt bad about invading it. By this time, Wendy and Michael had arrived with Nick and Matt, along with other relatives. The front yard was filled with cars.

"Yeah," Tim agreed. "And we need to tell Leigh and Paul before they hear about it from someone else." Leigh was in college at USC, Spartanburg, thirty miles away. Paul was playing basketball at USC, Union.

"And Mama and Scotty, and everybody else," I added.

After a half hour or so, I suggested we go back inside and see what Howard had to say. He had finished the questioning but wanted to talk to the family. We huddled around him and Susan.

"It would be best," Howard advised, "if everyone is in one place."

"We can go to our place," Tim offered.

"There's more parking space at our house," I said. They all agreed our house probably would be best.

Howard wrote down our phone number and said he would keep us informed about any developments.

I thanked Shirley McCloud for all her help and apologized for invading her home. She assured us that she was glad to help.

Walking to our car, Susan told me David was going to take her by her house to get her glasses and some clothes. "And Howard Wells said I need to get credit card numbers and information," she added.

"Okay, we'll see you at the house. Come on over as soon as you can get everything together."

"We'll tell Mama," Tim offered. "Paul should be home by now. We'll pick him up and then go to Mama's."

"Okay," I said, "Bev and I need to be home when Susan gets there."

Driving down Highway 49 toward Union, it all seemed liked a bad dream. I kept asking Bev, "Where are the children?

Where are the children? Who would do something like this? We've got to find them."

I thought about a locking-doors game little Michael and I played many times. Whenever Susan left my house with him and Alex, I reminded her to lock the car doors. My reminder became more urgent when a carjacker in D.C. took over a woman's car and dragged her down the road, killing her. "That could happen to you," I told Susan.

"Mama," she chided. "That won't happen in Union."

"It can happen anywhere," I warned.

I was so concerned that Susan wasn't taking the warning seriously, I got Michael to help me. When they came to visit, I would tell him that his mama should lock the doors of the car every time they went somewhere. Then when I stood outside their car to tell them good-bye, I would say, "Okay, Michael, what are you going to tell Mama?"

He would take the pooper (pacifier) out of his mouth and say, "Lock the doors, Mama," then giggle when she locked the doors.

My mother had already called Tim and Hedy's house before they got back. She was listening on a scanner and heard Susan's name and wanted to know why. They were all at my house within an hour; then Tim and Paul left for Spartanburg to tell Leigh. As it turned out, Leigh wasn't there. They had to leave a message with her roommate, Jennifer. The two of them came on when Leigh got home.

Relative after relative arrived, but Susan and David still weren't there. I was growing more impatient by the minute. "Where do you suppose they are?" I asked Hedy. "Were they going anywhere else besides Susan's house?"

"They didn't say they were."

Bev assured me they would be there in a minute, that they were just going to make a quick stop by her house.

I couldn't sit still. I went outside and paced up and down the driveway and down the road. I prayed desperately that the kids would be all right. "God," I begged over and over, "please don't let that man hurt Michael and Alex."

Bev was on the phone when I went back inside.

"Has Susan called?" I asked after he hung up.

"Not that I know of. But we've been on the phone calling everybody we could think of."

Finally, Susan and David came in the back door, carrying cokes and a sack.

"Where in the world have you been?" I asked.

"We stopped by Winn-Dixie," Susan replied matter-of-factly.

"Winn-Dixie?" I questioned. "Why in the world were you going by there at this time of night?"

"Some of our friends were working in the store. We got them to let us in to buy doughnuts."

"Doughnuts?" I must have had a puzzled look on my face. *Their kids are missing*, I wondered silently, *and they stop to buy doughnuts.*

"I thought someone might want doughnuts and coffee," she replied.

"How long does it take to buy doughnuts?" I asked.

She explained that they saw a bunch of kids hanging out at the stadium when they were leaving Winn-Dixie. Tiffany was in the crowd. Susan told David, "There's Tiffany. If you want to see her, go ahead." So David went over there and talked for a while. Then, on the way to my house, Susan told David that Tom Findlay might be coming down to our house, and she hoped he wouldn't get mad and that it would be okay if Tiffany came over here.

Going to Winn-Dixie and the stadium when your kids are missing. Buying doughnuts at midnight. It all seemed incredibly bizarre.

I didn't think about it at the time, but we have a custom in our family. When someone close dies, we take doughnuts and coffee. Susan had picked up on the custom. She thought we would need doughnuts to go with our coffee.

Left: Susan sticks her finger in the cake on her first birthday. As usual, a bunch of cousins, their parents, and other family members gathered at my house for the party.

Right: Birthdays have always been big for Susan. At her third birthday party, she holds a stuffed animal, a gift from one of her friends.

Left: Susan was six years old when her father killed himself. This picture was taken at Tim and Hedy's home while Scotty, Michael, and I were at the funeral home receiving friends and family who came by to express their condolences. At the time, she seemed to have no understanding of what had happened. Later, the tragic event would haunt her.

Left: Christmas of 1981. After opening presents, Susan's brother Michael, dressed as Santa Claus, clowned around with her (right center), her step-sister Tami (bottom right), and cousins Adrian (top), Leigh (left center), and Paul (bottom left).

Right: My brother Tim, our official family photographer, took this picture of Susan (left) and his daughter Leigh, just before we watched them perform at their dance recital. Susan was 8 and Leigh 6.

Above: Cousins at the beach (Susan, center). Several in our family occasionally got together and rented a house on Pawleys Island, off the South Carolina coast, a favorite vacation spot.

Left: Susan and a classmate in third grade. The two girls were winners of a contest to have their drawings on the covers of their class yearbook.

Right: Susan with her brothers, Scotty (left) and Michael, shortly before Scotty and Wendy married.

Below: Hedy, Joan, and I dressed the cousins for Halloween. From left: Susan, Adrian, Leigh, and Paul (in front).

Left: Susan with her cousins Leigh and Paul, at my mother's house one Easter. We always stopped by Mama's for a few minutes after church.

Right: Susan holds a dog Bev bought me for Christmas, a yellow Labrador named Bonnie. When Bonnie had puppies, we named one of them Clyde.

Left: Donna (right) and Susan during their senior trip. The two have been friends since they were children. Susan often went with Donna and her family to the beach on vacations.

Michael sits in front of a Christmas tree for a picture just before his second Christmas.

Alex at six months. He was such a good-natured baby.

Below: Michael helps Alex celebrate his first birthday. As usual, cousins, friends, and other relatives helped, too.

Right: Less than two weeks before everything happened, Susan made plans for Michael's third birthday party at McDonald's. Alex enjoys the birthday cake.

Left: Alex in a sea of colored balls at Michael's birthday party.

Below: Halloween 1993, Michael won a Keebler Elf contest. He was two. Susan and David took him trick or treating and stopped by Donna's house to show his costume to Barbara and Walt. Barbara grabbed her camera and took this picture of Michael and Walt. Barbara and Walt were like a third set of grand parents to Michael and Alex.

Left: Alex's birthday picture, the last formal photo Susan had made of Michael and Alex, shortly before their deaths. The photo was viewed around the world.

Right: Michael and Alex were special to Mitch, Donna's husband. He was disgusted and upset when the press speculated that he had something to do with their disappearance.

Right: When Walt and Barbara babysat the children, Walt often read to them. At times, he changed the story to tease them. Michael would quickly correct him because he had many of the stories memorized.

Left: Susan took this picture of Alex in her kitchen after Michael's third birthday party. It was on a roll of film that was still in her camera when we packed up her things. Alex "rides" a stick horse, Mitch's birthday gift to Michael.

Below: This photo of Michael also was in Susan's camera. He laughs as he often did when posing for the camera.

11

Searching for the Carjacker

By 12:30 a.m. the house was filled with people. I placed the doughnuts and soft drinks on the table in the breakfast nook and suggested Susan put her clothes in her old bedroom, then went into the living room to sit down.

I was barely seated when I looked up to see a TV reporter and cameraman standing in front of me. I had no idea who let them in, but I recognized the reporter as Cynthia Barnes from Channel 7 News, Spartanburg. She sat down beside me and asked if she could talk with Susan. "I don't know," I said. "I'll go see."

I walked down the hall to Susan's bedroom and knocked on the door. She was sitting on the floor when I opened the door. David was close by in a chair.

"A reporter from Channel 7 is here to see you," I told Susan.

A look of surprise, mixed with fear, flashed across her face. "What am I going to say to a reporter?" she asked, standing up and walking to the doorway. Before I could answer, the TV news duo was behind me. I moved out of the doorway, and Susan stepped into the hall to talk with them. Cynthia Barnes threw one question after another at her: How did it happen? What did the man look like? To one of the questions, Susan said something like, "I didn't have anything to do with the disappearance of my children."

Susan cut the interview short, saying she and David had to go to the sheriff's office. The team slipped out without saying so much as a thank you or even a good-bye. I didn't see their taped segment until the prosecution ran it on the first day of the trial, presenting it as strong evidence against Susan.

I don't know who gave Ms. Barnes permission to come into my home. I certainly didn't. I have asked everyone who was in my house that night if they let her in. No one remembers doing that. I suppose she sneaked in with all the people coming by. For this act of invading my home, she received an award and a significant promotion. This was the premiere event in the suffocating media onslaught on our family.

About the same time the news team exited my home, Kevin Kingsmore heard a report of the carjacking on a Spartanburg radio station. The announcer gave only a few details and no names. He simply mentioned that the car was a Mazda Protege and the ones involved were a young mother and her two little boys. He was shocked; he couldn't believe something like that would happen in Union. At the trial, he said it crossed his mind that it might be Susan, possibly because he had seen her the night before. They waved at each other as they both were leaving USC, Union.

Kevin and Susan met during their senior year in high school when they were in the same psychology class. They dated a few times and became good friends but never went beyond that. The last time he had talked to her was in 1989 when they went to a Christmas party together. After that, she got married and he went to college and established a computer business in Union.

Even though Kevin hadn't talked to Susan, he had kept up with what she was doing. People in small towns do that. He knew she was married and had two boys. At the trial, he described her as one of the most caring, honest people he knew. He found her to be basically shy but a lot of fun and able to carry on an interesting conversation when she got to know people. He knew nothing about her suicide attempts.

Kevin went to bed after hearing the news bulletin. Around 3:00 a.m. the phone rang. The caller confirmed his hunch. The young mother, indeed, was Susan Smith. He lay awake the rest of the night thinking about her and what he could do to help find the children. He remembered the Polly Klaas case in which a lot of her friends got together and developed a flier. He wondered if he and other friends could do the same for Susan.

Around six, Kevin called the sheriff's office and got permission from Howard Wells to develop the flier. He worked all morning designing it; but before he was finished, someone told him that Mike Stevens, a local publisher, was already printing fliers. Holly Russell Abee, Susan's stepsister, had gotten in touch with him. The fliers included the composite drawing of the alleged carjacker, a drawing of Susan's burgundy Mazda, and a recent photo of Michael and Alex. Kevin decided to redirect his efforts to organizing hundreds of volunteers to distribute Stevens' fliers all over the upstate. Eventually, they were broadcast on national television and sent all over the nation.

Two days later, Kevin came to our house to see Susan, just to let her know he was thinking about her and was helping to find the boys. When David Bruck asked if the Susan Vaughan he knew would harm her children, Kevin said, "She must have snapped. It wasn't Susan." And when asked similar questions by the prosecution, he said, "Her mind somehow was in a state of shock."

Susan Brown from Conso, who was the last person to talk with Susan before the tragedy, came by around nine in the morning. She sat down on the sofa with Susan and David and looked at pictures of Michael and Alex. At the trial, she said Susan got visibly upset, saying, "Oh, God, what will happen if my children don't look this way the next time I see them?"

Sharon O'Dell, personnel director at Conso, had called Tom Findlay around ten the night before to make sure he knew what had happened. "Have you heard about Susan Smith?" she asked. At the trial, he said his first thought was *Oh, my God, she's killed herself*! But he replied, "No." The next morning he called Susan to express concern about the children.

It seemed everybody in Union wanted to help. Friends from churches and the community brought food, prayed with us, and assured us they would pray for the boys' safe return. Leslie Henderson, from Conso, stopped by every day to tell Susan about friends at work who were praying for her and to relay messages.

Search teams were formed. Around ten in the morning, someone brought a big supply of fliers. People grabbed them up and flew out the door to their cars, leaving in a caravan.

The children in Judy Cathcart's day care wanted to help, too. They asked if they could pray for the boys. "Would you like to hold hands while we pray?" Judy asked.

My Daughter Susan Smith

"Can we get on our knees?" one asked.

Kneeling by the sofa, the children prayed that the man would bring Michael and Alexander back to play with them. Each child said a little prayer. They stopped a few times to dry their tears.

At lunch time, one little girl said, "We can't eat until Michael and Alexander get here. They're just late."

On Thursday, Judy helped the children hang two yellow ribbons on a tree in the front yard. When the parents picked up their children, many wore on their lapels a small yellow ribbon behind a laminated photograph of Michael and Alex.

****

Sitting around the table drinking coffee and watching news reports on TV in the den, we kept asking, "Where could the car be? Where could it be?"

Walt Garner couldn't sit still. He and his longtime friend Mike Lovelace set out to search for Michael and Alex. They walked from John D. Long Lake to Lockhart, hop-scotching as one drove the truck ahead of the other, left the key in the ignition, and then repeated the process. They walked down the highway and through the woods, tenderly calling for Michael and Alex.

Scotty, Michael, and Scott Kindricks drove down Highway 49 all the way to Charlotte. They carefully checked the Charlotte airport parking lot and everything in between. They met Dennis and Donnie on the way back from Charlotte. They had been to Chester searching for the children. All of them came back to our house.

When Walt went by his home in the evening, a man stopped him in the driveway. He talked about the abduction and how Walt was a close friend of the family. Walt told the man, "I was out looking all night, and I'll be going back out again. If I'm just standing around, I feel helpless." Choking back tears, he told the man he was holding Michael and Alex in his lap the night before they disappeared. Only later did he discover that the person in his driveway was a reporter from the Spartanburg *Her-*

ald-Journal, "I never would have talked to him if I had known that," Walt said. He already had his fill of the oppressive media.

In the days after the disappearance of the children, Walt had many encounters with media people who just didn't seem to care how much family members and friends of Michael and Alex were suffering. After Susan's arrest, reporters from one tabloid publication offered the Garners $1500 to allow them to photograph pictures of the children that were on display in their home. Walt and Barbara wouldn't allow that for any price. Eventually, the tabloid got photos from David and the Smiths. The Smiths removed virtually all of Susan's photos from her home, even the negatives. They showed up in one publication after another. Based on Walt and Barbara's experience, I guessed the Smiths were paid for them.

Walt looked for the children every day. Three days after their disappearance, I asked him what he was doing about his work. "I called them on Wednesday and Thursday," he explained, "and told them I wouldn't be in."

"They must be awfully understanding," I commented.

He told me he had no intention of going back to work until we knew something about the children. "There are things more important than a job," he said. "I finally told them I wasn't going to call every day, that I'll be there when they see me coming. Right here's where I'm going to be until we find the children."

We kept the TV turned to the news channel and waited for the phone to ring. Bev designated himself the official telephone man. He was like a robot with a booming voice, using call waiting to snag every call.

****

Susan and David left for the sheriff's office soon after the television duo scooted out. Sheriff Wells wanted to question them both and to have Susan meet with a police sketch artist. David says in his book that he was blind-sided the minute they arrived at the sheriff's office. Agents took him to one room and Susan to another. He says he still smarts from the fifth degree he was subjected to.

Wells and other agents questioned Susan continuously until 3:00 a.m. when Roy Paschal, the police sketch artist, arrived. Agent Jeff Stephens in the Union County sheriff's office had already briefed him about the alleged carjacking.

A sixteen-year veteran of the State Law Enforcement Division of South Carolina, headquartered in Columbia, Roy Paschal had extensive training in the techniques of composite drawing. As part of his training, he attended the Federal Bureau of Investigation Composite Artists School at the FBI Academy and took advanced forensic art courses that were sponsored by the National Center for Missing and Exploited Children.

Wells introduced Paschal to Susan and escorted them to the room where he would do his work. He explained the procedure to Susan and remained in the room for only a few minutes.

At the trial, Paschal said he remembered Susan being relatively calm under the circumstances. He spent a few minutes getting acquainted, then told her she would need to recall as much as possible about the abductor. He emphasized that the more she remembered, the better able they would be to find the man.

"I'm sorry," Susan blurted out. "I don't think I'll be able to help you."

"Oh?" he responded, trying to be calm. "Why is that?"

"I didn't see the front of his face. I really don't know what he looked like."

"Well, what did you see then?"

"I only saw the side of his face. I did see it a number of times, though," she added quickly.

"Then we'll draw it from the side. To begin, tell me what he looked like, what he had on, and so forth."

"He was a black man, thirty to forty years old," she began haltingly.

"And how tall would you estimate he was?"

"He was sitting down the whole time, so it's hard to tell. But I guess he was around five-foot-nine to six foot."

Once Paschal got Susan started, the details came out in rapid-fire order. He was amazed that she had such a good, overall view of the suspect.

"How much do you think he weighed?" he asked. "Did he have a large, medium, or small build?"

"As I said, he was sitting down the whole time, so I don't really know. I guess he weighed about 175 pounds."

"And his build—large, medium, or small? Was he heavy, slender, or what?"

"Medium build," she said, "and he had dark eyes."

Paschal drew as she talked. "What was he wearing?"

"He had on a toboggan-type cap and a plaid coat," she said.

"Color?"

"Blue. The cap was blue. And the coat was red, white, and blue."

Paschal's amazement grew as Susan continued to spill out the details. He drew as many as one-hundred-fifty composites a year. In his experience, traumatized victims generally had great difficulty remembering what somebody looked like. He usually found them to be in a state of shock and denial that the event even occurred; recalling details was very difficult. The process had always required a lot of prodding. This victim wasn't following the usual pattern.

He also was aware that victims usually start with specific items that catch their attention, such as eyes or mouth; then move to the general picture. Susan did just the opposite. She began with a vague, general picture; then, as she proceeded through the drawing, she got specific, struggling very little with details, even furnishing minute details in some instances.

He drew a nose, and asked her if it looked accurate. She said it did. He did the same for the other facial features.

"You're good," she chuckled. "That's what he looked like."

He was further surprised that she was so easily pleased with what he drew.

He set the completed drawing on the table in front of her. "Is there anything you would like to say about the drawing or the case in general?" he asked.

Her calm demeanor suddenly changed. She nervously examined the drawing for several seconds, then glanced up at Paschal with a faraway look in her eye.

"I feel like when the sun comes up," she began in a hopeful tone, "they'll find my children. I hope they're okay, but I know how they can be when they've been crying." Her manner was hesitant, her voice shaky.

"Please," Paschal urged, anxious to get her assessment. "If it doesn't look like the man, tell me. We are only trying to find the children. Tell us what you feel about the drawing."

"It looks just like him," she replied enthusiastically, her mood suddenly upbeat. "I like the way you draw. I'd like to get back in touch with you at Christmas to do a drawing, uh...."

He thought she was going to say a drawing of the children, but she stopped midway through the statement.

"How is your husband doing?" he asked, changing the subject.

"I'm separated and should be divorced in December."

"Do you have a boyfriend?"

"No," she replied self-consciously, embarrassed by the question.

"It's not unusual for people who are separated for an extended period of time to have a boyfriend and to have an agreement to date as a single," he said, trying to put her at ease.

"I do have a boyfriend," she acknowledged, obviously relieved that he thought it was okay. "As a matter of fact, this was his sweatshirt," she added, pointing to the Auburn writing on the front.

"Did your boyfriend go to Auburn?"

"Yes, he did."

"Oh," he responded. "That's a good school," he added as he stood up to end the meeting.

"Thank you, Susan. You were a big help. You remembered more than you thought you would, didn't you?" He then extended his hand.

"Yes," she said, smiling faintly as she shook his hand.

"These will be distributed right away," he explained. "They can be across the state and nation in minutes. I'll take this to the sheriff right now. He'll probably want to talk with you."

Paschal glanced at his watch as he walked down the hall to take the drawing to Howard Wells. It was 4:15 a.m. *Only an hour to do a composite*, he thought. *That is some kind of record.*

Part of a sketch artist's training involves learning to detect fabricated descriptions. He felt sure he had just drawn one. The short drawing time only added to his suspicions. But it wasn't his job to confront her.

With the drawing in hand, Wells went to the office where Susan waited. He sat across from her and placed the composite on the table. "Do you feel okay about the drawing?" he asked.

She said she did. "But could you really arrest someone from that picture?" she asked in a skeptical tone.

"It's done all the time," he replied.

She looked concerned. "How long do you think it will take to find him?"

"We've got people looking everywhere," he assured her. "The county people are involved; SLED is involved; and we've already contacted the FBI."

"The FBI?" she questioned, a surprised look flooding her face.

"Yes, in abduction cases, they are involved. We're doing everything we possibly can to find the children. We'll exhaust all possibilities."

Wells asked Susan to stay in the room for a while. He needed to get more information from her.

Paschal was waiting outside the room to report on his impressions. Wells suggested they go to his office to talk. Once he laid out his suspicions, the two of them decided it would be good to involve someone with a behavioral background. Wells asked him to contact SLED agent David Caldwell in Columbia.

Paschal talked to David Caldwell around 4:30 a.m., briefly telling him about the investigation and the concerns that had surfaced during the composite interview. Caldwell told him he was scheduled to be in Union regarding another matter and would come to the sheriff's office after taking care of that business.

Wells customarily recorded summaries of his interviews. In the summary of one of his first interviews with Susan, he noted an inconsistency in her description of the abductor. She told one officer the abductor wore a baseball cap, then told Wells it was a toboggan type. One time it was blue; another time it was dark. He knew the contradictions could be due to nervousness. He wouldn't allow himself to jump to any conclusions so early in the investigation.

****

Right after talking to Paschal, Wells told Susan and David they could leave, but he wanted them to come back at 11:30. Susan asked me to go back with them. When we arrived at the sheriff's office, David was immediately asked to go with an agent to one room. Wells wanted Susan to go to another room to look at mug shots until David Caldwell arrived. He said it was okay for me to go with her. While looking at the photos, she would make remarks like, "This sort of looks like him." She never went beyond that.

David Caldwell arrived at noon. After briefing him, Wells came to get Susan. He had arranged for Caldwell to interview her in Deputy Roger Gregory's office. I found a chair in the hallway to wait for her.

A seventeen-year veteran of the State Law Enforcement Division, Caldwell commands a strong presence, with his tall frame, sturdy build, and naturally aggressive manner. Making a special effort to put Susan at ease, he began the interview in a casual tone by securing general information from Susan: how old she was, marital status, how many children she had, where she worked.

Along with the information about her children and marital status, Susan told him she had lived in Union all her life and, for the last two-and-one-half years, had worked as assistant to the administrative assistant of the owner of Conso Products, a company in Union.

Caldwell asked her to recall the events of the previous day. He suggested that she start from the time she woke up that morning to the time the McClouds made the 911 call.

She said the day began at work like any other day and that some people from Conso got together for lunch to say good-bye to a co-worker from their English office. Without going into detail, she told about several conversations she had with co-workers in the afternoon before she left work. Then she began to tell what happened in the evening after work.

"About seven-thirty," she said, "I asked Michael if he wanted to go to Wal-Mart. He enthusiastically said, 'Yes.' He liked to look at the toys. I thought I might get some ideas for Christmas shopping.

"After leaving Wal-Mart around 8:40 p.m., I drove through Foster Park. Still driving around, I asked Michael if he wanted to go see Mitch, my best friend's boyfriend. He excitedly said he did.

"On the way to Mitch's house I stopped at the traffic light at Monarch Mills, just outside the Union city limits.

"That's when everything bad happened. Unfortunately, I never made it to Mitch's house."

Caldwell interrupted to tell Susan she didn't need to go into a lot of detail about the abductor, because she had already given that description to Paschal and others.

"He got in the car," she continued, "and he was out of breath and had a gun in his left hand. He told me to drive. I asked him not to hurt me or my kids.

"The man said, 'Shut up, or I'll kill you. Drive.'

"Michael asked, 'Who is that, Mama?' and started crying and saying, 'I want my daddy.' I told the kids it would be okay.

"He let me talk some," she told Caldwell. "I tried to look at him and he told me to keep my eyes on the road. He held the gun to my side.

"At one point on the road, he said, 'stop here,' and he pushed me out. I asked him to let me get my kids. And he said, 'I don't have time for that.' I was screaming; my kids were just screaming."

Susan abruptly stopped talking, obviously distraught. They sat in silence for a few minutes, Caldwell patiently waiting for her to continue.

"I wish I would have tried harder," she finally said, her bottom lip quivering. "Maybe there was something I could have done."

My Daughter Susan Smith

Caldwell asked her to describe the gun. She looked at a poster on the wall. "It looked like that one, about that size, too."

She went silent again and dropped her head in her hands, sobbing quietly.

"I'm scared," she said, looking up at Caldwell. "My mama always told me to lock my doors." Then shaking her head in dismay, she questioned, "What happened? My babies; I hope they're okay."

Caldwell asked her if she was familiar with any news reports of carjackings in the area, or maybe in Charlotte. She said she didn't keep up with the news and wasn't aware of any.

"In an investigation," he explained, "we have to be very thorough. A lot of people become suspects. The police have to go down every avenue and rule out every possibility.

"Information has come to us that you had a boyfriend in which you are quite interested, but he is not interested in pursuing a relationship, partly because of your children. I believe his name is Tom Findlay. Is that correct?"

"Yes," she acknowledged, surprised that he already had that kind of information.

"I hate to," he began in an apologetic tone, "but I have to ask. Would that have played any role in the disappearance of your children?"

She looked straight at Caldwell and smiled in disbelief. She then shook her head back and forth and looked down at the floor. "No man would make me hurt my children. They were my life."

At the trial, Caldwell said he noted with interest that his question didn't make her angry. In his experience, innocent parents usually got angry and asked why the police didn't go out and find the child, instead of harassing the parent.

Caldwell noticed that Susan looked very tired. He guessed she had been awake for more than twenty-four hours. He decided to conclude the interview. "I'm so sorry about the things that have happened to you," he said softly. "I think you've had enough conversation for one day. I'd like to speak with you again later. Would that be okay?"

"Yes," she agreed. "That will be okay."

Searching for the Carjacker

When Susan and David came to the place where I was waiting, I suggested we ask Howard Wells about where they were searching for the children. That was fine with them.

Sitting in the sheriff's office, I asked him if they were going to drag the lake. "We've already dragged that lake," he told us. "The car's not in the lake."

"What about other ponds?" Susan asked. "Are you going to look anywhere else besides the lake? You're not going to stop, are you? What if it's somewhere else?"

"We've got people looking everywhere," he assured her. Again, he emphasized that they would exhaust all possibilities.

After her arrest, Susan told me why she wanted to make sure they were looking for the car somewhere else. She thought the Lord had intervened miraculously to save her children. In her mind, the car never went down into the lake. The Lord had lifted it up and set it down somewhere else, and the children were safe inside. She thought the Lord was punishing her by hiding the car and keeping her children from being found. She reasoned that he would make her worry for a while and then let them be found. When she said, "Michael and Alex, I love you," on television, she had convinced herself that the children were somewhere alive. People just needed to keep looking so she could have her children back.

When we got home, Susan and David were exhausted and strung out emotionally. They slumped onto the sofa in the den, complaining that they had been put through a wringer. "Howard apologized for all the questioning," Susan said. "He wants us to come back tomorrow. I sure hope it won't be as bad as today." I felt sorry for her.

****

Wednesday evening, two hundred volunteers met at Monarch Elementary School to distribute fliers throughout the county and surrounding areas. At our house, we formed search groups, assigned a section of the county to each group, and went out looking for the car. Wendy, Scotty, and I were in one car, Paul and Michael in another. Bev's daughter Lori, Mitch,

Jennifer, and Leigh set out together. Walt and Tim were in the fourth car. Mama, along with Donna, Hedy, and Barbara stayed at the house with Susan and David.

As we searched, we kept running into each other, each time asking, "Y'all see anything?"

Scotty drove by the storage units at Monarch. "Someone could have pulled a car in there," Wendy remarked. "Think we ought to look?"

While we were parked by the units trying to decide what to do, Dennis Gregory, Susan's first cousin, pulled up beside us. He was conducting his own search. We asked him who owned the units. He called someone to see who they belonged to. In the meantime, we pulled one open. It was empty.

We rode and rode and looked and looked. Finally, exhausted and blurry-eyed, Wendy and Scotty dropped me off at my house and went to their home around the circle. It was almost two-thirty.

When I walked through the kitchen door to the den, I saw Mama and Bev asleep in recliners. Barbara and Walt were asleep on the sofa. Hedy was balled up on the love seat because it was too short for her five-foot-seven-inch frame. Paul was on the floor in front of her. Donna was lying on a comforter behind the sofa. A chorus of hard breathing and snoring echoed through the house. *This really looks like a flop house*, I chuckled to myself.

I wondered where Tim was. If Walt was there, he had to be somewhere. I found him in Michael's room on the floor with a blanket pulled down from the bed. I got pillows and covers for everyone. I put down comforters for Mitch and Leigh and Jennifer, who hadn't returned. I finally fell into bed fully dressed.

The next morning, when I went into the den, I noticed that people had changed their sleeping locations. Donna told me that she and Mitch lay down on the comforters in the den but soon moved to the foyer to get away from the snoring. Mama retreated to the washroom floor for the same reason. We all had a big laugh about the snoring. "I came in and everybody was snoring," Jennifer said. "I thought I'd never go to sleep, but I went to sleep when my head hit the floor."

Searching for the Carjacker

Another snoring event took place the next week. Walt told me about it after Susan's arrest. He and Mike Lovelace were sitting in the carport at our house, after returning from searching all day. Walt went to sleep. Clyde, our dog was lying nearby, fast asleep and snoring.

Mike had heard that a dog snores every eight seconds. He began to time Clyde's snoring and decided it was true. I chuckled, "Boy, that's a true friend! Here you are sitting around waiting, with nothing better to do than time a dog's snoring."

I was impressed that all these people were here because of love, concern, and friendship—even if they had to pass the time documenting a dog's snoring pattern.

12

Why the FBI?

Wednesday afternoon Wendy called the National Center for Missing and Exploited Children, asking for their help. They responded immediately. Margaret Frierson, executive director of the South Carolina Adam Walsh Center, a branch office of the organization, arrived Thursday morning. She was accompanied by Charlotte Foster, her case manager. They talked with Susan, David, Bev, Scotty, and me.

Ms. Frierson explained that the Adam Walsh Society was formed in the early eighties following the abduction and murder of a six-year-old named Adam Walsh who disappeared from a mall in Florida. His disappearance led to the first nationwide search in a missing-child case. As a result of the work with his parents, John and Rene Walsh, the National Center for Missing and Exploited Children was formed through a federal mandate in 1984 to serve as a national clearinghouse for all missing-child cases. The Center is most famous for the pictures of missing children on postcards distributed through the mail.

Frierson emphasized that their organization works closely with law-enforcement officials, but they are not an investigative or law-enforcement agency. Their role is to guide the family through the process. They often mediate between family members and the press. If requested, they go into the home and help answer the telephone and talk with family members and try to prepare them for the experience. Once they get involved, they notify people in the county and state and expand their efforts across the country.

The first thing the organization always requests is a clear photograph of the missing child. Bev and I gave several photos of Michael and Alex to Ms. Frierson. She told us they would create a missing persons poster for distribution through a volunteer base of people all over the United States—a trucking association, grocery chain, or whatever to help get the word out.

Frierson talked about the beauty of television and the fact that, with video imaging, it is possible to satellite the images of missing children all across the country. She asked if we had any videos of the children. Alex's birthday video was still in the VCR. It had been taped just before Nick's ball game that we watched the night of the tragic event. With the video they would create short public service announcements.

Ms. Frierson and her case manager spent the majority of the next day at a television station in Columbia, creating a thirty-second public service announcement based on the images in our home video. It was transmitted to all the national television networks, cable networks, and police agencies across the country and eventually was broadcast all over the world.

The Adam Walsh people also created a flier that featured a photograph of Michael and Alex, told of the circumstances regarding their disappearance, and asked anyone with information to call the Union County Sheriff's Department or the National Center for Missing and Exploited Children. They knew about the flier that was printed locally and suggested that their toll-free number be inserted at the bottom of it.

Frierson also offered to help in dealing with the media. Bev was happy to relinquish his position, and I was relieved because his booming voice and frantic attempts to catch every call got on my nerves.

****

After talking with Margaret Frierson, Bev and I went with Susan and David to the sheriff's office. The last thing I said to Susan before she went into Howard Wells' office was, "Try to remember anything that will help them find the children. We've got to get them back." She said she would try.

When I got a chance to talk to Howard Wells, I told him how it was tearing us all up rushing to the TV every time something came on about the children, that our emotions were constantly going up and down. "Y'all don't have to watch the news," he said. "If anything happens, you'll be the first to know." He promised to inform us of any news conferences. From then on, we kept the TV on but only on old movie channels and other non-news programs.

Susan was scheduled to meet again with SLED agent David Caldwell and FBI agent David Espie III. At the trial, Caldwell told about talking with her briefly while they waited for Espie to arrive. He asked her about taking a polygraph. "What if I fail?" she asked. He shrugged his shoulders in a neutral gesture, but his suspicions skyrocketed.

When David Espie arrived, Caldwell introduced him to Susan, explaining that he was helping in the investigation. Espie then took her to a witness room for the interview.

A certified interviewing instructor, Espie was a nine-year veteran of the FBI. Like Caldwell, he began the interview by getting to know something about Susan's background—how old she was, her family, her education, and so forth. Before she answered any questions, she wanted to know why someone from the FBI was there. Realizing that she had no idea the investigation would go beyond the Union County Sheriff's Office or possibly the South Carolina Law Enforcement Division, he reinforced what Wells had told her the day before. He said the FBI was simply aiding in the investigation and that it was routine in kidnapping cases. His purpose in being there was to help find the children.

At the trial, Espie testified that about seventeen minutes into the interview, he presented Susan with an Interrogation and Advise of Rights Form. Basically, the form was to advise her of her rights under the Miranda Warning. He explained that he had to provide the form for her to read to enable her to understand her rights at that time. She read the form and signed it. He also had her sign a form waiving her rights to have a lawyer present during the interview. She willingly signed that form, too.

Espie listened carefully as Susan recounted the events of October 25, beginning with her arrival at home from work. She went into detail about her visit to Wal-Mart with the children. She said she was hoping to get some ideas about what they wanted for Christmas and that they spent a lot of time in the toy section. Michael especially enjoyed watching the fish swim around in the fish tank, she told Espie.

He asked if she saw anyone in Wal-Mart she recognized. She said she saw familiar faces but no one she could identify by name.

She told Espie she left Wal-Mart around 8:30 p.m. and went to Foster Park, explaining that she thought it was very pretty there at night with the lights reflecting off the water. She drove around the park for about ten minutes but didn't get out of the car. She didn't want to go home; so she asked Michael if he wanted to go see Mitch Sinclair, Donna's fiancée.

Continuing her account, Susan told Espie that, after another stop at the Wal-Mart parking lot to pick up a bottle Alex had dropped, she drove down Highway 49 toward Mitch's house. At the traffic signal in the Monarch Mills area of Union County, she said a black man entered the passenger side of her car and ordered her to drive. He had a gun in his left hand. She continued to recount what she had already told Sheriff Wells and SLED agents—that the abductor pushed her out of the car near John D. Long Lake, and she went to the McCloud home for help.

At 1:15 p.m., Espie asked Susan if she was willing to take a polygraph test. She said she was. He gave a series of four tests, concluding the last one at 1:47 p.m. After the final polygraph, he knew she wasn't telling the truth. In addition to the test results, he felt her verbal and nonverbal behavior revealed she was lying. She responded to questions with short answers or no answers at all. She assumed a closed posture, crossing her arms and legs. She slouched in her chair. At times, she whimpered like she was crying, but no tears came. She cried at inappropriate places. Espie said he interpreted this behavior as an attempt to relieve tension and to delay the interviewing process.

As the interviewing dragged on, Susan became restless, according to Espie. She stood up and walked around the table, then around the room. She went to a corner and stood there, refusing to talk or to make eye contact.

Espie began the last hour of the interview with a warning: "Now is the time to relate the truth of this story for the good of your self respect and integrity of your children and your town.

My Daughter Susan Smith

Tremendous resources are being utilized in this investigation, and you are abusing it."

She stared blankly at him.

He continued, "It is my opinion and my strong belief that, without question, you have engaged in behavior that's led to the disappearance of your children, and you know where your children are now."

A shocked, angry expression filled Susan's face. "How could you believe that I could harm my children, my own children?" she asked. That was all she said in the last hour of the interview.

To conclude the interview, Susan moved to another corner of the room, turned to face Espie, and nervously demanded, "I need to leave." She then left the witness room and hurried down the hall. Caldwell, who was waiting in the hall with Union County deputy Rick Moore, caught up with her.

"Please tell me everything about what happened the night of October 25," Caldwell urged, "so we can resolve this matter. You know more about it than anybody."

She stopped, shook her head, and looked down.

"Why haven't you been completely honest with the police during the course of the investigation?" he probed.

"What do you mean?" she asked, still holding her head down.

"About going to Wal-Mart." She raised her head and turned to face Caldwell, a look of surprise and dismay on her face. He quickly suggested they go to a little room behind the courtroom to talk. She agreed to do that. Rick Moore followed but waited outside. Major General Christopher from SLED came into the room and left after a few minutes.

As they talked, Susan got up several times and walked around the room. She looked up at the ceiling, glanced out the window, and sat back down at the table across from Caldwell but refused to look directly at him.

"No one saw you at Wal-Mart that night," he said firmly. "How can you explain that in a town this small?"

"Okay, okay, I'll go ahead and admit it," she conceded, her voice rising. "I didn't go to Wal-Mart that night. I made the story up about shopping and coming back to pick up the bottle Alex dropped."

"Why are you misleading us on this, about this day of all days when your children were kidnapped? Why would you mis-inform the police? Why did you tell me that you went to Wal-Mart when you didn't? Don't you understand? We want to help you find your children."

"I was embarrassed," she said, barely above a whisper.

"Embarrassed? Why were you embarrassed?"

"Well, I was just riding around. I thought it would sound dumb to say I was just riding around." She abruptly stood up, then walked out of the room. Caldwell followed and suggested that they go to the sheriff's office.

Once in Wells' office, Caldwell stepped aside to let the sher-iff take over the questioning, along with Deputies Roger Greg-ory and Eddie Harris.

Around six that evening, Caldwell again interviewed Susan in Deputy Gregory's office. As she sat across the desk from him, he pounded away at the same theme: "Why haven't you told us the truth? You've told us some lies about phone calls that you made. You told me lies about Wal-Mart. You just haven't been truthful with me about that night."

"I told you why I lied about Wal-Mart," she snapped.

"You just haven't been truthful with me about that night," he snapped back. "I think you are involved in this thing. Can you see why we are so suspicious of you?"

"Yes, I can," she acknowledged. "I had had a bad day. I was just riding around. I was singing. Michael was singing."

"Hey, wait a minute!" Caldwell exclaimed, interrupting her. "You told me earlier that they were fussy. Your husband told me he could hear them fussing and screaming in the back-ground when he spoke to you earlier that night. Now, you're telling me they were singing. Which was it, fussy or singing. Fussy or happy? Which one was it? Which time were you ly-ing?"

She stared blankly past him, refusing to answer.

To press his point, Caldwell moved to the edge of the chair and looked Susan in the eye. "They were screaming, weren't they?" he suggested sarcastically. "And is that why you killed them?"

Slamming her hand down on the desk, she screamed, "I can't believe you think that. I can't believe you think I've hurt my children." She then bolted out of the chair and turned toward the door.

Caldwell quickly positioned himself between her and the exit; but when she angrily moved toward the door, he stepped aside to let her pass. "I just can't believe they think I did it. I can't believe they think I did it," she shouted as she stormed down the hall. Frustrated, Caldwell slumped into a chair.

Momentarily, a deputy stuck his head into the office, saying, "She wants to leave."

"She's not under arrest," Caldwell sighed with resignation. "She can go if she wants to." He didn't talk with Susan again.

****

After being questioned for hours, David stood on the courthouse steps and made a passionate plea for the return of his sons. "I plead with the man to return our children safe and sound," he told a mass of reporters assembled outside the courthouse. "It gets harder as time goes by to deal with this."

Sightings were called in from as far away as upstate New York. Thursday evening, a burgundy car was spotted in connection with a convenience store robbery in Salisbury, North Carolina. Law-enforcement officers searched fruitlessly until noon Saturday for the children in Uwharrie National Forest, a short distance from Union. Sheriff Wells later confirmed that a suspect had been arrested in the robbery, and there was no connection with the Union County carjacking.

By this time, the Union command center had received more than 1,000 calls offering information. Additional phone lines were installed at the Union County Courthouse to handle the huge volume of calls. When asked about the possibility of offering a reward, the sheriff said they would consider that later. He didn't want people giving information solely for a reward.

"We'll be looking in every direction," he said. "We're not

ruling out anybody, including the parents." He wouldn't say if Susan and David had taken a polygraph test but did indicate that he had ruled out a domestic dispute as the reason for the boys' disappearance. I didn't know it at the time, but Susan had already failed a polygraph test and David had passed.

Wells appeared on NBC's *Today* Thursday morning and CNN's *Larry King Live* Thursday night. "I hope the suspect will see this and notify us where to pick the children up," he said.

****

When we got home from the sheriff's office, Susan fell into my arms, crying, "Oh, Mama, they don't believe me. They think I did something with the children. I don't want anymore of this. You wouldn't believe how they're badgering me. I just can't take it."

My heart sank. If Susan wouldn't talk to them, we would never find the children. "Don't worry about it," I told her. "It'll be over soon. Just try to think of something that will help. We've got to find the children."

I felt sure, with a good night's rest, Susan would be willing to do whatever was necessary to find the children. She loved them too much to refuse to cooperate. Not for one second did the thought enter my mind that she had harmed Michael and Alex. Everybody knew she was a gentle, patient, loving mother.

About an hour later, as I was standing in the den talking to friends, I heard someone yelling at the back door. The sound then moved through the kitchen and into the den. It was David's father, charging in without a word of greeting. He and his wife, Sue, had arrived from California that morning. David had seen his father at the courthouse, but I didn't even know he was in town.

"They're treating Susan and David like dirt down at that sheriff's office," he shouted.

"Y'all come in here," I suggested, motioning toward my bedroom. Aside from his rudeness, I was shocked at his accusations and didn't think the whole world should hear. I also didn't think Howard Wells would mistreat Susan and David.

"What's the problem?" I asked, as I shut the bedroom door.

Dave went on and on about how Susan and David had been questioned relentlessly by one agent after another. He said something like, "If they're going to be treated like that, they do need a lawyer. You wouldn't believe what they're doing. David told me about it. They're accusing them, threatening them, treating them like criminals. David hasn't done a thing to his children. He's damn mad about how they're treating him."

"Susan is all they've got," I pleaded. "If they can't question her, we'll never find Michael and Alex. You can't expect them to exclude the parents from the investigation. They always look at the family. They would be derelict in their duties if they didn't look at them."

"But David's done nothing wrong," he insisted. "Why should they grill him like that when he had absolutely nothing to do with the children's disappearance? You tell me that. You don't know what's going on. You don't know how they're being treated."

"Any information they get has got to come from Susan and David," I insisted.

"All Howard Wells is thinking about is getting reelected," Dave snapped.

"Look," I explained. "Howard is godfather to Scotty's children. He's not just out for votes. He's doing what he has to do. It's his job. The last thing he wants is to hurt Susan and David."

"Okay! Okay!" Dave conceded angrily. He then stepped back and, in a wide-sweeping motion, drew an imaginary line on the carpet with his foot. "Today, we'll do it your way, but tomorrow it's your daughter and my son," he warned, shaking his index finger at me and pointing from one side of the line to the other. "If they are going to be treated like that, then I'll get David a lawyer."

"Fine," I said sharply.

I wish now I had listened to him. But, at the time, there was no way I could agree with someone who was acting like that. And I had no reason to think Susan needed a lawyer. Most of all I was haunted by thoughts of what might be happening to the children. Every single part of my being was focused on do-

Why the FBI?

ing something to find them. I was afraid we would never find the children if Susan didn't keep talking. I hoped that maybe, out of the blue, she would think of something she hadn't thought of before that would lead to them.

That discussion was barely ended when Leigh knocked on the bedroom door and asked me to come into the den. When I got in there, Susan and David were seated on the sofa with two people standing in front of them, one with a video camera.

Leigh suggested I sit beside Susan on the other end of the sofa. Other relatives and friends stood behind us. It was one question after another, mainly directed to Susan or David. Susan said something about hating it that she might never know what happened to Michael and Alex and that the children were her life. She appealed to the abductor to please bring the children home. David also appealed for their safe return. Susan told the reporter that she had been at the sheriff's office answering questions all day. She said she hated to go back but that she was going to do everything she could to help find the children. She then repeated parts of her story about the alleged carjacking. I said something about how many things in our house reminded us of Michael and Alex.

At some point during the interview, I realized the news team was from the tabloid television show *A Current Affair*. I wasn't happy about that, but there wasn't anything I could do without making a big scene. Later, I asked Scotty who let them in. He said he did, but he didn't know who they were. He had never watched the program. Actually, the reporter had talked to Scotty outside first, before she interviewed all of us. In agreeing to talk to her, he was just following Howard Wells' advice. Early on, Howard had told us the press could help in the investigation because they could reach so many people. All of us were simply going with the flow.

Soon after the people from *A Current Affair* finished interviewing us, Dave and Sue left. They were staying at Susan's house on Toney Road. David had suggested they stay there, and that was fine with Susan.

The same crowd was at our house for another night. Whatever happened, we all wanted to be together when we found out something. None of us really slept at night. We only collapsed when we were too tired to sit up or stand up.

By this time we had decided who would sleep where. Bev and I stayed in our bedroom. David and Susan slept in her bedroom. Michael kept his bedroom. Leigh and Jennifer shared a sofa. Donna and Mitch found a place in the foyer. And everyone else found whatever space was available in the living room and den. We all slept in our clothes, ready at a moment's notice to do whatever was necessary to recover the children.

****

Spartanburg's *Herald-Journal* reported that "the story of the young mother and the abduction of her sons, 3 and 14 months old, has become the talk of the nation with almost every major news organization airing stories Thursday." It went on to say that "after two days of the most intense police investigation in Union County history, police are no closer to learning who abducted two small children during a carjacking earlier this week."

When interviewed by a reporter Thursday morning, Susan said, "All I can do now is trust in the Lord and my family. I keep trying not to lose hope, but the more time passes, I get scared."

She paused to gain her composure, then said, "If they are lying somewhere dead, I want them home. Oh, God. I can't bear to think of that....I have a lot of hope. That's all I have. I can't imagine life without my children."

By now, Susan was into her story so deeply, she didn't know how to tell the truth. We unwittingly cooperated with the media people to drive her even deeper. They hounded us with persistent and endless telephone calls and a constant, suffocating presence outside. Every day, all day, they asked for any new word, pressuring us relentlessly for a statement. They especially wanted something from Susan or David. Over and over, we succumbed to the pressure, pushing Susan in front of the cameras, while urging her to try to think of something to help find the babies. We hoped the press could get the word to someone, somewhere who would send in a tip. We thought a plea from Susan might soften the heart of the abductor, if he could see how heartbroken she was.

Day by day, Susan could see our sadness increase. She knew it was going to kill us when we found out the truth. All we could do was talk about how precious Michael and Alex were. We looked at their pictures. We saw the wading pool filled with their toys that I kept behind the sofa in the den. Bev soon pulled it into Michael's bedroom to make room for all the people congregating at our house, but we still knew it was there. We wanted to hug them, to see them smile, to watch them play with their toys.

Susan told Dr. Halleck that during the entire nine days, she looked for a way and an opportunity to commit suicide. She planned to kill herself and write a note telling exactly what had happened. But she was never alone. We all made sure of that.

13

The Media Connection

Early Friday morning, a loud, mournful cry echoed down the hall from Michael's bedroom, through the den, and into the breakfast nook where Bev and Michael were drinking coffee. Bev hurried toward the sound. As he moved through the doorway, his eyes were immediately drawn to one corner of the bedroom. Susan was lying on the floor, face down, wailing uncontrollably. She had her right arm extended over the toys in the wading pool, while moving her arms and legs swiftly in fits and jerks.

Bev kneeled down beside her and tenderly placed his hand on her back, trying to console her. He then slowly eased her up. She leaned on his shoulder for a few moments, sobbing. Over and over, he told her everything would be okay, that they would find the boys.

At about the same time, Margaret Gregory, Susan's cousin, and her husband, Dennis, walked into the house, having repelled questions from reporters outside. At the trial, Margaret described Susan's cry as a mournful wailing, like something she had never heard before.

I was in the shower during all this activity. By the time I got out, Susan was calmed down and Bev was in our bedroom to tell me about what had happened. "Linda," he said, obviously alarmed, "you wouldn't believe the sound that came from Susan. It was awful. She's got to have something to calm her nerves." I didn't argue, but it seemed like a natural reaction for someone in Susan's situation. Almost any reaction would have seemed normal.

When Bev and I left our bedroom, Susan went in there and shut the door. A few minutes later, I walked by and heard her crying. I opened the door to see her lying on the bed on her stomach, kicking her legs up and down and pounding the headboard with one fist and then the other. How I ached for her! How I wished I could take her pain away. But again, I felt her reaction was normal, that she only needed to be left alone for a while.

In the early afternoon, I saw Susan go out to the screened-in porch. A little later I went to check on her. I found her on her knees, hanging over the handlebars of Michael's tricycle, trembling and whimpering. I helped her up gently and coaxed her inside. I was now convinced she needed medication. I got right on the phone to our family doctor and asked him to call in a prescription. He didn't hesitate.

From that point on, all of us were afraid Susan might try to commit suicide. We immediately took measures to protect her. Bev removed the guns from the display case in the den and hid them. I doled out the appropriate dose of her medication. We watched her constantly. The only time we left her alone was when she went to the bathroom or took a shower. Even then, someone made sure she came out in a reasonable length of time.

Leigh went into action to relieve the tension that was building up in Susan. A naturally friendly person with a contagious smile, she and Susan share a family resemblance with their brown hair, sparkling brown eyes, and outgoing nature. If anyone could cheer Susan up, Leigh could.

She talked Susan into playing cards. She says she felt a little guilty about doing that when the kids were missing, but she knew something had to be done; and it did help. She also tried to lighten things up by recalling amusing childhood experiences. She reminded Susan about a time when she was at our house and was striking matches in the bathroom to get rid of the smell. She was kind of overdoing it, though, striking one match after another. Susan looked through the window to tell her to hurry up. When she saw what Leigh was doing, she ran to tell me about it. Of course, I gave Leigh a mini-lecture on fire safety. She teased her cousin about being a tattletale for a long time after that. They had a good laugh about the remembrance.

With all the people around constantly, Susan and Leigh didn't have long conversations. But on Friday, they slipped out the basement door to avoid reporters and took a walk around the circle. Susan told her how sorry she was that her marriage was breaking up. She had always hoped she would get married and live happily ever after. Leigh wonders why she never got the nerve to tell her the truth about Michael and Alex. Like the rest of us, she thinks Susan got into something she couldn't get out of.

Leigh still talks about what a good mother Susan was. Susan's patience with the children amazed her. Recently, she told me about an incident when Susan and David were separated. A bunch of relatives were at our house for a holiday get together. When everyone started to leave, Leigh realized Susan would have to get the sleeping children into her house by herself. She offered to follow her home and help, but Susan insisted she would be okay. Leigh insisted back and followed her home. Once inside, the children woke up and started crying. Susan sat down in a rocking chair with both of them in her arms.

"I don't see how you do it," Leigh remarked.

In the most peaceful and calm way, Susan smiled faintly, saying, "Lord, sometimes all three of us just sit here and cry together."

From the time Leigh was old enough to know what was happening in Susan's life, she worried about her. She knew about her two suicide attempts. But she also knew she smiled a lot and seemed to rise above her troubles. And her children were a very stabilizing influence in her life. One time Leigh told a friend, "I always worried about Susan, but now that she has Michael and Alex, they are her life. I know she would never leave them."

****

The phone continued to ring endlessly, all day and into the night. Most of the time it was someone from the media. A crowd of reporters remained out front. No one could leave the house without a press tail. We had lost our privacy, and it was a horribly helpless feeling.

The Media Connection

Without a doubt, the press added greatly to our sadness and agonizing pain, with all their pressure-filled calls and endless questions: Had the abductor called? Had we heard anything more from the police? Were there any new leads? Had Susan thought of anything else that could help in the investigation? How were Susan and David holding up? What about the inconsistencies in Susan's story? Did she fail a polygraph test?

At first, Bev tried to answer a particular question, but he found that reporters never were satisfied with an answer to only one question. One answered question led to another and on and on until he was involved in a full-scale discussion. By the time we had learned their strategy, people were there to help us deal with the press.

Margaret Gregory took a leave of absence from her job to help us. As public information officer for South Carolina's Richland County Sheriff's Office, she related to the media on a daily basis. We were delighted that she wanted to help.

Being a family member, Margaret seemed a natural to be the official family spokesperson. Margaret Frierson from the Adam Walsh Center was happy to relinquish her leadership role and simply assist. Actually, as things worked out, there were so many media people calling and coming out to our home, it took two of them to take care of everything.

One of the first tasks we passed on to Margaret was dealing with Marc Klaas, father of twelve-year-old Polly Klaas who was kidnapped from a slumber party in her home and found dead sixty-five days later.

Bev took the initial call from Klaas. During their conversation, Klaas explained that police often suspect the parents; that was what happened to him. He offered to come out and help in whatever way he could.

Bev knew Klaas was connected with a tabloid TV show. After our encounter with *A Current Affair*, we wanted no more of that type of news reporting. Bev told him not to come, that we had plenty of people helping us.

I got involved in the Marc Klaas situation early in the morning before the two Margarets arrived. When I answered the phone, the caller identified himself as being connected with the

TV program *American Journal*. He said they were flying Marc Klaas to Union. "Don't send him," I said. "We already told him not to come."

"He's already on his way," the caller said.

"Well," I snapped, "he'll have to turn around and go back."

When Klaas and the *American Journal* crew arrived in Union, they located David's father and stepmother at Susan's house. Klaas convinced them he only wanted to assist, since he knew what the family was going through. Dave and Sue came to our house to talk with David, leaving Klaas waiting on our front doorstep.

A bunch of us were in the den. Dave and Sue went straight to David and explained how Klaas wanted to help. After convincing him, the three of them began to work on Susan. "Just talk to him," Dave urged. "He doesn't have a recorder, a piece of paper or anything. He just wants to help. He knows what you're going through. He knows how the police have been treating you, how the press hounds you, and everything. He's been through it."

When Susan balked, Dave motioned to me to join them. He then asked what I thought. I told them I had a very negative feeling about Klaas. I was disgusted with Klaas because he went to the other side of the family when he couldn't convince Bev and me to let him get involved. But I didn't tell them that.

While we discussed pros and cons about Klaas' involvement, Susan mumbled things like she wanted to do whatever she could to find the children, but she definitely was not enthusiastic about talking to Klaas and the *American Journal* reporters. Still, the Smiths kept pushing.

I finally asked Susan point blank, "Do you want to go out there?"

"No, I don't," she said.

"If you don't want to, you don't have to," I said firmly, then stepped over to the sofa and sat down beside Margaret Gregory. "Margaret," I said quietly but firmly, "tell that man to get off my doorstep right this minute. And if the Smiths can't act any better, they can get out, too." Margaret said she would take care of the situation.

Bev hadn't gotten involved in the discussion but did know what was going on. When he overheard my conversation with Margaret, he strode over to the Smiths. "This is enough," he told them. "You need to leave her alone. She's going through enough without this." It was quite a sight—six-foot Bev telling five-foot-four Dave to cool it. He and Sue stormed out the front door just as Margaret Gregory told Klaas and the *American Journal* people they would not get an interview.

****

Reporters kept pressuring Wells to reveal whether Susan and David had taken polygraph tests. He refused to tell them, saying it was the policy of the sheriff's office neither to confirm nor deny that a test was given. "We are talking with friends and family of the couple, looking for a motive," he said. "There have been no ransom demands, and we can find no one who was mad at the mother or the father."

Wells also noted that they had searched the area around John D. Long Lake to confirm that nothing had been thrown from Susan's car by the carjacker. A pacifier was found, but it wasn't connected to Michael or Alex. "In 20 years of law enforcement," he said, "I've never worked a case that had so little to work with, but there's not any more that can be done."

During a 5:00 p.m. news conference, Wells said investigators had talked to Susan more than one time and had found some discrepancies in her statement. He declined to elaborate.

With that information, the press lost no time in pouncing on our family. A reporter called Scotty to ask him about the discrepancies. Scotty downplayed them, saying the sheriff was just looking for additional details about the kidnapping. He said Susan became confused when investigators were trying to clarify her statements. He also said he thought news reporters were putting words into the sheriff's mouth about his sister's statements and her relationship to the male friend she was going to visit the night of the abduction.

Scotty's private thoughts were quite another matter. The discrepancies made him wonder about Susan's account of the carjacking. He said nothing to me at the time, but he had a nagging feeling that Susan had something to do with the children's disappearance. He thought she may have hidden them to keep them away from David, but the possibility that she had harmed the children never entered his mind.

An early morning call from the sheriff's office increased Scotty's concern. Howard Wells sent word that only David needed to come in for questioning in the afternoon. Scotty saw that as a signal the sheriff was stepping gently around the family because of personal relationships. He was well aware of the fact that Susan had been grilled at the sheriff's office, but he didn't want the questioning to stop. Like everyone else, he was convinced it was the only hope of finding the children. So he called the sheriff and urged him to ask whatever he had to ask and to do whatever he had to do. "We don't want to lose a moment," he emphasized. "Just find the children. Maybe Susan can remember something that will help you. We want those babies back home. We are all torn apart over this." Sheriff Wells assured him that he would do his job, even if he hurt some feelings along the way.

After Susan's arrest, Howard asked me if I knew Scotty had called and told him to do whatever he needed to do. By then, I did know, but Scotty didn't tell me at the time.

At this point, I had quit reading the newspaper; it upset me to read pure speculation about what had happened. I chose to listen only to what Howard Wells told me. He dealt in hard facts, not speculation.

All my thoughts were centered on having the children home. I envisioned holding them in my arms, watching them run in my yard, hearing them giggle. The precious memories are what kept me going and the hope that I would see them again. Susan and I looked at pictures of Michael and Alex and talked about how much we loved them. I was in my own little world, greeting friends when they came by, going with Susan to the police station, waiting for her to get through being questioned, and then returning home to wait for any new developments in the search. Mama remarked, "Everyone knows more than us, and we're in the middle of it." That probably was true of Mama and me but not of the others. Some eventually questioned Susan's story but never in my presence.

When describing to a reporter what was happening at our house, Margaret Gregory said, "I can't begin to imagine how many calls I have taken today, probably close to 100." She said the majority were from representatives of the media. "Friends and family members just stop by," she noted.

No one could have described all that was going on at our house. I didn't even know everything that was happening. I did know that many, many friends stopped by. Friends from our church and in the community and even businesses supplied food throughout the nine days. A constant stream of people came by to tell us they cared in a variety of ways. Many like Walt and Mike were in and out, reporting on their efforts to find the children.

Letters of concern poured in from all over the world, so many that we had to open a post office box. At times, Susan read letters to me. The love and concern expressed in them were truly touching. As an expression of our appreciation, we issued the following statement through Margaret Gregory:

"To all of you, our most heartfelt thanks. We are grateful to you all. We also want to thank the Union County Sheriff's Office, SLED, and all law enforcement agencies as we know you are doing all you can to find our children. This is an extremely difficult time, and we are pulling together as a family. We pray every moment for the safe return of Michael and Alex. We miss you, we love you and we want you home."

****

Late Friday evening, most of the people staying at our house decided to go home for the night and come back the next morning. Susan and David, of course, stayed here all the time, and Susan's best friend, Donna, her boyfriend, Mitch, Leigh, and Jennifer also stayed.

I started cleaning the house after everyone went to bed, purely from nervous energy. I put clothes in the washing machine, cleaned the bathrooms, and finally went outside to get the mop to clean the kitchen floor. I felt something move when I put the mop in the water in the sink. I lifted up one corner of the mop head near the movement. A tiny lizard was hovering there. I quickly dropped the mop back down over it. I was scared to death it would jump out and get in the house and maybe jump on Donna and Mitch, who were sleeping in the foyer.

I scurried into the bedroom and woke Bev. "You've got to help me," I told him. He sleepily trudged into the kitchen, reached down under the mop, grabbed the lizard, and took it outside. We both laughed about that, although muffled, to keep from waking anyone. It was almost three-thirty.

That little lizard relieved a bit of my tension. I was relaxed enough to go to bed. Once more, I slept in my clothes.

14

The Logan Interviews Begin

Saturday morning a rumor was afloat claiming Susan had taken a polygraph test, and it was inconclusive. Columbia's *State* newspaper reported that both federal and state law enforcement sources said Susan didn't pass a polygraph administered on Thursday, and they hoped to retest her. The report was out that David had passed. Wells refused to confirm or deny the rumors.

With this new information leak, the press came at us full steam, demanding more interviews. Margaret Gregory finally told them we weren't granting any interviews because we were "worn out."

Mixed in with the calls from the media was one from the sheriff's office. The deputy told Margaret Gregory that Major Christopher from SLED headquarters wanted to know if Susan would talk to a SLED agent named Pete Logan. He assured Margaret that Logan had a reputation for using a compassionate, non-confrontational approach and that Susan could leave when she got tired.

The deputy stayed on the line while Margaret talked to Susan. Momentarily, she told him Susan had agreed to go but very reluctantly. He set the meeting time at two in the afternoon at the National Guard Armory.

Margaret didn't ask why the meeting place was changed. She knew it was to get away from the media. The amount of media attention on the case made it difficult to get us in and out of the sheriff's office without being bombarded by reporters. For that reason, Wells had asked Eddie Harris, the SLED agent assigned to Union, to find another interview location. He selected the National Guard Armory. He was the sergeant major in the National Guard battalion stationed there and had a key.

Before the deputy hung up, Howard Wells came on the line

to ask if members of both the Russell and Smith families would meet with him at the Armory at eleven to talk about further questioning of Susan. We agreed to do that. Susan hadn't been questioned since Thursday. All of us were concerned that the children would never be found if they didn't get more information from her.

A horde of media people were stationed out front; so, when the time came to leave for the Armory, we went out the basement door and across the backyard to Scotty and Wendy's house. We quickly realized there weren't enough cars. Luckily, Walt came around the circle in his pickup, and Scotty asked him to take Bev and Michael. Walt lingered outside at the Armory, explaining to SLED agent Eddie Harris that he wasn't family. Harris asked him to go on inside so reporters wouldn't see him. We gladly included him in the discussion.

We all sat around the conference table as Sheriff Wells explained that they were at an impasse in the investigation because of the accusatory tones the two agents took in questioning Susan earlier. He assured us Logan had a less confrontational and more personable approach. He thought Logan could keep her talking so they could find the children.

We liked what we heard and agreed to have him talk to Susan as much as necessary. Again, I didn't entertain the thought of having a lawyer with her. And no one else said anything about a lawyer, either.

Looking back, I realize Howard Wells was using us to put pressure on Susan. We readily agreed because we felt it was the only way to get the children back. Susan could have refused to go along, but she was willing to do what we felt was best.

****

Major Christopher had called Pete Logan Saturday morning and asked if he would talk to Susan Smith. Logan wanted to know who all had talked to her and what had happened in the investigation so far. Christopher told him Susan had walked out on a couple of interviews, but he thought she would respond favorably to his approach. Logan asked the major to have

The Logan Interviews Begin

someone check with Susan to see if she would talk with him before he made the trip to Union. "If she wants to talk to me," he said, "I'll come up." After our meeting with Howard Wells, Major Christopher called Logan to tell him Susan would meet with him.

Bev, David, and I went to the Armory with Susan. Howard Wells and Pete Logan were waiting for us in the reception area. My first impression of Logan was positive. He struck me as a gentle, grandfatherly type. He stood tall, had snowy white hair, and spoke in a calm, friendly tone, quite a contrast to Caldwell.

Logan told us he probably would give Susan a polygraph test, if she felt okay about it. He emphasized that it was strictly up to her and she could leave at any time. At the trial, he described his interviewing approach this way: "I don't think in my thirty-five years I have ever hollered at anyone or raised my voice. I try to take a compassionate and understanding approach. That happens to work for me. That's not the only viable approach to people you want to talk to, but generally that's my approach."

As Wells and Logan proceeded to take Susan to the conference room, I caught her by the arm. "Tell them anything you can think of, so we can have the children back home," I urged. She assured me she would. "I will, Mama," she said. "I want them back, too."

The sheriff stayed in the room with Logan and Susan for a few minutes, then returned to the reception area to talk to us. He told us a little more about Logan. He said he began his law-enforcement career with the FBI and was with that agency for twenty-seven years. One of his first major cases was the Kennedy assassination in 1963. He was assigned to Dallas as part of a special investigation. He had been a SLED agent for the past eight years.

Pete Logan stated at the trial that he was determined to start fresh with Susan, with no preconceptions of guilt. His intention was to get her to tell him what had happened, what the facts were.

Seated opposite Susan at the conference table, Logan began the interview by telling her something about his background

My Daughter Susan Smith

and why he was there. He emphasized that he wanted to get as much information as possible so that they could find the children. "If some of the questions are repetitious," he said, "I apologize for that."

He told her she didn't have to be there if she didn't want to. No one could tell her to be there—her mom or dad, law enforcement, no one else. And she didn't have to answer every question. "If I ask a question that embarrasses you or makes you mad, you don't have to answer," he assured her.

"Now I know you've been through a couple of interviews," he acknowledged, "and that you became upset. I want you to know that you can get up and walk out the door any time, if you want to. I won't be upset at you, and I won't holler at you. You are free to leave at any time." He then warned that the interview might last a while because they had a lot of ground to cover.

"Later on, if you want to do a polygraph," he continued to explain, "we can do that, but you can decline it." Again, he told her she did not have to sit there and be interviewed and polygraphed. She could leave, and it wouldn't make him mad.

His gentle manner and personable approach put Susan at ease.

"Right now," he said, "tell me a little about your background—your name, date of birth, height, weight, members of your immediate family." He used this open-ended approach throughout the interviewing process, asking questions like: Tell me about your educational background. Tell me about what you do. Tell me about what you like. Tell me about your friends.

He had a definite purpose for using this approach. First, he wanted to establish a rapport with Susan. Second, he wanted to determine if she would be suitable for a polygraph test. He had learned over the years that many people aren't suitable when they first come in for an interview, especially when involved in a trauma of the magnitude she had experienced. At this point, he felt she wasn't ready for a polygraph.

When Logan asked Susan about her educational background, he discovered that she had graduated from high school and that during high school she was active in Junior Civitan and was president of the club during her senior year. He was impressed

The Logan Interviews Begin

with her desire to help people and decided it was one of the things that would help him determine how to approach her.

He asked about places she had worked. She told him about Winn-Dixie. She told about wanting to buy a car when she got her first job after high school. She said she went down to buy the car with Bev and me. The payments were $800 a month. Shortly after the purchase, she took the car back, because she knew she couldn't afford it.

She told about getting her job at Conso and how proud she was about starting in the credit department and being promoted soon thereafter. She said she was taking courses at USC, Union, along with her work.

He asked her about her mother and father. She told him about Harry's and my separation when she was only three. She became emotional as she related her father's suicide. She said she loved him very much and was extremely upset about his death. It was obvious that her father's death still was a very painful memory.

He asked about her boyfriends. She didn't hold anything back. She revealed that she had an affair with a married man in her senior year in high school and that she had sex with his co-worker while they were going together. She told how ashamed she was and that she couldn't understand why she did such a thing. She talked about her suicide attempts. She told Logan she was two months pregnant when she married David. She knew she had let her mother down when that happened, and she was sorry. She described troubles that developed in her marriage, how she was mentally abused, how David didn't want her to go out at any time, how he complained that she went by her mother's house too much, how he constantly made her choose between him and her family.

She told about the two separations in her marriage before the final one when she filed for divorce. She mentioned that she had filed for divorce on grounds of adultery and had hired an investigator to verify the charge. She told about David's claim that he had her telephone tapped and his threats to reveal embarrassing facts about her life. She said she was terrified that a lot of people would be hurt if he carried through on his threats.

When questioned about possible physical abuse in her marriage, she told Logan about the time David dragged her out of bed and left her on the porch in the cold.

After she told him about her affair with Tom Findlay, he asked, "What did you like about Tom Findlay?"

"He's different from the average man in Union," she explained. "He's very intelligent and financially well off."

She related in detail her conversation with Tom when she admitted being involved with his father and that she was afraid he wouldn't want to see her again. Over and over, she talked about how she had let people down.

Periodically, Logan asked her if she was tired or upset. Each time, she took a short break, then chose to continue. He made no effort to run a polygraph test during this first interview.

Around five-thirty, he asked if she was tired. She said, "Yes."

"Would you like to go?" he offered.

"Yes, I would," she replied quickly.

"Would you be willing to come back tomorrow?" he asked. "We have a lot more to cover. I would like to hear about the events just preceding the abduction."

"Yes," she agreed, "if it will help in finding the children, I can come."

"I believe it will," he said.

Logan walked with her to meet us in the reception room. She was calm, a sharp contrast to how she looked after the interviews on Wednesday and Thursday with Caldwell and others. "He said I didn't have to be there, that I could leave at any time," she told us on the way home. She thought he was a kind and understanding man.

Shortly after we returned home, I decided I wanted some bacon and eggs. People had continued to bring all kinds of food, and we had several pounds of bacon and several cartons of eggs.

"Anyone else want bacon and eggs?" I called to the den. One after another said, "No, thanks." But when the aroma of the bacon floated through the house, they all changed their minds and descended on the kitchen. The supply ran out faster than I thought. I called Mama and told her to pick up some eggs and bacon on the way to our house. By the time everyone ate, I had cooked four pounds of bacon and I don't know how many eggs.

In spite of the heavy burden hovering over us, we were able to engage in light-hearted conversation and enjoy one another's company. For the brief time we were eating, we put the sad event out of our mind, or at least kept it from coming to the surface.

****

All Union was focused on expressing love for the children and giving us loving support. Yellow ribbons were displayed everywhere—tied to trees, telephone poles, and doors of businesses and homes. Many wore them in their lapels. "I've never experienced anything like this," one woman told a reporter from Spartanburg's *Herald-Journal*, as she placed a big yellow ribbon on her front door. "I'm keeping this up until the children come home."

My heart overflowed with feelings of gratitude for all the expressions of concern and love. I am still grateful.

Churches all over Union County organized special prayer vigils. Susan came into the kitchen about ten o'clock in the evening and said Mitch wanted us to go to one at his church. I assumed one was planned there, and I think Mitch did, too. So, fifteen of us piled into three cars to go down to the church, with Mitch and Donna leading the way.

To our surprise, the church was closed. Mitch suggested we check with the pastor who lived nearby. When we pulled up to Rev. Cato's house, he was in the driveway getting something out of his car. Mitch walked over and explained that we thought there was going to be a prayer vigil at the church. Rev. Cato said people were praying around the clock in their homes rather than at the church, but he graciously invited us into his home. He didn't appear the least bit upset that we had dropped in without notice but did mention that his wife had already gone to bed.

My Daughter Susan Smith

We filed into the living room from the kitchen entrance and sat in a circle. Mitch asked Rev. Cato to lead us in prayer. He said he would be glad to and suggested that we silently express to God what we had on our hearts; then he would close the prayer.

I opened my heart to God, telling him how much we loved the children and asking him to please bring them safely back to us. It was a solemn, touching, uplifting experience.

It was almost eleven-thirty when we left Rev. Cato's home. We were barely settled in bed when the phone rang around twelve-thirty. A police sergeant from North Carolina told me a woman in a bar in North Carolina said she knew something about the children's disappearance. She was working on a road crew there but claimed to be from Buffalo, South Carolina. Someone overheard her say, "Yeah, I saw that car go by. It was a black man, with two white kids jumping up and down in the back seat." The men in the bar got so excited they organized a search party. More than two hundred volunteers searched all over the area where the woman said she saw the children.

I asked the officer, "Who is she? I grew up in Buffalo. If she's from there, I may know her."

I didn't recognize the name but said I would see if I could find out something about her.

I was out of my mind with excitement. This was the first person to say she had actually seen the children. There had been supposed sightings of the car and vague descriptions of the occupants but none so specific about the children.

Bev recognized the name. He called the woman's father, who lived down the street from Mama, and asked if he thought they could believe her. "If she was drinking," the man acknowledged, "I don't know."

Disappointed and discouraged, I called the officer and told him what the woman's father said. North Carolina law officers didn't pursue it any further.

Once again, I was left with the puzzling question: Where

could Michael and Alex be? I couldn't understand how the car could disappear from the face of the earth, but it seemed that it had.

15

Tuesday Recalled

The house was strangely quiet. The crowd of relatives and friends were gone for the day. I was glad for a little privacy but missed their loving support.

In the afternoon, Bev and I went with Susan and David for her two-o'clock meeting with Pete Logan. She didn't seem to dread it.

At the trial, Logan said he began as he had the day before, reminding Susan that she didn't have to be there and that she didn't have to take a polygraph. And if she decided to take a polygraph, he would review all the questions with her and go over everything they would do. He showed her the polygraph waiver form she would have to sign if she decided to take the test. Susan said she understood and would sign it when that time came.

"What I would like to do right now, Susan," Logan said, "is go over your activities of the weekend before the children disappeared. Let's begin with Friday morning."

She said David came by about six o'clock in the morning, took the children to day care, and came back for sex. After sex, he cleaned the carpet in her car. She could tell he had something on his mind when he came back inside. He wanted to talk about their pending divorce. After telling Logan how angry David was about her filing for divorce on grounds of adultery, she explained that he informed her about the evidence he had that would prove she also had committed adultery. She said David named one embarrassing thing after another that he was going to expose.

She told Logan about my being upset when I found out she had been going with Tom Findlay. She said it was because I didn't want her to do anything to make it possible for David to get custody of Michael and Alex. "Mama loves those kids like they're her own," she emphasized.

She paused, a sad look filling her face, then continued. "I don't know why I did anything so stupid as getting involved with Cary Findlay. I've messed my life up so bad. I've let everybody down."

They sat in silence while she gained her composure. Logan patiently waited for her to continue.

She next related events of the weekend: going to a friend's wedding on Saturday, Walt and Barbara keeping the kids, and her Sunday-evening conversation with Tom Findlay. She told about the Monday night aerobics class she missed and going instead to Hickory Nuts restaurant to see Tom Findlay and other friends from Conso. She told about waking up Tuesday morning feeling guilty about almost everything, especially worried that David was going to expose all the bad things in her life and hurt a lot of people she cared about.

Step by step, she recounted the conversations she had Tuesday afternoon at work. She said she was sure Tom hated her after she told him about her relationship with his dad, even though he said they could still be friends.

She said all she could do was cry when she got home from work, because she was upset about the mess she had made of her life. She really didn't know how things could have gotten so bad. When David called and tried to get her to tell him what was wrong, it was a final jolt. He was the last person she wanted to talk to. She said she had to get out of the house and clear her head and get control of her emotions.

After getting the kids in the car, she said she intended eventually to go to my house; but she had to stop crying first. She didn't want me or anyone else to know how upset she was.

She recounted her erratic driving that night, working up to the black man jumping into her car and ordering her to drive. She repeated in detail the story she had been telling from the beginning: that she asked the man to let her have her children when he pushed her out of the car near John D. Long Lake, that she ran to the McCloud home to get help.

After she told Logan everything that happened Tuesday evening, he asked her if she would be willing to take a polygraph test. She said she would. He gave her a form to sign, explained what questions he would ask, and said she could quit at any time.

"I need to go to the bathroom, first," she requested.

When she returned, Logan slowly moved her through the first chart of the polygraph. He noticed that she was getting more nervous as he asked one question after another, but not to the point of losing control. That really didn't surprise him; a polygraph makes most people a bit nervous.

He paused before beginning the second chart. Susan said she needed to go to the bathroom again. This time, he walked down to the restroom with her and waited nearby. When they got back to the room and sat down, she was visibly upset.

"I'm not sure I can continue with the polygraph right now," she said.

"Fine," Logan assured her. "You certainly aren't required to go forward with it, if you don't want to." He paused, then asked, "What's wrong?"

"I was thinking about my children. I want to have my children back at the end, if God will let me."

Logan excused himself and went out in the hall to find Howard Wells. He briefed the sheriff on what had happened. Wells went in to talk with Susan while Logan waited outside. She seemed calmed down when he returned to the room.

He decided to take another approach to get the information he was looking for. He asked Susan if she would prepare a written statement for their next meeting about the events leading up to and following the carjacking. He suggested, "Maybe you can recall some additional details that will help us know what happened, so we can find the children." She said she could do that. He then asked her if she could meet with him the next day. She couldn't; she had some things to do.

"That's fine," Logan agreed. "Maybe we can get together the next day, and you can bring me the write-up at that time. I'll be in touch with you to work it out." She said that would be okay. He escorted her down the hall to the reception area where we were waiting.

Tuesday Recalled

****

While Pete Logan was interviewing Susan, divers from the South Carolina Wildlife and Marine Resources Department checked John D. Long Lake again, and dozens of horsemen rode through surrounding woods and along the roadways. Wells told reporters that investigators had returned to the lake because they wanted to go over the area more thoroughly. He said they found nothing relevant to the case.

Others continued to help, too. Edward Lear and his wife drove over from Rock Hill. They wanted to get involved because, twenty years before, a friend's fifteen-year-old daughter disappeared and was never found. "I run a heavy equipment and machinery repair business," Lear said, "and a lot of times vehicles will get off in the water. I've been looking for oil slicks that would have come from the car. But I can't find any clues."

Church marquees carried messages of hope and comfort. Congregations took turns praying for our family in round-the-clock vigils. On Sunday morning, people prayed for the children in Bible study classes and in worship services. After church, crowds of people flocked to downtown Union to find out how the search was progressing. They gathered at the courthouse to talk to reporters. Nearly everyone wore a yellow ribbon.

When interviewed by the local newspaper, Sheriff Wells said his office hadn't ruled out the possibility that Susan Smith's carjacking story was a hoax, but they had no evidence to support that viewpoint. "This has been a very intense investigation," he said, "and we are just wanting to bring this case to an early close and put this family back together."

16

Halloween Celebration

For most people in Union, Halloween has always been a special fun time for children. Hedy loves to decorate for such special occasions and already had her Halloween decorations up before the children disappeared. She had ghosts and goblins in the front yard and small sacks with sand and candles on the front porch to keep the ghosts and goblins away, of course. This year the decorations were a painful reminder of Alex and Michael's absence.

The Halloween outfits hanging in Susan's closet were other painful reminders. Susan had bought a clown outfit for Alex and a pirate suit for Michael and trick-or-treat bags for both of them. She was prepared for Halloween two weeks early.

I stopped by her house one evening to see the outfits. "I can hardly wait!" she exclaimed, taking each one out of the closet to show me. She talked about painting Alex's face like a clown and how cute he was going to be. She put the pirate hat on Michael and told him to show Grandma. She planned to take them trick-or-treating by my house and Tim and Hedy's and Barbara and Walt's and other family members and friends. She even got me excited.

Union had to make a decision about Halloween. People debated about whether it was appropriate to celebrate the event with Michael and Alex missing. It was finally decided that the downtown merchants' annual trick-or-treat outing for children would go on as planned. For more than an hour in the evening, children descended on stores and businesses collecting the goodies. Television crews and reporters mixed with the young trick or treaters all over town.

On the north end of Main Street, one young mother expressed her feelings about the situation as she watched her children going door to door. "You can't just focus on this all the time," she said. "The children are having fun. It's not that we don't care, but life can't stop in Union. We have to go on."

Another woman told a reporter, "These children have to go on; they can't continue to be sad. They have to feel like children, but they just have to be more careful. We are still praying and thinking about the little children; but at the same time, we have to get on with our lives."

****

On the television show *A Current Affair*, broadcast Monday, a reporter revealed that Mitch Sinclair was the friend Susan was going to visit when she was carjacked. While being interviewed for the program, Mitch stated that he had taken a polygraph test and didn't do well. When reporters asked Sheriff Wells about the test, he wouldn't confirm or deny it, only that Mitch had been questioned to see if he could shed any light on the case. Probing further, they asked about Mitch's statement on the same program that "the truth would come out" about the carjacking, Wells said, "I think we have more to talk about." Later, Mitch clarified what he meant. He thought the sheriff was doing a good job of investigating the case and would get to the truth.

Mitch's brother Patrick said he was sure Mitch had nothing to do with the carjacking and the children's disappearance. "I think the kids are hidden somewhere," he speculated, "but my brother didn't do it."

Mitch was at our home from the time the children disappeared until they were found. Not for one minute did we suspect that he was involved in any way. But, like the rest of us, he was hounded by the press. Reporters followed him everywhere, asking whether he was a suspect. On many occasions when he got out of his car, they ran behind him, belting out one question after another. He was very upset about the suggestion that he would do anything to harm the children he loved so much. To get away from the press, he finally packed a bag and moved into our house.

Reporters asked Howard Wells repeatedly if the kidnapping

could be a hoax. He said nothing had been ruled out but that authorities were still treating the case as an abduction and were doing everything possible to find the children. He said he had no children of his own and had been drawn close to Michael and Alex. "I have had very little rest," he said. "When I lie down, I think about where they are and wonder if they are all right."

Despite Wells' refusal to confirm or deny whether Susan had taken a polygraph test, speculation mounted about the truthfulness of her story. Residents of Union went from not taking sides to skepticism to staunchly defending her. At our house, we were all incensed about reports that pointed a finger at her. "How could anyone suggest that she had hurt the children?" one after another protested, saying things like, "She loves Michael and Alex more than life."

Margaret Gregory told reporters our family didn't talk about rumors that the carjacking is a hoax and that Susan is somehow responsible for the abduction of her children. "We talk about how to bring the children back," she emphasized. She said our family felt law enforcement was doing everything it could to make sure Michael and Alex were returned.

When asked if the family had hired an attorney, Margaret said that to her knowledge, we had not. Questions like that never raised the possibility in my mind that Susan needed a lawyer. How I wish they had. But all of my emotional energy and thoughts were focused on getting the children back home. That's all anyone thought about. And I just could not conceive of my daughter needing a lawyer.

During an afternoon conference Monday, the sheriff said efforts to find Michael and Alex would proceed "full bore" and that authorities might offer a reward. We were encouraged by the intense efforts.

It had been six days since the disappearance of the children. David's half brother, Billy, hadn't called or come by. I wondered why. He lived only thirty miles away in Spartanburg. I asked David where Billy was. "I guess he's at home," he replied matter-of-factly. Scotty asked David about him, too. All he could tell Scotty was that he had a lot of guilt feelings about the way he had treated Billy when they were growing up.

Halloween Celebration

****

Pete Logan called in the late afternoon to talk to Susan. He asked if she could meet with him the next day. She agreed to do that, and he set the time at twelve o'clock, explaining that it needed to be earlier because of an activity at the Armory later in the afternoon. He checked to make sure Susan planned to bring the written statement. She told him she had spent most of the day working on it and that it was finished.

Her account of the carjacking was six pages long. She began by telling what had happened when she got home from work and how she rode around for a while with the children, finally asking Michael if he wanted to go to Mitch's house. The remainder of the account went like this:

"Unfortunately I never made it to Mitch's. I had stopped at the red light in Monarch Mills. While I was waiting for the light to change, a black man jumped in my car, put a gun to my side and said, drive or I'll kill you. I went into hysterics and started screaming why are you doing this? What do you want? He just told me shut up and drive or he would kill me. Michael asked me who that man was and what was wrong. I tried to comfort him and tell him that everything would be okay.

"The black man had allowed me to talk to Michael and Alex for a couple of minutes, but then he told me that was enough. I continued to drive, was praying to the Lord to take care of me and my children. Out of nowhere the black man told me stop. It was odd to me that he was asking me to stop right there in the middle of the road on that highway. I questioned him about stopping, and he told me to stop the car right now. I was going to pull over beside the road and stop but he told me no, to stop right here. He then told me to get out of the car or I'm going to kill you. And I opened my car door and told him that I have to get my babies as he was moving over to the driver's seat. He was pushing me out of the car and he told me he didn't have time. And I screamed and begged for him to please let me get my children. and he said again he didn't have time, but told me that he would not hurt my children. He shut the door and took off. I dropped to the road like a ton of bricks, screaming for someone to please help me. I went totally numb. I then jumped up and started running up the road and continually screamed for help. I ran up to the closest house that had any lights on. I could barely see because it was so dark. I got on the front porch and I banged on the door, continuing to cry for help. A lady or a man opened the door and saw that I was in trouble, but I couldn't hardly tell her what was wrong. She took me into her house and tried to calm me enough so I could tell her what happened. Once they knew what had happened, they immediately phoned the police. And as I sat in that lady's house, I prayed and prayed that my children would be okay. I was devastated. I was hysterical. I couldn't understand why."

Margaret Gregory helped Susan write the statement, and we all encouraged her to tell everything she could about the carjacking. As always, we hoped she could remember something that would help the police find the children. Unfortunately, her detailed account was another step deeper into the paralyzing maze of lies.

17

A Wish to Turn Back Time

From the moment word leaked out that Susan had failed a polygraph test and her story was being questioned, reporters were parked in front of our house day and night. As we sat in the den drinking coffee on the morning of that seventh day, most of us knew her account left many unanswered questions. Even so, the idea that she would harm Michael and Alex was something none of us could believe. We couldn't think the unthinkable.

Margaret Gregory came into the den and told us the press was pounding her for a word. "Why don't we give them a statement about how we feel?" she suggested. We agreed that might satisfy them. So she and Susan went into the bedroom to write something.

When they came out, Susan read the statement aloud to us. Leigh and I looked at each other, shocked and exasperated. It sounded like something a little girl would write, little more than a sweet thank you for your cards and letters.

"We'll go write this again, Susan," Leigh offered. "I'll help you." She then ushered Susan into the bedroom, and motioned for Margaret to come, too.

"Put something in there like it's hard to eat each day knowing they might be hungry," I called to them.

They worked on the statement for more than an hour. Margaret Gregory read it at a press conference late Tuesday morning as a message from our families. Here is that statement:

"No one here can begin to imagine how upside down our lives have been turned since last Tuesday night. Our children have been ripped out of our lives, and it is so unfair that Michael and Alex have been torn from us. We cannot begin to describe how much hurt and agony we are going through and how scared and frightened Michael and Alex must be.

"It is so difficult not knowing where they are. We can't feed them; we can't wipe away their tears; we can't hold them; we can't hug them. The things we take for granted as parents, taking them for walks, giving them a bath, playing with them—it hurts so much not to be able to do these things.

"It is so hard to explain how much we love these two little boys and how much we miss them. The hardest part of all is not knowing where they are. It is torture; it is a nightmare that seems to have no end. So what must it be like for Michael and Alex?

"We remember their first smiles, first words, first steps; but we need more than memories. We need Michael and Alex home where they belong. We can only hope and pray that the man who took our precious babies can find it somewhere in his heart to return them safely to us. We pray the Lord will help you realize how much we miss Michael and Alex and how much everyone loves them and that you will bring them back to us.

"We want to ask that anyone who knows anything at all or has any information that would help us find Michael and Alex that they would please come forward. No one can understand the pain we are going through or how much harder it gets as each day goes by without them being here.

"We know from all the cards and letters we have received that many people are praying for our families and for Michael and Alex, and we are grateful for those prayers. We know that everyone will continue to do everything they possibly can to find them.

"Michael and Alex, we want you to know that we love you and miss you very much. Not one minute goes by that we aren't thinking about you and praying for you. It's hard to eat each day thinking that you might be hungry. It's hard to be warm thinking that you may be cold. It's tough to laugh thinking that you may be crying. We have put our faith and trust in the Lord that he is taking care of you both, and hopefully soon you will be back home with Mama and Daddy. You both have to be brave, and you must hold onto each other because we are doing everything in our power to get you home where you both belong. "We love you."

Little did we know that this statement would be used against Susan in the trial to show she was mentally okay. Had we let her release her own brief, childlike statement, would things have gone differently? I can only wonder.

****

Since Tuesday was a regular working day for employees at the Armory, something had to be done to maintain secrecy. Again, Eddie Harris made the arrangements. He talked with the battalion commander and battalion A. O. and arranged with Columbia headquarters to excuse full-time guard members from duty on that day. They would make up the time later.

At breakfast we talked about getting to the Armory without the press on our tail. We decided to have Bev and David leave in the car and head toward Scotty and Wendy's house. Susan and I would go out the basement door and sneak across our backyard to meet them.

We knew it was very important for Susan to be there on time. Howard Wells didn't appreciate tardiness. Once when Susan and David were thirty minutes late for a scheduled meeting, the sheriff was preparing to send someone after them.

About twenty minutes before twelve, I knocked on Susan's bedroom door to make sure she would be ready on time.

"Y'all ready?" I asked when she opened the door.

"He's not going over there," Susan explained, pointing to David, who was sitting on the floor in front of the bed, looking rather hostile.

"Why aren't you going?" I asked. He said he was tired of sitting there forever.

I turned back to Susan and said, "They're going to come looking for you, Susan, if you're not on time."

"I know," she agreed.

"Remember, the sheriff said you needed to be calm, so you could pass the test."

My Daughter Susan Smith

"I know," she said again, but made no move to get her things together.

"Susan, you've got to go," I insisted, without looking in David's direction. "If David doesn't want to go, leave him here."

With that remark barely out of my mouth, David jumped up, accusingly pointed his finger at me, and screamed, "I ain't going nowhere with that thing!" He then stomped back and forth across the room, his mouth puffed up with rage and his eyes bulging out.

"Well, stay here," I snapped. "But Susan has got to go."

Susan picked up her purse from the bed and joined me. I signaled to Bev that it was time to leave. Susan and I then sneaked out the basement door and across the backyard to Scotty's house. Once safely out of the neighborhood, we cheered at the fact that, once more, we had fooled the media people.

Walking through the front door of the Armory, I took hold of Susan's arm and again urged her to tell them everything she could think of so we could find the children.

"But what if they don't believe me?" she asked.

"Don't worry," I said, chalking up her question to nervousness. "If you're going to take these tests, just tell the truth. Maybe you can think of something that will help find the children."

"If I fail, how am I going to prove I'm telling the truth?" she asked, pressing her previous point.

"Just tell the truth, and you won't have to prove anything," I said, puzzled by her persistence. "We want Michael and Alex back home. Tell them what you know."

"I will, Mama," she replied. "I will. I want them back home. They're my life."

At the trial, Logan told about Susan sitting down at the conference table that afternoon and handing him her six-page statement. He asked if she wrote it all herself. She said she did with some help from Margaret Gregory.

He scanned the statement and saw that it was the same story she had been telling all along—a black man jumped in her car, stuck a gun in her ribs, and told her to drive.

"Is there anything else you can remember about the car-jacker?" he asked.

"Not really," she replied. "I can't give you much, other than the fact that I only saw his eyes and teeth."

He set the statement aside and proceeded to go through the routine he had followed for the previous interviews—telling Susan she didn't have to be there if she didn't want to, that she could leave at any time. He then went over the questions he would ask on the polygraph and asked her to sign the appropriate forms. She willingly complied.

"Did you have any contact with Tom Findlay after the car-jacking?" was one of the first questions.

"Not that night," she said. "He was out of town, but he called me on his car phone when he heard what had happened. I tried to apologize to him for what I told him about his father, but he didn't want to talk about it. He said I had more serious things to consider and I shouldn't worry about that. It was a very short conversation. He acted like he hated me, and I couldn't blame him. I saw him in the hall at the sheriff's office later, but I haven't talked to him since the phone call."

"If you had one wish, what would you wish?" Logan asked.

"If I had one wish," she replied, "I would turn back time. I wish I had never said anything to Tom Findlay about his father."

Logan moved to his next question. "What are your five greatest concerns right now?"

The answer came quickly. "The first would be not knowing where my children are. And I'm concerned about not knowing if my children are alive or not alive, whether they are being taken care of. I would rather know that my children are in heaven than someone hurting them or torturing them. Just basically not knowing what has happened."

After completing the polygraph, Logan turned to a list of Susan's relatives. He asked about each of them—where they worked, how close she was to them, whether any of them had recently traveled outside South Carolina. He went into considerable detail about relatives on both sides of her family.

Near the end of the interview, he asked, "Would you mind

telling me or showing me where the carjacking occurred.?" She said she could. They then returned to the reception area, and Logan told us they would be back in a few minutes but didn't say where they were going.

Driving down Highway 49 toward John D. Long Lake, Susan said, "Mr. Logan, there's something else I haven't told you."

"Oh, what is that?" he asked.

"It's about my stepfather, Beverly Russell. We have been attracted to each other. He used to come into my bedroom and fondle me when he thought I was asleep. I wasn't really asleep, but he didn't know that. Because of that, I went to counseling with Social Services." He let her tell what she wanted on this subject without asking any follow-up questions.

They rode straight to the proposed carjacking site and back to the Armory. When they returned, Logan told us they would be through shortly; all they needed to do was decide when they would meet again.

Back in the conference room, Logan showed Susan a waiver form. "Would you mind if we obtained some of your records—medical records, telephone records, things like that." That was okay with her. She signed the form.

"We also need to search your home to see if we can find anything that would help in locating the children. Would that be okay?" She agreed to that request and signed the form.

She suddenly looked troubled and nervous.

"Is something wrong?" Logan asked.

"Well, I feel bad that my family has to wait so long each day."

"Would you like for me to talk to them and have them at least consider maybe not coming?"

"I would appreciate it if you would do that."

"You wait here right now, and I'll go down and talk to your family."

He found Sheriff Wells, and the two of them came to the reception area to talk to us. Logan said Susan had failed the polygraph test. When my mouth flew open, he quickly explained that people sometimes fail because they're nervous and traumatized by the experience. He had seen a case where the person was so emotionally distraught it took forty days to get him calmed down enough to pass.

Changing the subject, he said Susan felt bad about us having to wait so long while he interviewed her. He said we could make our own decision about whether or not to come back each day; but if we chose not to come, they could arrange for Susan's transportation. We said we wanted to do what was best for Susan and would talk about it and let him know our decision right away.

The sheriff told us the next interview would have to be somewhere other than the Armory, because employees were returning the next day and would need the conference room. He would contact us as soon as they made the arrangements.

With these matters settled, Logan went to get Susan. When she came to the reception area, we told her David had reconsidered coming and was there, but he was in a waiting room on the opposite side of the Armory.

"I better go get him," she said. She returned in a few moments and told us David didn't want to go back to our house. Instead, he wanted her to go with him to his apartment.

I asked her if that was where she wanted to go. She said, "No, I want to be with the people I love and who love me."

"You don't have to go with him," I said.

"That's the way David has always done me," she lamented. "He always tries to make me choose between him and my family." She said she would go with us.

Later, David called Susan and said he was coming back over. He thought they should be together.

Barbara Benson, David's mother, and his brother Billy were at our house when we returned. Barbara explained why she hadn't come sooner. "David's my son," she said, "but you've been closer to the children than me. I thought I could do more good giving interviews and putting out fliers."

I talked to Billy for a little bit about how things were going with him and where he lived and worked and went to school. "I'm sorry for what y'all are having to go through," he told me.

My Daughter Susan Smith

The sequence of events in Billy's appearance made me suspicious. He hadn't been to our house since the children disappeared; then he showed up the day after I had asked David about him. Also fresh in my mind was something Susan told me about David and his friends following her. The suspicion formed in my mind that David had followed her, kidnapped the children, and took them to Billy's apartment.

The next morning, I asked Walt and Mike Lovelace to drive to Spartanburg to check around Billy's apartment to see if the car was stashed there. They gladly did that but found nothing suspicious. Another false hunch.

Around midnight, Tim got a call about a wrecked car at a junk yard in Inman, just north of Spartanburg. My nephew Eddie Pettit, Michael, Walt, and Tim headed over there. The car didn't match Susan's. Disappointed once more.

Spartanburg's *Herald-Journal* reported that Wells was out of his office for most of the day Tuesday and that he declined to say where he was, only that he was out checking leads.

18

The Unraveling

Sheriff Wells called around ten and asked for me. He calmly said he had received a call from the law enforcement people in Washington State. They had found an abandoned child fitting Alex's description.

"Howard, is he all right?" I asked excitedly, my heart pounding.

"Linda," he said firmly, "I want you to listen to me closely. I need a good description of what Alex had on, any identifying marks, and a description of the car seat. Get all that information and call me back right away."

The minute I hung up the phone, I thought, *If it is Alex, where is Michael*? I forced the thought out of my mind and went to tell Margaret Gregory the good news. We slipped out to the porch to talk. She suggested we get Susan and David and go into our bedroom. We didn't want to say a word to anyone else until we got all the information together.

Margaret took notes as Susan described the outfit Alex had on. She said it had red and white stripes. "You know which one it is, Mama," she said, smiling faintly. "That knit one he looks so cute in. And he had on his little blue and red jacket," she added.

About identifying marks, she said, "Tell them he has the most sparkling brown eyes you ever saw, and he's a chubby little thing. But can he ever get around fast!" It was as if she were reminiscing about Alex, picturing him at his birthday party in August. His eyes did sparkle as he plunged his hand into his own little cake and stuffed a big piece in his mouth. He was having a great time with Michael sitting beside him, helping him eat the cake. Balloons flew over their heads. When the children went outside, Alex ran up and down the driveway, trying to keep up with his cousins on their bikes and Michael on his tricycle. Did Susan remember telling Nick and Matt to be careful not to run over him? I thought maybe she did. I held back the tears.

Susan told Margaret that Alex's car seat was a gray tweed with gray straps and a gray buckle. "And, oh yes," she noted, "they were both real clean because Mama had cleaned them for me."

When I called the sheriff to give him the information, he asked us to come on down there. I then went into the den and excitedly announced, "They think they might have found Alex! Howard wants us to go down there." Everyone gathered around me, asking for more information.

I went to take a quick shower. As I dried off, the thought once more crossed my mind, *If it is Alex, where is Michael?* Again, I forced it out.

While we all stood in the den deciding who would ride in what car, David was beaming from ear to ear, but Susan looked surprisingly sad. "Smile, Susan," Margaret urged, "we may have found them."

"I hope so," Susan said softly but still didn't smile. I felt sorry for her. I thought she had given up hope.

We drove to the sheriff's office in a caravan, with the press right behind us. They gathered together in front of the courthouse while we went inside.

Wells was in the reception area to greet us. Before he said a word, the disappointed look on his face told it all. The child had been identified, but it wasn't Alex. My heart sank.

We talked for a minute about other possible leads, then Howard walked outside with us. The crowd of reporters pounced on us. They wanted to hear from Susan, David, and the sheriff.

Susan and David made another appeal for the safe return of their children. Susan spoke first:

"To whoever has my children, please, please, bring them home to us where they belong," she began. "Our lives have been torn apart by this tragic event. I can't explain how much they are wanted back home. We love them; we miss them; they are our hearts. I have prayed every day. There is not one minute that goes by that I don't think about these boys. And I have prayed that whoever has them will realize that they are missed and loved more than any other children in this world. Whoever has them, I pray every day they are taking care of them. And know we will do anything, anything, to help you get them home to us. I can't express it enough that we have got to get them home. That's where they belong—with their mama and daddy.

"I want to say to my babies, your mama loves you so much, and your daddy, this whole family loves you so much. You guys have got to be strong. I just know, I feel in my heart, you're okay. You've got to take care of each other. And your mama and daddy are gonna be out here waiting on you when you get home. I love you so much.

"I am putting all of my faith and trust in the Lord, that he is taking care of the children and will bring them home."

Next, David made a brief, moving appeal:

"To the American public, please don't give up on these two little boys and the search for their safe return home to us. As we continue to look for this car, for our children, and for the suspect, continue to keep your eyes open. If there is anything that you see, please call and let it be known."

About the latest lead in the search, Wells told the crowd that it "turned out to be not as promising as we first thought. There were a lot of similarities that drew us close and our hearts soared for a while."

Margaret Gregory expressed the deep disappointment for our families: "It gave us hope to hang onto. We are disappointed by the fact that this child who has been located is not one of Susan and David's children, but we are extremely hopeful new leads will develop, and we will continue to cling to the hope the little boys will be home very soon."

One of Susan's neighbors was there hoping to hear some good news. "They are good neighbors," she said of Susan and David. "They love their children, and the babies were always so happy."

"We are hoping to hear good news," said a woman whose daughter went to school with Susan. "We want those children back."

Before we left, I told Howard we wouldn't be coming with Susan for the Logan interview. He said Eddie Harris would be available to pick her up and that he would be there at twelve-thirty.

Eddie had selected the Family Life Center of First Baptist Church for the interview. He was a member of the church and could easily get a key. The location was close to the courthouse and easily accessed from the back, well away from the attention of the media. The church itself faces Main Street, with the Family Life Center about fifty yards behind it and a parking lot in between.

In addition to being used as a recreation center, the building has classrooms. Eddie selected one in the back. Since it was his job to prepare the room properly, he made sure there was a conference-type table and no pictures or other visuals on the walls. He took down a poster that had inscribed on it "Jesus Loves the Little Children."

Police officer Bobby Hicks, our family friend, was out front when Eddie arrived to pick up Susan. It was his responsibility to protect us from the press horde. Luckily, they had not returned from downtown.

Eddie came in to see if Susan was ready. Margaret Frierson from the Adam Walsh Center talked to him for a minute about efforts to find the children. He said they were checking all leads.

As Susan and Eddie left, I gave her my usual urging to try to think of anything that would help find the children. And she gave her usual answer. "I will, Mama; I will."

****

Before beginning the interview, Pete Logan explained why the meeting location was changed. He said the employees had returned, and it would have been too noisy. She said that was fine.

Logan then went over the usual ground rules, assuring Susan she didn't have to be there, that she could refuse to answer any question she didn't like, and that she was free to leave anytime she wanted. As before, he told her he would be running a polygraph and would go over the questions with her before starting.

The first questions on the polygraph related to the written statement she had brought in the day before: Was there anything else she could tell him that she hadn't written down? Had she falsified or fabricated any of the information in the statement? She said no to both questions. The graph showed she wasn't telling the truth.

When they finished the polygraph, Logan wanted to talk about the stop light at Monarch where Susan claimed the abductor jumped into her car. He showed her a form indicating the traffic light had an eleven-and-a-half-second cycle before turning. He explained that, if a car approached the signal on Highway 49, the light would stay green, unless a car entered the intersection from the side street. If that happened, there would be an eleven-and-a-half-second delay before turning. Logan had checked the intersection that morning to make sure the signal worked as intended.

"I know you were under a lot of stress at the time," he said, "and you might not know for sure if you were there. Is it possible that this took place somewhere else?"

She got a funny look on her face. "Mr. Logan," she admitted, "it didn't happen in Monarch; it happened in Carlisle. I didn't want to tell you before, because I didn't have any good reason to be that far away from home at that time of night."

"Would you ride with me to the new location and show me exactly where it is?" he asked. She said that would be fine.

Logan excused himself to ask Eddie Harris to follow them to the site.

"Are you familiar with this area?" Logan asked, as they drove down Highway 215 toward Carlisle.

"Not really," she replied.

"Then why did you come to this area?"

"I do know a little about it," she replied quickly. "There's where I used to park with a boyfriend," she added, pointing to a side road.

"Sometimes when people are upset or confused, they get in the car and just drive," Logan suggested. "I know people who have done that. Maybe that's what happened with you that night."

"I guess so," she acknowledged. "I didn't have any plan. I was just driving."

Shortly after entering Carlisle, Logan pulled up to a stop sign at the Carlisle-Chester Highway. On the opposite side of the highway was a service station and mini-mart with pay telephones outside.

"This is where it happened," she said. "Right here across from the service station."

Logan turned around and headed back to Union. Susan told him the abductor ordered her to turn around that night, too.

Back in the interview room, Logan asked Susan if he could get some more details about what had happened in Carlisle. She said she was getting tired.

He looked at his watch. It was almost five o'clock. "I can understand why you're tired," he assured her. "We've been here more than three hours. Why don't you just go home and write a short statement about what happened and bring it tomorrow."

"Yes, I can do that," she agreed.

"Tomorrow will be a short day," he promised. "You bring the statement, and we'll discuss it briefly. I'll tell the sheriff about this new information. I'm sure he'll want to investigate the scene."

Eddie Harris wanted to pick Susan up at eleven the next day. She said that wouldn't work. "How about one?" she suggested. He said that would be okay.

****

We had lived for a week with a house full of people, all filled with anxiety and sadness. Everybody's nerves were beginning to fray. Billie Grace, Harry's sister, was helping me with the dishes after supper when Barbara Benson came in there to tell us good-bye. While she was standing beside me at the sink, Margaret Gregory came in and said the press was pressuring her for a statement from the family. "What about the grandparents saying something?" she suggested. "Maybe they'd be satisfied with that. Linda, would you be on one of the morning shows?"

"Oh man, Margaret, I don't want to do that. But I'll do whatever it takes to get the children back."

"And maybe Sue could be on there with you," she suggested.

Before I could say anything, Barbara shrieked in my ear, "I can't believe they would have that woman do something on TV." She then pointed to David's stepmother in the dining room and yelled, "She's not their grandmother. I'm their grandmother. You don't know what that woman's done to me. If..."

"I don't care! I don't care!" I screamed, then turned around to face Barbara squarely in the face. "All I want is those babies, Barbara. I don't care about that crazy TV show."

Barbara stood there dumbfounded as I flew through the den past David's sister Becky and the room full of people and down the hall to Susan's bedroom.

I charged past Bev and Margaret, who were sitting in chairs, to the bed and grabbed Susan by the shoulders. "Susan," I pleaded, my arms trembling and my voice choking with emotion, "I want the children. Do you know where they are? Have you hurt them?"

"Mama!" she said, "You know I would never hurt Michael and Alex." Her incredibly sad eyes and hurt expression stunned me to the core of my being.

As I stood there frozen in place, Susan turned to Bev. "I can't take anymore of this," she said, her voice trembling. "Get her, Bev. Do something for her."

Without saying a word, Bev stood up to leave; and Susan followed him out of the bedroom.

I slumped down on the bed, crying. Margaret got up from the chair, sat down beside me, and put her arm around my shoulder.

"Margaret," I sobbed, "I can't believe I said that to Susan."

She tried to console me, saying, "It's all right, Linda; it's all right." While I cried, she kept telling me Susan would understand, that things would be okay. She even cried with me.

I don't know whether you would say my blowup was because I doubted Susan or only that I had reached a point where I had to know. At the time, I couldn't understand why I took my frustration out on her. I hadn't suspected her for a minute. It was deep concern, not suspicion, that made me keep urging her to think of something to help investigators locate the children. It was because she was the only one who really knew what happened, the only one who had seen the abductor, the only one who could provide the clues that would crack the case. Now I realize there were many signs that made others suspect Susan, but I couldn't see them. Maybe the thoughts were festering in the deepest recesses of my subconscious. I just don't know. I do know I simply couldn't entertain the thought that the daughter I love dearly and the mother who loved her children with all her heart could harm her children.

When I finally pulled myself together, I walked back down the hall and into the den. By then, Barbara was gone and Susan was sitting in the den in our rocker-recliner, leaning back with her eyes closed. She looked exhausted. I eased into the recliner with her and lay my head on her shoulder. "This is so comfortable," I sighed, trying to be upbeat. "I can see why Michael and Alex liked for you to rock them."

She opened her eyes and smiled lovingly.

I took a deep breath, then said, "I'm so sorry, Susan, that I blew up at you. I just couldn't take Barbara anymore."

"Mama, what I want more than anything in the world is to have my babies back in my arms and to rock and rock and rock them. I could rock them forever." I felt guilty and relieved at the same time.

Barbara called back later to talk to David. Before I told David his mother was on the line, I apologized to her.

"I needed to get away," she explained. "I needed to get with my support group. I wasn't getting any support there. You just don't know what that man's done to me. You just don't know. And I can't believe I still love him."

Later in the evening, a friend of Susan's from Conso came

by. When she was ready to leave, Hedy walked outside with Susan to tell her good-bye. As the friend drove off, Susan pointed to the lawn chairs on the porch and said, "Come and sit down with me, Hedy."

They sat there quietly for a moment, then Susan said, "Hedy, I wish I could turn back time."

Hedy silently questioned whether she should ask her to explain that strange statement. *No*, she decided, I *can't do that. Susan is in so much pain. I don't want to hurt her any more.* She would listen and let her say whatever she wanted. But Susan said nothing more on that subject.

Hedy told me later that she would have probed if she had suspected Susan, but that possibility didn't enter her mind. At the trial, she told how she felt when she learned the awful truth: "Knowing Susan like I knew her, there was no way she could ever have done anything like that.... Something had to have happened to her." The Susan Hedy knows could never have harmed her children.

19

How Could I Do Such a Thing?

Barbara's outburst changed Margaret Gregory's plan for dealing with the press. Instead of grandmothers, she asked Susan and David to appear on the TV morning shows to make an appeal.

I ran into Susan in the hall outside her bedroom early the next morning. "Mama," she said, "I don't want to do this."

"Susan, they're going to be here soon," I replied. "It looks like it's too late to back out." I hurt for her, but I wanted to keep the children before the public. It was the only way to go.

She and David appeared on the morning news programs of all three major networks, appealing passionately for the return of Michael and Alex. Susan urged the carjacker to return the children that were so loved. She urged the children to be brave.

At a news conference later that morning, Sheriff Wells told reporters there were no new developments in the case. Margaret Frierson said a car similar to Susan's was sighted in Atlanta, Georgia, Wednesday night; but the lead didn't pan out.

A foot search was scheduled for Saturday, November 5, two days away. It was to begin in Lockhart, two miles from John D. Long Lake, around 10:00 a.m. Walkers would scour the roadsides in Union, Chester, and York counties. Kevin Kingsmore, who helped to organize the search, planned for walkers to cover thirty miles, with six designated areas. Search organizers had received around four hundred calls from people wanting to participate, some from as far away as Jacksonville, Florida. Buffalo Baptist Church and Tabernacle Baptist Church offered vans to transport volunteers. Bell Atlantic Mobile had supplied a telephone number and voice mail. Law enforcement people would give strategic support.

****

Since we weren't going with Susan to the interview, I told Bev there were some places I wanted to check out. "They've looked everywhere," he protested impatiently. "Where do you want to look?"

"Let's get in the car," I insisted. "I'll show you."

I directed Bev to the home of an older woman Susan worked with. She was the one who had brought Susan to Hedy's house after a party at the Findlay estate. Driving by slowly, I saw a woman I didn't recognize place a child in a car parked in the driveway. The child wore a jacket similar to Michael's. The driver pulled out of the driveway and quickly drove in the opposite direction. The swiftness of the getaway raised my suspicions.

"Let's go back," I told Bev. "I want to check this out." I walked to the front door and knocked. No answer. I peaked in the small glass opening in the door and saw toys. I next went to check out the garage to see if Susan's car was there. Disappointment gripped me as I pulled up the door to see nothing that pointed to Michael and Alex.

I suggested we go by the home of David's great-grandmother in Buffalo to see if Susan's car was there. We looked in a barn behind one of her houses. No car.

Snatching at any possibility, I allowed myself to consider, for the first time, that Susan might somehow be involved. I silently wondered if she had hidden the children to keep them from David. Maybe someone from work had helped her. I reasoned that, even if she were involved, the children were somewhere. And if we found the car, we would find Michael and Alex. Not for a second did I think she had hurt them.

Suddenly, guilt consumed me. How could I possibly suspect my own daughter? I refused to go any further with that thought, pushing it out of my conscious mind. I said nothing to Bev or Susan or anyone else about my feelings.

****

Susan held a coke in one hand and a brown envelope in the other when Eddie drove up to Scotty's driveway. The envelope contained the statement Logan had asked her to write about the details of the carjacking in Carlisle.

She placed the coke in a beverage holder and reached for the seat belt. Her hands trembled as she adjusted it. She explained that the press made her nervous. "I'm so tired of them being everywhere," she said. "I'll be glad when all of this is over."

"I'll make sure they don't see us this time," Eddie assured her. He then drove around the circle and out to Highway 176. "We're okay now," he said, pulling up to the stop sign. "They didn't see us when we went by your street."

"Thank goodness," she said, then turned upbeat. "By the way, did you see me on TV this morning?"

"Yes, I did," Eddie replied, a bit puzzled by the sudden change.

"How did I look?" she asked.

"You looked fine," he replied.

At the trial, Eddie said Susan's upbeat manner seemed inappropriate, given her situation. That wouldn't have surprised any of us who know her well. She can act happy, even when things are very bad.

"It's a beautiful fall day," Eddie observed, changing the subject. "I'm sure the mountains are pretty now."

"I don't really care for the mountains," she said. "I enjoy the beach. When this is all over, I would like to go to the beach and get away from all of this. They do the shag on the beach. Do you know how to shag?"

"Yes, I do," he replied.

"Well, maybe you can teach me sometime. How old are you?"

"I'm forty-four."

"You look good for your age."

"I have a daughter that's the same age as you—Christie. You were in school together."

"Yes, I knew that. She works at Conso, but I don't know her very well. I remember her in high school. And I've been seeing you around Union all my life."

"Yes, I've been around Union all your life," he acknowledged, but he didn't tell her he was one of the investigating officers when her daddy killed himself. At the time, he was employed by the Union Police Department.

Close to downtown, Eddie told Susan he possibly would have to take a different route to the Family Life Center to avoid the media. She was grateful. She couldn't stand the thought of talking to one more reporter.

At about one-thirty, Pete Logan greeted them just inside the entrance and escorted Susan to the classroom where they met the day before. She handed him the envelope with the statement, sat down, and placed her coke on the table.

He opened the envelope, took out the papers, and began to read.

"Why don't you take it home and read it," she suggested.

"That's okay. I won't read every word. I know we agreed this would be a short day."

"Yes, I'm bushed. David and I were on TV early this morning."

"Is this written statement basically what you told me yesterday?" he asked. She said it was.

After briefly discussing a number of points about the statement, he excused himself.

Logan always had an understanding with law-enforcement officials that, when he conducted an interview, he called the shots. It was his policy to be the only one who had contact with the person until he decided it was time to get someone else involved. He had decided it was time to bring in the sheriff.

Susan didn't know it, but Howard Wells was also in the building. He had been informed about her change of carjacking location the day before and had gone to the new site that morning. Logan also had alerted him to the possibility that he might be called in sometime during the interview.

Logan escorted Wells into the room, handed Susan's statement to him, and suggested he sit in the chair next to her.

"Are you upset or mad at me for not telling you the right place at first?" Susan sheepishly asked him.

"No, I'm not mad at you, Susan," he said with a half-smile.

My Daughter Susan Smith

"Now, just tell me what happened."

She repeated what she told Logan the day before about the carjacking happening in Carlisle rather than Monarch. When she had finished, Logan left the room.

Wells turned his chair to face Susan. Holding up the written statement and pointing it at her, he said firmly but gently, "Susan, this could not have happened as you have said."

"Why do you say that, Sheriff Wells?" she asked nervously.

"When confronted with information that the red light at Monarch could not have been red," he began, "you changed your story and identified a location in Carlisle. It couldn't have happened there either, because the intersection you named with the stop sign and the yellow median next to a service station . . ."

"That's the one," she interrupted.

"That's Dehart's Service Station," he explained. "There is a telephone booth in that lot. At the time in question, the Union County sheriff's office had that location under surveillance for drug activity in the area. It's directly across the road from the post office. Right?"

"Yes," she acknowledged.

He looked her straight in the eye. "Susan, if this did not happen as you say, and a black man was not involved, I am obligated to release this new information to the media. Tensions have risen in Union because a black man has been implicated. If it was not so, I am obligated to tell them."

She lowered her head and said nothing. That morning after appearing on TV, she told me she didn't know how she could possibly go in front of the TV cameras again. This threat meant another bombardment by the press.

Slowly, she raised her head and looked sadly at the sheriff. "Would you pray with me?" she asked, tears forming in her eyes.

"Yes, I will," he said softly.

"Would you say the prayer?" she asked, placing her hands in his.

He told God it had been an extremely hard time for all the family members, for law enforcement, and for everyone involved about not knowing where the children were, whether they were all right. He said something like, "The family has been burdened, and it is time that it be revealed. I pray, Lord that you will be with all of those who are involved and strengthen us and give us guidance and forgiveness."

They both quietly said, "Amen," when he concluded the prayer.

The sheriff raised his head and looked Susan in the eye. "Susan," he said softly. "It's time. You will need to tell me exactly what happened."

She dropped her head into her hands and began to cry. Tears ran down her face and dripped off her chin. Her hands started shaking. Within moments, she was trembling all over and rocking back and forth in her chair. Wells thought she might be hyperventilating.

"I'm so ashamed," she gasped. "I'm so ashamed. I am so ashamed. Please give me your gun, Sheriff Wells, so I can kill myself."

"Why would you want to do that?" he questioned.

"You don't understand. My children are not all right."

"Susan, don't say anything else," he cautioned, then stepped out of the room.

"I need a Waiver of Rights Form," he told Logan, asking for what is popularly known as the Miranda Warning.

When Wells returned to the room, Susan was leaning on the table with her head in her hands, still sobbing and rocking back and forth. He sat down beside her and said calmly, "Susan, I need to get your attention." He patiently waited for her to pull herself together. He then read the Advise of Rights Form to her:

"Your rights," he stated with emphasis. "Before we ask you any questions, you must understand your rights. You have the right to remain silent. Anything that you say can and will be used against you in a court of law. You have the right to talk to a lawyer for advice before we ask you any questions and to have him with you during questioning. If you have no money to pay a lawyer's fee, then the court will appoint one to represent you without cost, if you wish. If you decide to answer questions now without a lawyer present, you will still have the right to stop answering at any time. You also have a right to stop answering at any time until you talk to a lawyer. I have read this statement of my rights and I understand what my rights are."

"Do you understand your rights?" he asked.

"Yes, I do," she replied, her tone hesitant, her voice shaky.

He asked her to sign the form. Her signature was recorded at 1:55 p.m., November 3, 1994. The sheriff signed as a witness.

He next asked her to read the Waiver of Rights Form:

"I'm willing to make a statement and answer questions. I do not want a lawyer at this time. I understand and know what I'm doing. No promises or threats have been made to me. And no pressure or coercion of any kind has been used against me."

She signed the Waiver of Rights Form without protest.

Wells handed her a handkerchief to wipe the tears that were streaming down her face. "I need you to talk to me, to listen, and to answer my questions," he said.

His tone was sympathetic but professional. "Susan, right now there are heavy burdens on your family, on law enforcement, and I'm sure on you. But the Lord will lead us through this. But it's time that this is revealed. It is time. You will need to tell me exactly what happened."

Her trembling body gradually quieted; her voice turned steady. "That night," she said, "I was riding around, thinking about what a mess my life had become, how many bad things had happened to me, that I couldn't be a good mother. I didn't want my children to be without a mother. I felt so alone and depressed. There was no one I could talk to. I just couldn't understand why things had turned out so badly in my life. I wanted to die."

The words rolled out fast, one sentence bumping into another.

"I went to John D. Long Lake with the intent of killing myself. My children were asleep when I came up to the lake and stopped at the ramp. I can't believe that, after I got there, I allowed my children to go down the ramp without me in the car. At the time the car was rolling into the lake, I wanted to go back. I didn't hear it go down into the lake, but I knew it was too late. I sank to my lowest when I let my children go into the lake without me.

"All this time, I've known, deep down, that I would have to tell what happened. But I still can't understand why it happened the way it did. I don't deserve to live."

"No, you don't deserve to die," Wells said decisively.

When Susan finished telling what happened October 25, 1994, Wells said he needed to leave for a minute.

"Susan has confessed," he told Logan. "I want someone else to hear the confession. I need you to come back into the room so she can repeat this to someone else. It was not taped, and it was not recorded by any means."

The two men entered the room to find Susan on the floor between two chairs with her head face down on one chair. A stream of tears flowed onto the chair. She looked to Wells like a child at prayer.

He pulled a chair beside her and sat down. "Susan," he said, "look up and tell Agent Logan what you told me."

"I'm so ashamed, Mr. Logan," she began. "You don't understand. How could I have done this? I'm so ashamed."

She then told Logan what she had told Wells. When she finished, Wells asked her if she wanted to go out to the lake to show him where everything was. She didn't want to do that. "But I want to tell you something," she said, looking him in the eye.

"What is that?" he asked.

"When you didn't find the car the first day, it was as if it didn't happen, as if the Lord had lifted the car up and swept it away to punish me. I thought he was going to let me suffer for a while and then the car and the children would be found."

Her sincerity mystified him—she really believed what she said!

Responding only with a sympathetic but puzzled look, he left the room to talk to Carol Allison, a senior supervisor in the FBI office located in Greenville, South Carolina. She had been in the building for sometime.

Wells asked Allison to sit with Susan and Pete Logan while he made arrangements with other law enforcement officers about plans for the rest of the day and about the manner in which they would go down to the lake. He emphasized how important it was that Susan not be left alone at any time. He was convinced she would try to commit suicide if not watched. He then left to make arrangements for the retrieval of the car and the bodies. It was around two-thirty.

When Carol Allison entered the room, Susan was sitting in a chair, sobbing and rocking back and forth. Logan was sitting beside her. She sat in a chair on the opposite side of Susan.

"I don't deserve to live," she sobbed to Logan. "How could I have done this? How could I have done such a thing? I don't deserve to live."

"Yes, you do," Logan said.

He directed her attention to Carol Allison and introduced her as a special agent with the FBI and a mother. Looking straight at her, Susan sobbed, "I wanted to die. I wanted to die, but I didn't want them to grow up without a mother. I drove down the ramp and was going to go, but didn't, and then I was, but didn't. Then I released the hand brake and ran. How could I do that?"

She told Susan it wasn't the first time something like that had happened.

"I'm such a terrible mother." she cried.

She told Susan she had seen videotapes of her with the children and they looked well fed, clothed, and cared for. She assured Susan that everything she had heard about her showed she was a good mother to her children.

"I'm so sorry," Susan sobbed. "I'm so sorry." The pathos in her voice was heavy.

"Do you want me to tell your mother?" Allison asked.

"No," she answered decisively. "Please ask Sheriff Wells to advise me on that."

How Could I Do Such a Thing?

Sheriff Wells came back in and asked Susan if anyone else knew what had happened or was involved.

"No," she replied emphatically. "No one else knew, and no one was involved. I'm so sorry. I don't deserve to live."

"Susan," Allison said. "They've searched the lake twice. Do you know which direction the car went or how long it floated?"

"No. I covered my ears and ran. I didn't see anything or hear anything."

The tears flowed down her cheeks and onto her chin. Allison held some tissues out to her. Susan reached for the tissues and dropped her head in Allison's lap. "Can you explain how I could have done this?" she cried.

"I don't know, Susan. I don't know."

"I've hurt everyone so badly," she sobbed. "David and my mother will never be able to forgive me. Do you think God will forgive me?"

"Yes, I do," Allison said softly.

"Is it really true that this is not the first time something like this has happened?"

"Yes, that's true."

"Didn't any of those other mothers have any remorse or feel any remorse?"

"I don't really know. I suppose they may not have. Why do you ask?"

"Because I'm full of remorse. I can't imagine anyone doing something like this and not feeling any remorse."

At a pre-trial hearing, Allison stated that she had viewed Susan's TV appeals for the safe return of her children and never was moved by them. She suspected her involvement from the first day she was brought into the investigation. She thought Susan was a bad actress. Her crying was forced; nothing appeared genuine. It just wasn't real. But watching her on this ninth day, she saw something different. It was not a performance. The pretense was gone. The tears were real. The sorrow was deep.

When Allison had calmed Susan down enough to answer a question, Logan asked her what her actual route was that night.

She told him about leaving home around eight intending to go to my house but wanting to drive around long enough to stop crying. She told about going to Carlisle and thinking about suicide at the Broad River Bridge. She verbally traced the route from Carlisle to Monarch Mills, then finally to John D. Long Lake.

She paused and stared ahead blankly. "I don't understand how I could do such a thing when I loved those children so much. I wish I could die. I don't deserve to live. I don't understand why I didn't go into the lake with my children."

For the next two-and-one-half hours, the two agents and Susan talked about what happened the night of October 25. Allison later described that time as "an intense, emotional, draining experience."

The sheriff was in and out of the room the rest of the afternoon to check on things and to talk with Susan. Around three o'clock, she asked him if his statement about the drug stakeout was true. He admitted it was not, that it was simply part of his strategy to get her to confess.

Just after four-thirty, Logan asked Susan if she would like to write down on paper what happened concerning her children— the events and her feelings at the time. She said she would.

Logan showed her an Advise of Rights Form and asked her to read it. She read and signed it.

Next, he gave her a Waiver of Rights Form. Susan read and signed it. Pete Logan and Carol Allison signed as witnesses.

Logan handed her a legal pad and a pen, and she began to write the confession that was read at the trial and has been in newspapers all over the country. The tearful account is in the second chapter of this book.

20

A Public Funeral

The car was retrieved from the lake Thursday night, with the children inside. The morning newspapers carried the report, along with a photo of the car. I didn't read the report or look at the photo. I could barely face the new day, much less deal with something so very sad.

I don't know what I expected to happen next with Susan. I was too numb to think. It never entered my mind to go to the bond hearing on Friday, and nobody said anything to me about it. I suppose they knew what condition I was in and wanted to give me more time to face what had happened. I didn't realize it at the time, but Bev must have stayed home to take care of me. He took advantage of that opportunity to tell me Susan absolutely needed a lawyer and that Robert Guess had talked to David Bruck about representing her.

Scotty, Wendy and Bev's daughter Lori went to the bond hearing. Afterward, Scotty came by to give Bev and me a report. "Everything up there was out of control," he said. "Then David Bruck walked in and took control." He was definitely impressed with Bruck.

After the bond hearing, a law enforcement car was waiting at the courthouse to transport Susan to the Women's Correctional Center in Columbia. Spectators angrily shouted, "Baby Killer" as the car drove away. I was glad I wasn't there to watch.

Surrounded by members of the Smith family late Friday afternoon, Margaret Gregory read a statement from the courthouse steps:

"An unimaginable event has ripped our lives apart, but we do stand here together as a family. And we stand here in remembrance of Alex and Michael. We hope everyone in this community who has prayed for us, who has sent us their thoughts and concerns, who has shared our hopes, will continue to do so. It will be a long time before any of us can even begin to think about overcoming what has happened to us. We have no answers as to what happened; we do not understand why it happened; and I don't know if we ever will.

"We thank the nation for everything, and we thank the media for helping us in the search for Michael and Alex."

David's Uncle Doug also spoke:

"Our hearts go out to Susan's family as they come to grips with the grief that has fallen on them. They will need your continued support and prayers. During all the ordeal, the community of Union, South Carolina, provided an unprecedented amount of support for David and the family."

All over Union, one merchant after another removed yellow ribbons from their doors and windows and replaced them with flowing ribbons of blue and white. "The blue is for the little boys, and the white is for their innocence," one store owner said.

****

I didn't know how to get in touch with Susan or even if they would let me talk to her. And I guess our family could deal with only one monumental task at a time. I know it sounds unfeeling; but, in a sense, we had to put Susan on hold while we took care of the funeral arrangements. The process of burying the children virtually required all our emotional and physical energy. I could think of nothing but the two little boys and that I would never see them again.

I assumed that decisions about the funeral would be left up to David, the next of kin; but he hadn't said a word about it to us. Friday morning, Bev decided it was time to check. He called William Holcombe, the funeral director, and asked him who would be in charge. He said whoever accepted financial responsibility. Bev told him we certainly were willing to help.

A Public Funeral

Less than an hour later, David called and talked to Bev. He said he was going to need our financial help and asked if we could meet him at the funeral home at noon. I was terribly relieved.

Scotty, Wendy, Bev, Michael, and I went to the funeral home. David, his father, stepmother, mother, and Uncle Doug were already there when we arrived, seated on a sofa in one of the conference rooms. William's father, Billy, was in charge of the meeting.

Right away David said he would let us do whatever we wanted. His only request was that the children be buried beside Danny in the cemetery at Bogansville Methodist Church.

David had barely finished stating his request when his father jumped up from the sofa, raised his right hand in an emergency-stop gesture, and exclaimed, "Wait a minute! There's something we need to get straightened out about the money you have. Why don't we leave the women out of this and the men go in the hall and get this money thing straightened out."

"What are you talking about?" I asked, with a puzzled look on my face. "What money?"

"The money people have sent and that you all have."

"Where is it?" I asked. The only money I knew about was $250 that came in the mail from people wanting to help.

Wendy explained it had been agreed that she would open an account and deposit the money, just to do something on a temporary basis. She had opened the account under "Michael and Alex Trust Fund."

"Whose name is on it?" I asked.

"Mine," Wendy said, "because I opened the account."

I asked David if he could meet Wendy at the bank and put his name on the account with hers. He said he could do that. Two days after the funeral, David called Wendy to see if she could meet him at the bank. He needed money for postage. Scotty told her to give all of the money to him. She had the account transferred to David and never was involved with it again.

With the money matter settled, we turned back to the sad task facing us. I asked David if it would be okay to have the service at Buffalo United Methodist Church, since that was where Susan took the children when she made it to church. He said that would be fine.

We talked about the coffins. Billy said he had two small ones. *Two!* My mind raced ahead to visualize two little coffins sitting in the church. Somehow two didn't seem right, because they would be separated. They needed to be together as they always were—not Michael, then Alex, but Michael and Alex, as if they were one.

David was in full agreement with my suggestion. I asked Billy if that would be okay. He said they could do that, if he could find a coffin the right size. It had to be shorter and wider than coffins usually are. He made some calls and found a white casket with gold trim. That sounded good to all of us.

We turned next to the subject of pallbearers. There would be six. I knew how much Walt Garner and Mitch Sinclair loved Michael and Alex. For the third, I wanted Mike Lovelace. He had been at our house day and night from the first day. David picked close friends as his three choices.

We discussed ministers. Of course, my family wanted Dr. Mark Long, pastor of Buffalo United Methodist. Then I thought about Harry's side of the family. The Vaughans are a large family, and most of them attend Tabernacle Baptist Church. I suggested we ask their pastor, Dr. Joe Bridges. Since Walt and Barbara Garner are members at First Baptist Church, we discussed having their pastor involved. It turned out that he had a death in his church family and wasn't able to attend. We finally settled on Rev. Bob Cato, Mitch's pastor, because he had been so gracious and helpful to all of us. I am ashamed of myself for not thinking about the pastor at Bogansville, where Michael and Alex are buried.

We were discussing a family wreath when Betty Jo Holcombe, Billy's wife, came into the room and said she had received a call from a florist in Spartanburg. The owner wanted to provide flowers free of charge in memory of her ten-year-old son, whom she had lost the previous year.

"Betty Jo," I said, "I don't want to have donated flowers. We can afford to do this for them."

A Public Funeral

"Linda, this lady is very sincere," she explained. "She said she didn't even want anyone to know about it."

I thought for a minute, then said, "If she wants to do this for her son, then it's okay with me, if it's okay with everyone else." Everyone agreed that would be fine. We decided on yellow roses.

The final matter to take care of was visitation arrangements. Holcombe Funeral Home had four or five other funerals in process. I thought about all the people the funeral home would have to accommodate and about how large our family is. I suggested that we receive friends at our house and let David and his family receive friends at the funeral home. The group agreed that would be a good way to go.

I suppose I am naive, but I never dreamed so many out-of-town strangers would bombard David at the funeral home. I guess he survived with Tiffany's help. I couldn't believe he had the gall to have her stand in the receiving line beside him. When I found out she was there, I was glad we had made other arrangements. It would have been pure agony to watch them standing side-by-side, receiving condolences from people for the children they helped to put in their graves.

As we prepared to leave, David's mother asked, "What about clothes? Don't we need to get clothes for them?"

I stared at her in shocking disbelief. Could this woman possibly think the children would have an open casket after being in the lake nine days?

Billy quickly answered in his gentle, sweet voice, "If you want to bring clothes, I can lay them on the children." I never heard any more about that.

When we returned home, Walt and Barbara were there, along with the rest of the family and many other friends. "I asked for you to be a pallbearer," I told Walt. "Think you can do it?"

"Linda," he said, tears welling up in his eyes, "I wanted to do that so bad, I almost asked. But I thought it wouldn't be right."

"I was wondering if you could do it emotionally."

"Oh, I'd be honored," he assured me. "I can do it."

"I don't know of anybody I'd rather carry them for the last time than you."

Our organist, Reba Bogan, and our choir director, Zora O'Dell, also were there waiting to talk to us about music for the service. Reba asked if there were any special songs I would like to have played.

"Whatever you choose will be fine," I said. Then a picture of Michael flew into my mind. I could see him sitting on the clothes hamper when I dried his hair with the hair dryer. He would get the cord to Bev's electric razor from the vanity drawer, close the plug-in end in the drawer, and use the razor end for his microphone. He sang several songs but none was as sweet as when he looked up at me with those beautiful brown eyes and sang, "Jesus loves me, this I know, for the Bible tells me so."

Susan had bought a "Mr. Microphone" for Michael's birthday in October. She could hardly wait to see him sing into it, but she discovered at the last minute that it didn't work. When she went to exchange it, they were out, and she had to buy something else. She later exchanged the microphone and saved it for Christmas of 1994. It was still stored in her attic.

I reached out and touched Reba's arm. As she turned to me, I said, "Reba, there is one song. Will you do 'Jesus Loves Me'?" She nodded her head and patted my arm. "Yes, we will do 'Jesus Loves Me,' and it will be pretty."

Susan called from prison while everyone was still there. I can't describe how glad I was to hear her voice. She said we only had ten minutes to talk. The first thing I said to her was, "I love you." Then I told her about the funeral arrangements.

"Mama," she said, "can you get two red roses for them? No one will have to know they're from me; but I will know and you will know, and somehow I think they will know."

She paused, then continued. "Mama, I don't understand how any of this happened. I can't believe they're gone. How can I live without them? I just want to die."

The phone went dead without any warning. Our ten minutes were up! I felt like dying. For the first time in my life, one of my children needed me and I couldn't get to her. My heart ached; I wanted to put my arms around her so badly. She was alone and scared, afraid I didn't love her anymore. I loved her more at that moment than I had ever loved her. I knew my child's heart was broken, and she was all alone. I wanted to go get her and bring her home and take care of her. I wanted my daughter back. I wanted Michael and Alex back. I wanted this to be a dream.

Saturday morning I called Billy Holcombe and asked him to have the florist in Spartanburg bring three red roses, with one of them to be "From Grandma." He said he would have them for me at the funeral home.

****

Representatives from the media contacted Holcombe Funeral Home early Saturday morning to request permission to have cameras inside the church. They prefaced their request with the familiar refrain, "The public has a right to know."

William Holcombe told them the decision was for the family to make. He came to our house Saturday afternoon to discuss the matter. He said a press representative had promised to leave us alone outside the church, if we would allow one camera inside. That compromise must have come from the Smiths, because David says in his book that he, his father, and his Uncle Doug felt that a single camera in the back of the church, not anything obtrusive, would be okay.

The pretended compromise flew all over me. "Who do they think they are?" I questioned angrily. "That sounds like blackmail." There was a chorus of agreement.

For nine days, members of the press had dogged our footsteps, spied on our family, misquoted us or took statements out of context, and totally misinterpreted our feelings—time after time. These people, who had invaded our home, who ran roughshod over our feelings in getting their stories, who manipulated the truth to fit their biases, now wanted to further torture us with a pretended compromise.

What did the public need to know? Did they need to see the tears flow freely to know how we were grieving? I think not.

My Daughter Susan Smith

No, they weren't out to let the public know of our sorrow. Who wouldn't know that? They were out to catch the most sensational picture or word possible. They wanted to zoom their cameras in on our tears, our gestures, our expressions to get just the right angle for a story or a comment. They wanted to report their story, not ours.

We all said we preferred obstacles outside the church to obstacles inside. We wanted time to grieve without a microphone stuck in our face and a camera zoomed in on us. It was an incredibly sad time; we needed some semblance of peace.

I told William to go back and tell them that the church is a sanctuary, a refuge from members of the press. We didn't care if we had to go over, under, around, or through them on our way to the church door, we didn't want cameras inside. He agreed to communicate our decision to the press representatives. We assumed that was the end of it.

Over four hundred people came to our house on Saturday. One of Susan's co-workers started shaking so badly when she told me how much she thought of Susan that I had to find a place for her to sit down. A friend helped me take care of her.

The message from person after person was the same, "Tell Susan I love her." All these friends knew Susan wouldn't do something like this in her right mind. They knew how kind she was, how much she loved Michael and Alex, what a good mother she was. Many knew how David had treated her. A number knew about Bev's sexual abuse.

Initially, some in Union were hostile toward Susan; but when people found out about everything that led up to the tragedy, the majority were sympathetic. By the time of the trial, there were none who screamed, "Baby Killer." Instead, many hoped Susan would get the psychological help she needed all along.

Several of us went to the funeral home on Saturday evening to get the flowers I had requested. I placed the one "From Grandma" with the yellow roses on top of the casket. I arranged the two red roses from Susan in front of a picture of Michael and Alex displayed on a table near the casket.

By eleven, all the visitors were gone, and we were ready to

collapse into bed. Then the phone rang. It was Dr. Mark Long, pastor of Buffalo United Methodist Church. He told Bev that David's Uncle Doug had called and said the Smith family wanted to have cameras in the church. He said they reasoned that the public had followed everything from the beginning and needed to share the remembrance of Michael and Alex. They didn't want America to forget the children. Dr. Long told them he understood the Russells didn't want cameras, and he didn't, either. He said he would not allow the funeral to become a media event.

Uncle Doug threatened to move the funeral to a location where they could have cameras. Dr. Long advised us to let it ride until they made that move.

In the event the Smith family took that drastic measure, Bev and I had decided we would have a memorial service at Buffalo and let them have the funeral with the casket. As it turned out, they chose not to push the camera matter any further.

I slept very little that night and dreaded getting up Sunday morning. I was weary to the bone. I wondered how I was going to make it though a funeral for two babies who were so much a part of my life and whom I loved so dearly?

When I went into the washroom to get a blouse, I looked outside and saw that it was raining. Watching the slow, gentle drops, I thought, *Even the angels in heaven are crying. The rain drops are their tears.*

While we waited for the family limousine to arrive, I felt an overwhelming need for God's help. I abruptly stood up from the sofa, went into my bedroom, and shut the door. Hedy was right behind me. "Linda, are you okay?" she asked as she came in and shut the door.

"Hedy," I said, "I have to pray. Will you pray with me?"

We got on our knees beside the bed and poured out our hearts to God. We prayed that He would please give us the strength to make it through the day. We prayed for understanding. We prayed for Susan. When we returned to the den, I noticed that the sun was shining. I thought, *Lord, is this a sign that the sun will shine for us again*? At that moment, I couldn't imagine one ray of sunshine making its way into my life, ever again.

Someone said the family limousine had arrived and it was time to go. I didn't know it at the time, but David and his family came to our house in another limousine so we could all go to the church together. I never saw him, but learned later that Tiffany was with him. I still can't believe he had the audacity to bring that girl to my house.

Approaching the church, the scene was overwhelming. We couldn't believe how many people were standing outside. The police estimated the numbers at more than five thousand. People had arrived at the church early to get a seat. Most were total strangers. Friends who should have been inside were forced to stand outside. They came dressed all kinds of ways. Some came in T-shirts. Some brought barefooted children. One couple wore cut-off blue jeans with keys hanging from their belt buckles.

A black man from North Carolina showed up in a clerical robe. He wanted to participate in the service. Bobby, a deacon of the church, said he couldn't do that. "Where I go to church," the man angrily insisted, "everybody who wants to participate can."

The man fell in step beside me when we got out of the limousine. Bobby took him by the arm and led him away. He called Bobby a racist and threatened to talk to the bishop. "That will be fine," Bobby said. "He is sitting in the front pew, and he is a black man. He'll agree with us." The bishop planned to visit Susan in jail the next day. Sadly, he died in his sleep that night.

The church was packed. Chairs were set up in the social hall, which also was full. We sat on the second pew, just behind David and his family. David's grandmother Sarah arrived late. Someone brought a chair for her and placed it at the end of the pew. I later learned that *Inside Edition* paid for her transportation from California. She had even requested a police escort from the airport and asked that the funeral be delayed to accommodate her late arrival. I pictured her going down the highway in a limousine with little flags on the front of the car, being escorted by siren-blowing police cars, as if she were some important dignitary.

The funeral service was a soothing, peaceful lull in the

storm. Reba was right. The rendition of "Jesus Loves Me,"
played on a keyboard, was beautiful. Afterward, everybody
talked about how beautiful it was, along with "Away in a Man-
ger." Rev. Bob Cato's words were so comforting. About the
boys, he said, "They're home where there's no more pain, no
more anguish, no more people screaming across the street trying to get in a word edgewise. And yes, no more media asking
us for statements."

The usual onslaught of reporters confronted us as we came
out of the church to go to the cemetery. The Smith family didn't
seem to mind. David wasn't crying until he saw the TV cameras; then he broke out in tears for the nation to see his grief. I
guess he wanted to keep the cards coming with the money; for
he sure went to the post office faithfully.

What the nation doesn't know is that evening after David
buried his children, he went out for pizza with Tiffany. Our little town talked about that for quite a while. Everybody wondered how he could he take his girlfriend out for pizza at such a
time. When someone mentioned it to David's daddy, he said,
"Well, they had to eat, didn't they?"

A long line of cars followed us the short distance from Buffalo Methodist to the Bogansville Church cemetery. At the
close of the grave-side service, David stood at the grave, crying
and saying he didn't want to leave the children. I could hardly
control myself. Sitting between Bev and Scotty, I mumbled,
"Wonder why you never minded leaving them before." They
each put a hand on my arm to restrain me. Later, Mama told
about seeing David when he stood up and walked to the grave.
She said he looked around for the cameras before he started
crying. His grandmother Sarah joined him and put on a show of
kneeling and kissing the coffin. Bev and Scotty really restrained
me that time, too. I've never wanted to hit anyone as badly as I
wanted to send that woman sailing. How dare that selfish
woman put on such a show when she had denied Susan and
David and Michael a small four-room house to live in.

We were all drained when we returned home. We rested a
short while, then went back to the cemetery to see the flowers.
There still were so many people around that Billy Holcombe

My Daughter Susan Smith

had to make a path for us to get to the grave. I removed some of the yellow roses, one each for Barbara, Mama, Wendy, and Hedy, and two for me. Leigh picked one for herself. I had already taken Susan's two red roses from the church. The wife of a co-worker of Walt's enclosed Barbara's in a glass dome and offered to do the same for Susan and me at no charge. She arranged them in two domes, Susan's red roses in one and my two yellow roses in another. I placed the two domes on top of my TV.

On Monday morning, Bev, Michael, and I wanted to make a video of the flowers at the cemetery. A newsman was there when we arrived. I was close enough to the man to hear him talking; still it was like he didn't exist. But when he said something about Susan killing her children that almost took my breath away, I moved out of hearing distance. I didn't want to hear another word from him.

While walking to our car to leave the cemetery, a girl gently touched my arm to stop me. "You don't remember me," she said, "but I'm a friend of Susan's from grade school. Tell her Dee Ann loves her." I did remember the girl. She was in the same class with Susan when Harry died. Her father died during that same school year.

My thoughts flew back to that sad time. I was with Susan when she picked out the card to send to Dee Ann. I think she looked at every card on the shelf, trying to find just the right one. Dee Ann obviously remembered that kindness.

Some in the press corps tried to stir things up over Susan's accusing a black man. They failed, because people in Union know blacks and whites get along. This fact was brought home to me when Bev and I went by the funeral home after our trip to the cemetery. William Holcombe had asked us to come by to make a decision about what to do with the flowers.

A black woman walked up to me when we got out of the car in the funeral home parking lot. "Oh, Linda," she said tenderly, "I've just prayed and prayed to Jehovah that I could see you. And now my prayers are answered. Here you are in the parking lot with nobody around." She hugged me and told me that she had prayed many times for our family. I thanked her for her kindness and asked her to continue to pray for us.

Another black woman stopped me downtown a few weeks later. "Are you Mrs. Russell?" she asked. "I want to hug your neck. I told a friend that, if I ever saw you anywhere, I was going to hug your neck."

Two days after the funeral, Scotty made a public announcement to apologize for Susan's accusation. "On behalf of my family," he began, "we want to apologize to the black community of Union. It is really disturbing for us to think that anyone would ever think that this was a racial issue. I am thankful especially to many of my black friends who called me to comfort me and tell me they still loved me. It is a terrible misfortune that all this happened. Had there been a white man, a purple man, a blue man, on that corner that night, that would have been the description Susan used. We apologize to all of the black citizens of Union and everywhere, and we hope that you won't believe any of the rumors that this was ever a racial issue."

At an inter-denominational, interracial community meeting at First Baptist Church Monday night, pastors from nearly a dozen churches spoke about the need for the town to heal its wounds. Joe Bridges, pastor of Tabernacle Baptist Church, urged: "I hope that we all forget about our differences and forget about our hurts and that we all get closer to one another." At the same gathering, Rev. Dale Lynch praised Sheriff Howard Wells for the way he handled the investigation. Wells had done his best to downplay any racial implications.

****

Bev and I were scheduled to meet with David Bruck on Monday afternoon. With no time to grieve and not a single day to recover from the heart-wrenching ordeal of burying two beautiful babies, we entered a legal system we knew nothing about. No one in my family, Bev's family, nor our extended families had ever had any dealings of this magnitude with the judicial system. I had no idea what to expect.

From the beginning of our relationship with David Bruck,

we were all impressed with his skill, his professional manner, and his compassion. Up front, he said his obligation was to represent and defend Susan. All decisions would be between him and her.

Before we got very far in our discussion, Bruck told us what the fee would be. What a shock! We didn't have that kind of money, and we didn't know where we would get it. But we knew we had to figure out something.

I slept on the couch that night, trying to think of possibilities for raising the money. I remembered the trust fund Bev had inherited from his mother. "Maybe we can borrow the money," I suggested to him, "and use the interest income from the trust to pay it back." We passed over that possibility. It wasn't enough.

Bev decided to ask for advice from a friend who is high up in the judicial system. He told Bev that this wasn't a capital case because of Susan's state of mind and the events leading up to the tragedy. His advice went something like this: "Don't hire an attorney for Susan. Let a public defender represent her. If she gets a death penalty, which I don't think will happen, spend your money on an appeal. A higher court will overturn such a verdict, given the mitigating circumstances."

Neither of us felt comfortable taking that risk. We would have to raise the money. We ended up taking out a second mortgage on our house, which raised our monthly payments from $267 to $1,250. Bev also sold an office building he owned.

On Tuesday, David Bruck met Bev and me at the prison in Columbia. I had never even been to a prison. The regimented atmosphere was overwhelming. In order for the guards to bring Susan to us, they had to lock everybody in. The onus was on them to make sure nothing happened to her. The prison was to be her "safe keeper."

To be put in a safe-keeping status meant one of three things: She was a high-escape risk; she was very violent; or they were concerned with her protection if she were held in a local facility. Susan fell into the third category. Immediately upon her arrival at Columbia, she was isolated in an observation cell to guard against a suicide attempt. Ironically, their method of pro-

A Public Funeral

tection—complete isolation—contributes to thoughts of suicide. Susan was always shackled when she left her cell to see us. The procedure followed was to close the compound, shackle her, and bring her up to the room where we would meet. The guard took off the shackles and handcuffs before coming to get us. One time they took us to the room before they got Susan. It killed her for us to see her with those chains.

On the first visit, Bruck stayed in the room with us for a few minutes, then left Bev and me alone with her. At first, all we could do was hug and cry. I couldn't get over how awful she looked. Her face was puffy from crying and broken out from stress. I ached for her. Heartbroken and suicidal, she couldn't understand why she did it. I couldn't either, hard as I tried.

As Bev drove out of the prison grounds that day, I started crying. I cried all the way from Columbia to Union. Through the tears, I told Bev the only reason I was still in the marriage was that I had not been able to figure out how to get out of it. He said nothing.

It would have appeared to an outsider that Bev and I were handling everything as a normal married couple. But that had not been the case for a long time. I had planned to finally divorce him when the doctor said Michael was okay. That was only a month away when this tragedy happened. I had to put my plans on hold, pretend our marriage was normal, and focus on helping Susan through this.

Strange as it may sound, though, I couldn't have gotten through it all without Bev. He's made some big mistakes in his relationship to Susan, mistakes for which I find it difficult to forgive him; but he has done everything within his power to right the wrong. I realize now that he has a problem that requires specialized professional treatment. He knows that, too, and wishes he had faced up to it years ago—before he caused Susan so much harm and destroyed our marriage.

21

The Solicitor's Decision: Death

Less than two weeks after Susan's arrest, David was interviewed on *Dateline* by Katie Couric. He called Bev after the taping and told him he thought we would be satisfied with what he said about Susan. On November 15, we watched him tell Katie Couric, "Susan, she was wonderful....She was a very dedicated, devoted mother to those two children. They were her life, just like they were mine."

Even with the bragging, I reacted very negatively to the interview. There David was on TV conning people into thinking he was a loving father and receiving all kinds of sympathy. All I could think about were the times he was so mean to Susan and that he didn't have time to come to Michael's last birthday party. He wasn't the perfect father he pretended to be; he wasn't even close to being a perfect husband.

Shortly after I went to bed that night, everything connected with the tragedy descended on me in one big fell swoop. I felt like I was in this world, yet carried to another dimension. I was sinking, sinking, sinking. It was as if I were in danger of disappearing, going into nothingness. I couldn't see anything. I couldn't hear anything. I couldn't feel anything. I was surrounded by a thick fog, isolating me from everything. Bev was lying right beside me, but he didn't exist. It seemed I was completely, utterly alone.

"Everything in this world is upside down," I moaned. "Nothing is right." I knew I was talking to Bev, but strangely, he wasn't there. He was far, far away.

"It's crazy," I said. "Everything in this world is crazy. Everything's upside down. Susan wouldn't intentionally hurt anyone, and she's in chains. And one of the meanest people I know is on TV, and everyone feels sorry for him. The world's upside down. It's not a good place to live."

The Solicitor's Decision: Death

I grabbed for something, anything to stop my descent into madness. I had to hang on to sanity, because I knew my children needed me. I felt like I would go crazy if I turned loose.

Only later did I learn that Bev attempted to console me, telling me everything would be okay, that we would get through this. I couldn't see him. I couldn't feel him hug me. I couldn't hear him. Finally, I fell asleep from sheer emotional and physical exhaustion.

Bev was gone to work when I got up. I wasn't alone long, though. Hedy, Leigh, and Jennifer were on my doorstep around ten o'clock. I sleepily went to the door in my housecoat. Hedy made some excuse about needing a vacation day to explain why she was there. We sat around all day, talking, crying, and even laughing. Hedy, with her boundless energy, did all the cooking. Those three precious friends will never know how much they did to lift my spirits. Much later, Hedy told me Bev had called her because he was worried about me.

A few days after my traumatic experience, I reflected on its meaning. I thought Susan must have felt like that at the lake. Consumed by despair and a feeling of isolation, she lost her grip on sanity. In the pitch darkness, she couldn't hear anything; she couldn't see anything. I couldn't see anything; I couldn't hear anything; I couldn't feel anything. Bev was there right beside me, but he wasn't. Susan's children were there, but she had no consciousness of them. She knew something was wrong with her, but she didn't know what it was or why she felt that way. She lost her battle with madness. I came close. *Maybe*, I thought, *the Lord let me feel that way so I could understand how she felt*.

That same day, I wrote a letter to the editor of the *Union Daily Times*. I thanked everyone for all they had done to help our family during this tragic and heartbreaking period in all our lives. I extended sympathy first to David and his family. Then I thanked every person, black and white, who spent hours looking for the children, who brought food, called, sent flowers and cards, showered us with prayers and love. I gave a special thank you to our church and to Holcombe Funeral Home and their staff. I thanked Howard Wells and his staff for doing their job with compassion, love of God, and professionalism.

Bev took the letter to the newspaper office with the request that it be published as a letter to the editor. The staff of *The Union Daily Times* chose to run it on the front page with a mug shot of Susan.

****

A week or so after Susan's arrest, David told both Scotty and Wendy that he still loved her and, if there was any way he could, he would take her somewhere and start over. I wondered what he would have done about Tiffany.

Scotty and Wendy also talked to David's father about the situation. He was sympathetic to her. He thought "something in her head snapped." The other Smiths agreed, including David. They didn't think Susan was evil. They thought something happened to her at the Lake, that she was too good a mother for her act to make sense. David's sister Becky said Susan was her role model for an ideal mother. Before Tommy Pope got to the Smiths, they gave no indication they wanted Susan to receive a death sentence.

Rumors circulated about a possible plea bargain. Sheriff Wells indicated a plea bargain was the best route to take. He thought it would be best for the families and for Union County to be spared the trauma of a long trial. David Bruck wouldn't discuss that possibility with the press, but he did talk privately with the solicitor and proposed twenty years for Susan. Tommy Pope rejected the offer.

The solicitor told the press that he was going to wait until after the first of the year to make a decision about whether or not to seek the death penalty. He said he wanted everybody to enjoy the holidays.

Those of us on Susan's side of the family wondered how Pope thought anyone could enjoy the holidays, not knowing what was going to happen to her. For our peace of mind, we had to talk to him. We couldn't wait until the new year for his decision.

When I first called the solicitor's office, Pope tried to put me off. I kept calling, insisting that we had to talk with him before Christmas. He finally agreed. Susan's immediate family—Bev and I, Scotty, Wendy, and Michael met with him. We were waiting in the outer office when a lady came in, looked at me, and said, "Mrs. Smith, the solicitor can see you now."

"I'm not Mrs. Smith," I said sharply. "I'm Mrs. Russell."

She looked a bit embarrassed but motioned in the direction of Tommy Pope's office.

"Boy, Mama," Scotty said, "you let her know right quick you weren't Mrs. Smith." I figured she should have known better with all the publicity the case had generated.

Pope and his assistant, Keith Giese, took us to a room with a conference table. Pope sat across from us. Giese slumped into a chair next to him with a plug of tobacco pushing out his cheek. In his left hand was a Styrofoam cup, positioned below his bottom lip. He spit into it periodically. He didn't utter one word during the meeting. My daughter's life was at stake, and all he could do was spit.

We tried to tell Pope that something was terribly wrong with Susan. I emphasized that she was a good mother up until the time this happened, and everyone she knew would testify to that fact.

Pope listened with little feeling, but he did let us have our say. Then, when he felt that we had been allowed enough time to state our case, he dropped his pen to the table and blurted out, "I'll just tell you what I think is the appropriate sentence. I think they ought to lock her up and throw away the key."

My mouth flew open. Pope then quickly explained that the death of one or more children under the age of ten made it a capital case in South Carolina.

"But this was a disturbed young mother who loved her children," I reasoned. "Have you found anyone who has said she wasn't a good mother?"

He admitted that he hadn't. "But," he argued, "she was there. We have to hold her responsible."

"She was absolutely insane," Scotty said. "The Susan I know would never have done this."

"She's sane now," he replied. "Under South Carolina law, there's no way to find someone temporarily insane."

"Why couldn't you go for life," Bev probed, "instead of the death penalty?"

"Because life in South Carolina doesn't mean life," Pope snapped. "It means twenty years, and that ain't enough."

He told us this case had had an effect on his five-year-old son, that he had asked him what he was going to do for Michael and Alex. I found it absolutely incredible that Tommy Pope's five-year-old son would help determine the fate of a disturbed young woman.

"What if this had been your sister?" Scotty questioned. "You'd say, 'My sister would never have done this.' That's what I'm saying. The Susan I know would never have done this."

Obviously, what Pope told the public and what he told us were two different things. Long before January 1, he had decided to go for the death penalty. His political drive propelled him to appear tough on crime. In Pope's thinking, it had to be death for justice to be done. I thought executing my emotionally disturbed daughter would be vengeance, not justice.

Bev asked him if he had talked to David. He said he hadn't been able to talk to him. "Right now," he said, "he doesn't make much sense." I guess making sense to Pope meant agreeing with him on the death penalty.

I called David Bruck after the meeting. "No doubt in my mind," I said. "Pope is going to seek the death penalty. He can say all he wants about getting input, but his mind's been made up since November 3. He's waiting until the first of the year to announce it to give him time to get David's support."

David Bruck thought there was a chance David wouldn't go along with Pope if we kept quiet about him. He didn't specifically tell us not to attack David, but he did say the last thing he needed was a public fight between the Smiths and the Russells. He designated Scotty and Wendy to keep the lines of communication open with David.

Reporters kept pressuring us to make a statement about the situation, asking questions such as "Don't you want to defend your daughter? Has David Bruck got you under a gag order?" We wanted to defend Susan, but the only way we could defend her was to attack David. My daughter's life was in his hands; and he knew it. We stuck together as a family, and it took all the self-control we could muster to restrain ourselves from striking out at David.

Susan told David Bruck that she wanted to see David. I didn't think it was a good idea; I didn't trust him. But I was overruled. Shortly after Thanksgiving, accompanied by David Bruck and his lawyer, David went to see her.

David tells about the visit in his book. He relates that Susan started crying when he and the two lawyers came through the doorway into the visiting room. He walked over to where she was sitting, sat down, and hugged her. Right away, he asked her why she did such a thing. She said she didn't know why.

Tearfully, he told her he would never be able to show his kids how to ride a bike. He would never get the chance to take them fishing or teach them how to play ball. She had ripped all that from him. Why did she do it, he wanted to know. Again, she said she didn't know why.

He said that one minute they were grieving parents who had just lost their kids. The next minute, he saw Susan as the murderer of his children and he the husband she had betrayed. He would ask her why she did it; then they would cry together and talk about how much they missed Michael and Alex. He even wiped the tears off her face a couple of times.

David said what chilled him the most during that visit was something Susan said about "after we get through all this." He says that was what made him decide to throw his lot with Pope and go for the death penalty. Susan has a different account of the conversation. Her recollection of what she said is, "I wish we could start over, erase all that has happened."

What amazes me most about David's visit with Susan is what he concluded about the depth of her sorrow. He didn't think she seemed really sorry, even though she said she was, again and again. He said, if the roles had been reversed, he would have been stretched out on the floor and wrapped around her ankles, while bawling his head off that he was sorry and wailing for forgiveness. David's assessment stands in stark contrast to those who were with her when she confessed. They all testified that she had great remorse.

And David said he couldn't see sorrow for the deaths of Michael and Alex in Susan's written confession. Incredible! It is filled with sorrow. Obviously, he took everything she said and twisted it to suit his purposes. He was looking for an excuse to go along with Tommy Pope.

David said another factor in his decision to support Tommy Pope was the possibility that Susan would one day get out of prison. The only way he thought he could keep her from living a free life again was to put her on Death Row.

David knew it wasn't all up to him. At the same time, he felt the solicitor would have been out on a limb if he had opposed him. He was quite aware of the fact that he had a certain degree of power in the situation.

Just before his public announcement, Tommy Pope called David Bruck to tell him what he had decided. He wanted the defense attorneys and all of us to know before it came out in the papers. It was his way of acting like a considerate person. He was going to announce his decision at a press conference the next day. Incensed about the decision, David Bruck beat him to the punch. He called a press conference immediately after hearing from Pope.

I know David Bruck, the judge, and Tommy Pope had a three-way telephone conversation about bringing Susan to Union for the reading of the indictment. It could have been handled by certified mail, but Pope insisted she be present. It was his way of getting back at David Bruck for taking the wind out of his sails. And it was all for the cameras.

On January 16, 1995, Pope formally announced in the courtroom that he would seek the death penalty against Susan. While Susan and Bruck stood facing the judge, Pope proudly read the indictment out loud to her: "If it please the court, Your Honor, indictment 94-GS-44-906, the State versus Susan Smith, indictment for murder. It's alleged that Susan Smith did in Union County on or about October 25th, 1994, feloniously, willfully, and with malice aforethought kill one Alexander Tyler Smith by means of drowning. And said victim died as a result thereof." This reading was followed with indictment 94-GS-44-907 concerning the death of Michael Daniel Smith.

Susan broke into tears, and David Bruck had to help her to her seat. He then entered no plea for her; he wasn't yet ready to make that decision. Circuit Court Judge Costa Pleicones entered a plea of not guilty in her behalf.

All of our family was present for the reading. Since we knew what the indictment would be, we had been able to at least deal with the fact, but we couldn't agree with the decision. Yes, we accepted the fact that Susan was guilty of causing the death of her children, but she wasn't guilty of premeditated, first-degree murder. The mitigating circumstances argued against that.

Bev and I saw Susan before they took her back to Columbia. The three of us sat in the visiting room and cried and cried, letting out all the emotions we had held back because of the cameras. My heart was broken for her. I knew how much she loved Michael and Alex and how sorry she was that she had caused their deaths.

During a press conference after the hearing, David Smith stood at Tommy Pope's side while the solicitor told the gathered crowd about his decision. He said he had met with members of the Smith family and that he had their support in going for the death penalty. So, the man who said he would have taken Susan somewhere and start over, if he could, had gradually settled on revenge, with a lot of pressure from Tommy Pope.

We will never know exactly what happened to the Smiths to turn them against Susan, but we do know the solicitor played a major role. After he got hold of them, they did a complete flip flop. I think he kept hammering away at the idea that I was going to defend my daughter and someone needed to defend Michael and Alex. David bought into that viewpoint and made it his own. By the time the trial started, he and his father were passionately for the death penalty. All the earlier statements from them about Susan being a good mother and not being in her right mind went by the board. They had moved to premeditated murder.

On February 28, 1995, David publicly announced, "I am in support of the solicitor's decision. I'm backing him up. I'm behind him 100 percent." He said he did it for Michael and Alex.

Not all the Smiths agreed with David's decision. His mother, Barbara Benson, publicly broke from the family. On the television program *A Current Affair*, broadcast after Pope's announcement, she told the reporter that she pitied Susan and wouldn't want to see her sentenced to the electric chair. She emphasized, "You can't get Michael and Alex back.... Killing Susan, it's another death in the family." Concerning Pope, she said he had not been in contact with her at any time concerning his decision and didn't even return her phone calls.

Barbara told David Bruck to tell Susan she loved her and that she had nothing to do with the decision to seek the death penalty. She also wrote a letter to Susan, telling her that she loved her, that she knew she was a good mother, and that she would pray for her.

David's sister Becky also was against the decision. Before the trial, she told me she didn't support David in this decision and asked me to "tell Susan I love her."

****

On January 27, Judge William Howard conducted a hearing to act on the solicitor's request that Susan undergo a psychiatric evaluation by state doctors and that Bruck be ordered to reveal whether he planned to use an insanity defense. Bev, Scotty, and I attended the hearing. David was there, too, accompanied by a victim's advocate.

Bruck had objected to a court-ordered evaluation because of the possibility that Susan's answers to questions about the deaths of Michael and Alex could be used against her in the penalty phase of a capital murder trial. The judge gave him until February 28 to announce whether he intended to use an insanity defense. He said he wouldn't order an evaluation until it became an issue. He didn't want to violate Susan's Fifth Amendment right to remain silent.

At the February 28 deadline, Bruck entered no plea for Susan but said in absence of further notice to the court, the defense would rely on an insanity defense and a plea of guilty but mentally ill. He said he would consent to having Susan evaluated by state psychiatrists. The court order for this evaluation was issued on March 23, 1995. At the time, the defense team had already arranged for Susan to be evaluated by two private experts. Sociologist Dr. Arlene Andrews and psychiatrist Dr. Seymour Halleck were in the process of conducting a thorough evaluation of Susan, her family, and her background.

Dr. Donald William Morgan was chosen by the state to evaluate Susan as to her competency to stand trial. In a hearing on July 10, Solicitor Pope questioned Dr. Morgan to establish him as an expert in forensic psychiatry. When Pope moved that he be qualified as an expert, David Bruck agreed that he was "eminently qualified."

Accompanied by Dr. Geoff McKee, a forensic psychologist, and Dr. Tracy Gunter-Justice, a forensic psychiatrist, Dr. Morgan had interviewed Susan five times for approximately two hours each session. His guidelines for determining competency were the South Carolina statutory requirements. He expressed his understanding of those requirements as follows: That the person must have a rational as well as factual understanding about the charges and proceedings against the person; and that the person must be able to cooperate with their attorneys in their defense.

When asked by the solicitor if there was any indication that the defendant had any mental illness, Morgan said, "Yes, she did have a mental illness, and she does have a mental illness." His current diagnosis of Susan was that she suffered from major depression.

My Daughter Susan Smith

When Pope asked what was causing Susan's depression, Morgan replied, "There is no way to sort that out. She probably has a biological component. She had depression before when she was eighteen. Clearly, she has the stress of the situation. She clearly has the reality of the crime itself."

David Bruck began his questioning of Dr. Morgan by referring to his diagnosis that Susan presently suffered from major depression. Morgan confirmed that a diagnosis of major depression requires, among other things, that the symptoms exist over a fourteen-day period, minimum. He diagnosed Susan as having major depression in April and May and in July at the time of the court hearing. In May, Dr. Morgan recommended that Susan be started on an antidepressant and remain under constant observation. His team considered her at "great risk for taking her own life."

Bruck asked if he looked for deception on the part of Susan as he did in every forensic evaluation. He said he did. He then stated that Susan tried to cover up the amount of distress and pain she felt and the depth of her depression, rather than exaggerate her distress or her mental illness. She wanted to appear more in control.

Dr. Morgan said Prozac, the antidepressant medication, had helped her, and she was less depressed in July than when the evaluation team saw her back in late April or early May. Her mood had lifted, and she was dealing more with the reality of the situation. But that sense of reality had made her more suicidal. He stated that the most critical time for people to actually complete suicide is in the phase of coming out of a serious major depression, which she was in at that time. He emphasized that she was still in a major depression and had a major mental illness.

Bruck asked Dr. Morgan if he had concern about Susan's present competency to stand trial. "I have concern," he said, "in that she is so helpless. She feels so helpless. She feels that she doesn't care and that she would like to die. And that if she could figure out a way to die, that she would in fact do that. I believe that." He said Susan had a fantasy of reuniting with her children. She told him she would take her life as rapidly as possible if she were not in prison.

Dr. Morgan told Bruck, as he told Pope, that he felt Susan had a biological predisposition to depression, that to some degree, she had inherited a risk of depression in her genes from her parents.

Bruck asked if Prozac or some antidepressant medication would have made a difference if Susan had been taking it in October.

"Had Susan Smith had help," Dr. Morgan replied. "I think that would have made a big difference."

"Is it possible that we wouldn't be here?" Bruck asked.

"It's possible," Dr. Morgan replied.

After Bruck's cross-examination of Dr. Morgan, Judge Howard said he wanted to make sure he understood what Morgan was saying about Susan's competency to stand trial at that time. "You are saying," he began, "that you have had an opportunity today to evaluate her to the extent, that although you see a marked increase in her current state of suicidal tendency or ideation, that you still feel that she is able to fully cooperate with her attorneys, to make those choices that are best for her, to make at least rational, valid choices with regard to the defense of this matter?"

"The troubling part for me," Morgan emphasized, "would be if she chose to take the stand. That is to say, if she took the stand and described herself and described her feelings and told people that she was really guilty and that she deserved to die. I mean, I think that would be troubling if I were her lawyer, but I'm not her lawyer. I'm her doctor."

The judge probed further. "Well, I'm asking you from a medical, from a doctor's standpoint. Is she competent, given this what you described as an increased suicidal tendency? Is she competent at this time to stand trial, in your opinion, to a reasonable degree of psychiatric certainty?"

"Absent her testifying, she is," Dr. Morgan replied.

"But what I want to make sure that I understand," Judge Howard told Dr. Morgan, "it sounds to me like what you are saying is that as long as she's got her lawyers making the decisions for her, that she will be self-protected, because they will be protective, but she will not be self-protective. And that, therefore, she can't participate, in reality, in the defense of this matter. Is that what you are telling me, in your opinion?"

"In my opinion, yes, sir. In my opinion, as long as she does not have to testify, I think she's competent. That is, she has a rational, factual understanding. She trusts her lawyers. But should she choose to testify, I think she would then no longer be self-protective." In other words, he felt that Susan would sabotage her own defense if she testified.

Judge Howard asked for questions as a result of his questioning of Dr. Morgan. Tommy Pope came forward and asked Dr. Morgan a series of questions designed to show that Susan met the narrow definition of competency, according to South Carolina law.

When the judge asked for a response from David Bruck and his co-counsel, Judy Clarke, Bruck responded, "I think it's a close call. Yes, Dr. Morgan went through the legal formula.... But the testimony is that she has a major mental illness. And that is the core of her suicidality....We have a mentally ill defendant before the court."

Judge Howard said he would review the report and the case law before he made a decision in view of what the doctor had to say. In the court session the following day, July 11, he ruled that Susan was competent to stand trial. In the course of his explanation as to why he was declaring her competent, he said, "I conclude that she, with the diagnosis of this mental condition, and, as I recall, Prozac as the medication that is helping her with regard to that, as I understood his [Dr. Morgan's] testimony, it does give her a better understanding of the circumstances in which she finds herself and the issues that are to be presented in this case.

"In that sense, as the cases that I have researched involving the medicated patient....I believe Ms. Smith is rendered more rational and has a better understanding of the proceedings with this current treatment. And I believe Dr. Morgan related that indeed. And to that extent I do not feel that that in any way undermines her competence to stand trial."

Finally, in regard to this matter, Judge Howard said, "Based upon these conclusions, I find that Ms. Smith is competent to stand trial, and we will proceed with this matter at this time."

One courtroom observer stated that Dr. Morgan did more for the defense than the prosecution, stating that the doctor came close to having Susan declared incompetent. The only thing Dr. Morgan did for the prosecution was to acknowledge that Susan met the narrow South Carolina definition of fitness for trial. In order to be declared insane under South Carolina law, a person has to be totally incapable of understanding what is going on.

Susan would never have made it through all the activity before and during the trial if she had not been on medication. Without antidepressants, she would have been incapable of giving her lawyers any help in her defense. She was and is a disturbed young woman.

Sometime after Pope announced that he was going for the death penalty, Bruck proposed a plea bargain in which Susan would get thirty years, instead of the twenty he had previously offered. Pope declined.

There was no reason for Susan, nor us, nor Union, nor America to go through the agony of her trial. We all feel strongly that it was politics that drove Pope to hang on to his decision. The high profile nature of the case was too good an opportunity to lose to a plea bargain.

22

The Trial

February 6, 1995, Bev called me from his office in Spartanburg. He wanted to know if David Cox, his counselor, could come over in the evening.

"I guess it'll be okay," I told him, wondering what he had in mind for David's visit. Since he seemed to be in a big hurry; I didn't ask for any details.

Bev was unusually quiet when he got home. He said he was tired. That wasn't surprising. It was income-tax time, his busiest season of the year. And it was obvious that he didn't want to discuss anything.

Around seven, Bev met David at the front door and ushered him into the den. Bev suggested he sit in the recliner and then sat down beside me on the sofa. After small talk, they both turned serious.

"Bev has something to tell you, Linda," David said softly.

A look of dread filled Bev's face. He slowly opened his mouth to say something, but nothing came out.

Tears suddenly flowed down his cheeks.

"I'm so sorry, Linda," he sobbed. "I'm so sorry."

Possibilities flashed through my mind: Was it about him and Susan again? Was he involved with another woman? The emotional display disgusted me.

I stood up abruptly and asked David if he wanted a cup of coffee. He said, "Sure," then followed me into the kitchen.

"Linda," he offered, with a somber expression on his face, "do you want me to tell you?"

"No," I said angrily. "He at least owes me that, whatever it is. He needs to tell me, not someone else."

Bev was still crying when we returned to the den. "I'm so sorry, Linda," he sobbed, then tried to say more. Again, the words wouldn't come out.

The Trial

"Tell her, Bev," David coaxed; "you've got to tell her."

Bev tried again, but still nothing came out.

"You've got to tell her, Bev," David urged.

"Bev," I blurted out, "was Alex your child?"

He stared at me in shocked disbelief. "No," he said, as if he would never do something that terrible.

"There's something David Bruck felt you should know," he began haltingly, "before it comes out in the papers."

My chest tightened and my heart raced.

Another bomb, I thought, *How much more can I take?*

Slowly and self-consciously, he explained that David Bruck had to give certain information to the solicitor the next day. Bruck knew it would turn up in the press because that had happened every other time he had given him supposedly confidential information.

He paused, an incredibly sad expression forming on his face. He took a deep breath.

"I'm so sorry, Linda," he continued; "I'm so sorry. My sexual relationship with Susan didn't end with the two incidents you know about. There were two more. One happened two months before the children's deaths."

Sadness, rage, shock, disappointment, disbelief all converged on me with the force of a giant boulder hitting me broadside. My mind was in a whirl. My head was spinning. I thought all of that was behind us. After all his promises, Bev had crossed the line again, not once but twice.

"How could you do that?" I questioned. "How could you?"

"It wasn't intercourse," he quickly assured me, as if that fact made him less guilty.

He kept saying he was so sorry, that he never meant for anything to happen. How many times had I heard that pitiful refrain? It was like an alcoholic saying he would never drink again and then came home drunk.

How could he do this to me? How could he do this to me? The haunting question echoed through my mind.

"Was anything like that going on while Susan was living with David?" I asked.

"No," he said. "Absolutely not!" He was deliberately vague about exactly when the incidents started again. Not until the trial did I learn that the relationship resumed when Susan left David and moved back home.

"You went into that with your eyes wide open," I snapped. "It was just getting started, and you got it stopped for you. You didn't stop it." He knew what I meant. Only Susan's tragedy stopped it.

The laborious dialogue dragged on and on. Bev kept saying he was so sorry. David Cox kept saying he was truly sorry. Bev even asked if I would ever forgive him? I responded with a blank stare.

"Can you forgive him?" David asked.

I curtly replied, "I don't know; he never asked for forgiveness before."

Somewhere in the conversation, Bev even suggested, "We can overcome this."

To that ridiculous remark, I silently asked, *What is wrong with this man? How many times do you forgive a man for committing the same heinous act?*

After several hours of repetitive conversation, David asked to use the phone. He said he needed to call David Bruck. When I heard him say, "He's finally told her." I strode into the kitchen and asked David to let me talk to David Bruck.

"Why didn't you tell me about this?" I asked.

"Linda," he replied calmly, "it wasn't my place to tell you."

"You're right," I agreed. "It was Bev's place."

When David and I returned to the den and sat down, Bev turned to me.

"I can go ahead and move out tonight. I'll get some clothes and go to Aunt Ren's."

"As far as that goes," David offered, "you can go home with me."

"It's so late," I said sharply. "Wait 'til morning. Go on in the bedroom, and I'll sleep on the sofa."

I wasn't making that concession to be nice. I was simply too upset to deal with anything else at that late hour. It was practically midnight.

Bev was gone the next morning when I got up. I heard him walk through the den on his way out but said nothing. That night he came in around twelve. I was already asleep on the sofa.

We lived like that for almost a week. Every day, Bev followed the same pattern of going to work early and coming in late. I knew when he left and when he came in but made no attempt to talk. He didn't either. By Saturday morning, I had had enough.

"I can't stand this anymore," I told him. "I'm going to see Susan tomorrow afternoon. I want you out of here when I get back." Most of his things were gone when I returned.

With the trial coming up, Bev and I had to talk to each other for Susan's sake. I needed his help, and David Bruck needed his help. Bruck wanted him to help gather information for Susan's defense. I couldn't jeopardize that. Further, I didn't know how I could possibly handle the trauma and notoriety of a divorce on top of a trial.

Bev made a special point of telling me that he would help in any way I wanted. He even took me to lunch to tell me. He dealt with this problem as he had every other problem. He showered me with kindness. The Sunday before the trial I had to pack up all the stuff in Susan's house because I was renting it. Bev found out a bunch of us were doing that and came by to help.

It didn't take long for the press to learn that Bev and I had separated. Less than a month after David Cox's visit, a reporter from Spartanburg's *Herald-Journal* stopped me outside the courtroom during a pre-trial hearing. With Scotty by my side, he approached me in a very pleasant and friendly manner.

"How are you today, Mrs. Russell?" he asked.

"Okay," I replied with guarded reserve.

"I wanted to ask you about you and your husband's separation. Was it the stress of the trial that caused you to separate?"

"I have nothing to say to you," I snapped and walked on at a fast pace.

The reporter called Scotty at home in the evening, trying to get more information.

"I heard my mother tell you she had nothing to say about that," Scotty said impatiently. "What makes you think I would tell you anything?"

Not to be deterred, the reporter called my mother. She, too, told him she had nothing to say.

****

I went to every hearing related to the trial, but without Bev. I didn't want him there. Most people assumed he couldn't take off work because of the trial expense. I let them think that. But I was never alone. My family made sure of that. Tim was in court with me. Hedy took work home at night so she could be there. Walt took vacation days. Barbara turned down teaching opportunities.

June 30, 1995, just before jury selection began, Judge Howard ruled against cameras in the courtroom. I was relieved. When that ruling came down, I turned around to one of the cameramen, smiled, and coyly quipped, "Bye." He didn't smile back.

It is amazing how the atmosphere changed the minute the cameras were removed. With the cameras there, people were stiff and tense, or they performed for the camera. Thinking the judge would allow cameras, the clerk of the court went all over town shopping for clothes to enhance her wardrobe; she told people she was going to be "on camera." She must have been disappointed when they weren't allowed.

The day before the cameras were removed, members of my family were sitting right behind Susan, as we had done every day to that point. When court resumed in the afternoon, I leaned over the railing and hugged her. I looked up to see the solicitor glaring at me. The next day SLED agents occupied the front row, and we had to sit behind them.

I sat through every day of the tedious jury-selection process. When the jurors were finally selected, the court learned that one

The Trial

was father-in-law to a girl David dated after Susan moved back home. He was replaced with a woman who later was Michael's doctor. The convened jury was made up of five white men, four black men, and three white women, with one white male as an alternate.

The pre-trial evidentiary hearing followed jury selection. This is the time when the judge decides whether certain evidence is admissible in the trial itself. The testimony basically was a presentation of evidence gathered during the investigation.

The Smith family was there in force. They came into the courtroom with pictures of Michael and Alex pinned on their clothes and sat down behind the prosecution team. A framed picture of Michael and Alex sat on the solicitor's desk, a gift from the Smith family. Pope picked up the picture and held it over his left shoulder so we could see it.

Before adjourning for lunch, the judge noted that some people in the courtroom were displaying things that "pertain to the case, pictures of children, and so forth." He then said, "I cannot allow any kind of statement by people in this courtroom about this case, by either side....So I would ask you, please, not to do that, and to assure that you don't do that through the trial of this case." They put the pictures away and never brought them back to court.

Sheriff Howard Wells was the first evidentiary-hearing witness and others followed in chronological order. As one investigator after another testified, I thought about all of us urging Susan to tell them something, anything that would help in finding the children. I thought about the meeting with Howard Wells when we told him to continue questioning Susan, even without a lawyer present. We trusted Howard's judgment, and I'm not mad at him. He was doing his job. We just were terribly naive.

The most gripping testimony during the hearing centered around the events connected with Susan's confession. SLED agent Pete Logan and FBI agent Carol Allison dramatically described the depth and sincerity of her remorse.

Carol Allison said, "I have never had any situation quite like this, but I would say in my personal experiences of people that are grieving losses, that this was genuine." She said Susan repeated over and over that she didn't deserve to live. She told about holding Susan's head in her lap as she questioned, "How could I have done something like that when I loved them so much?"

David Bruck never told me about the effect this testimony had on Judge Howard, but an inside source did. I can't divulge who it was, but the source told me that the judge called Tommy Pope, Keith Giese, David Bruck, and Judy Clarke into his chambers after the evidentiary hearing. He asked Tommy Pope if he knew what the nature of Logan and Allison's testimony was going to be. He said he did.

According to my source, Judge Howard suggested Pope go back to the Smith family to see if they would agree to a plea bargain, which, at this point, would have been thirty years. My source said the solicitor did go back to the Smith family, but they were adamant—no plea bargain.

Then the trial began—what we had dreaded for so long.

DAY 1

Before the proceedings began on the first day of the trial, I turned around to Scotty. "Never in a million years," I said, "would I have thought any of us would be sitting in here like this."

"Mama, I know," he replied. "Its like this can't even be real."

Keith Giese, Tommy Pope's tobacco-chewing assistant, presented the opening statement for the prosecution. After introducing himself and Tommy Pope, he described the State's case against Susan. His first point was this: "For nine days in the fall of 1994, Susan Smith looked this country in the eye and lied." He told the jury that the way he and Pope intended to present their case was to "start back at the beginning, at October 25, 1994, and recreate the nine days that everybody lived through."

He stated that the basis of the charges against Susan was

The Trial

"malice aforethought," then explained that malice aforethought doesn't mean you have to plan an act out weeks or months in advance or lie in wait for somebody. "If you have got that evilness at any time before the fatal act." he emphasized, "it is malice aforethought." Earlier, Pope had labeled the nine days the "malice aforethought" that justified going for the death penalty. I am convinced that the nine days of telling the same story over and over is the primary reason Susan received such a harsh sentence.

A second key factor in Giese's opening statement was Susan's relationship to Tom Findlay. He presented Michael and Alex as the "stumbling block" to her snagging Findlay. The media emphasized this claim, but it is so far from the truth. Tom didn't tell Susan it was because of her children that the intimate part of their relationship was over. He said it was because of her sexual relationship with his father.

Judy Clarke, one of Susan's lawyers, began the opening statement for the defense by acknowledging that "Michael and Alex Smith, the most precious people in the life of Susan Smith and David Smith are dead. And they are dead at the hands of their mother." She said Susan wasn't there to blame anyone, that she took full responsibility for her actions. Clarke noted that Susan "tried to cope with a failing life, and she snapped." She told the jury that they needed to know why and how this happened and they would be talking a lot about Susan's life and about her mental illness and how it affected her judgment and her life.

Clarke noted that the solicitor told the jury they would start the case the night of October 25. "But I want to tell you," she said, "this case goes way back well before the night of October 25, 1994. And I tell you that because it is essential you need to know about the life of Susan Smith so that you can judge her responsibility and judge her actions and judge her life. So we must take you back. We must talk with you throughout this case about Susan, because she is on trial."

Clarke emphasized that Susan's act of letting the car roll into John D. Long Lake without her was a failed suicide. She described Susan as part of the walking wounded. "Suicide became an option for Susan," she said, "when her father committed suicide."

Following opening statements, Shirley McCloud, the first person to see Susan after the tragic event, was called to the stand by the prosecution. Sheriff Howard Wells followed her. Both recounted what happened the night of the tragedy.

The prosecution team intended to recall Wells later and use his testimony to reenact the events of the nine days leading up to Susan's confession. But David Bruck denied them that opportunity by doing it himself in his cross-examination of Wells. One lawyer concluded that Bruck cheated the prosecution "out of the drama of chronologically reenacting the nine days."

About 4:07 p.m., Judge Howard asked the jury to leave the courtroom. He then told the courtroom crowd that there had been a bomb threat. Everyone calmly but hurriedly left through three exits. After a thorough search, no bomb was found.

DAY 2

On day two of the trial, SLED agent David Caldwell, FBI agent David Espie III, and forensic artist Roy Paschal were called to the stand. They testified that they were skeptical of Susan's story from the very beginning.

Several Conso employees followed the law-enforcement officers, including Tom Findlay. Tom's testimony refuted the prosecution's claim that Susan killed her children because they were a stumbling block to her relationship with him. He emphasized that Susan loved her children very much, that they were her world. He supported the defense claim that Susan intended to die with her children.

One of the last witnesses of the day was Steve Morrow, a sergeant with the South Carolina Department of Natural Resources. After Susan's car was located in the lake, the responsibility fell to him to verify that the children's bodies were inside.

The minute Steve Morrow's name was called, David's mother left the courtroom. I certainly understood how she felt.

The Trial

It took everything within me to sit there and listen to Pope lead Morrow through a series of questions designed to describe the scene. I had already been through that horror in my mind's eye. I cringed at the prospect of reliving it again.

Morrow related to Pope that, after verifying the identity of the car, he began a slow search around the vehicle. He said he placed his light against a side window and saw a small hand pressed against the glass. With this statement, a collective gasp went up from the courtroom crowd, followed by sobbing. I fought back tears. Susan dropped her head and began to rock back and forth in her chair, sobbing.

Pope pressed on. He asked what direction the hand came from. Morrow stated that his best guess was that the children were hanging upside down in the car seats. He asked Morrow to verify that fact twice.

David Bruck chose not to question Morrow. I was grateful and relieved.

After court recessed, David's mother and I ran into each other in the hall. She hugged me and whispered in my ear, "I'm so sorry." She then quietly told me she didn't support her son.

When I told one of the secretaries in Bruck's office about Barbara hugging me, she said she wasn't surprised. She had called their office and wanted to know if she could sit with us.

DAY 3

On Thursday morning, July 20, 1995, the state called Dr. Sandra Conradi to the stand. She is the forensic pathologist who performed the autopsies on Michael and Alex. When the solicitor asked about her external examination of the children, I gasped silently. Before Dr. Conradi could answer, David Bruck objected on grounds of relevance, saying it had already been established that Michael and Alex died by drowning and nothing else.

After lengthy discussion outside the presence of the jury, Judge Howard ruled that he would sustain Bruck's objection to the extent it "would go into any description or discussion of the

My Daughter Susan Smith

observation." Pope had to limit the discussion to the fact that drowning was the cause of death and what happens to the body as a result of drowning.

When Pope resumed questioning Dr. Conradi, he told her, "I don't want you to go into specifics on what you visually saw of the boys."

In his cross examination of Dr. Conradi, Bruck made two points. First, her examination revealed that the two boys were well nourished. Second, there was no evidence whatsoever of recent or old injury—no broken bones, no trauma. She concurred on both points.

After Dr. Conradi's testimony, the prosecution rested its case. That announcement surprised David Bruck, because two prosecution witnesses had not been called. They were SLED agent Pete Logan and FBI special agent Carol Allison. Pope obviously knew they would help the defense.

David Bruck asked the judge for time to regroup, since the defense team hadn't expected to begin their case until the afternoon.

As it turned out, Pete Logan was the first witness for the defense, with Carol Allison coming a little later. When asked if Susan showed remorse during her November 3 confession, Logan said it was "probably the greatest I've seen in thirty-five years." He said she planned to go down in the car with her children.

Dr. Arlene Andrews was the last witness called on Thursday. She noted that, during her exhaustive study of Susan's family, she had interviewed ninety-seven persons—family members, friends, teachers, doctors, and psychologists. She guided the jury through a presentation of Susan's family tree that was designed to highlight family members who had attempted suicide or suffered from some form of depression. She emphasized that her discoveries indicated "a lot of depression to find in a family tree."

When cross-examined by Pope, Dr. Andrews forcefully stated that she felt Susan's two suicide gestures as a teenager were serious attempts to end her life. Pope couldn't make her budge from that assessment.

DAY 4

Psychiatrist Seymour Leon Halleck was the third defense witness on Friday, July 21. He described Susan as one who is able to present a pleasant exterior that conceals serious mental illness. He said she has "about as severe a dependent personality disorder as I've ever seen." It was shocking and painful to hear someone say my daughter is mentally ill. I thought about the many times I tried to get Susan to stand on her own two feet, how I wondered why she didn't defend herself against Bev, how I tried to get her to defend herself against David. What I interpreted as a need to develop backbone was, in fact, mental illness.

Based on his interviews with Susan, Halleck concluded that her actions at Broad River Bridge and John D. Long Lake were serious suicide attempts. Referring to a psychological term called disassociation, he said it was probable that, for a few moments after she jumped out of the car, it was as if her children weren't there. He explained that someone experiencing "as agonizing a stress as she was experiencing are capable of blocking things out."

DAY 5

When the testimony and evidence portion of the trial concluded on Saturday, July 22, Judge Howard dismissed the jury, saying that the attorneys had some legal matters to discuss. During this discussion, the defense team argued that the jury should be given three options in deciding Susan's sentence: not guilty of murder, guilty of murder, or guilty of involuntary manslaughter. The prosecution team disagreed, saying involuntary manslaughter didn't apply in this case. After both sides argued the point forcefully, Judge Howard ruled that he would allow the jury to consider the charge of involuntary manslaughter, which carried a maximum sentence of ten years.

After this discussion, the jurors were brought back into the courtroom, and Judge Howard gave the charge to them. At 5:30 p.m., July 22, 1995, they were instructed to begin deliberations.

At 7:57 p.m. that same day, the jury returned to the courtroom to report its verdict. As we sat there waiting for the reading of the verdict, someone told me to look across to the prosecution side of the courtroom. There was Tiffany sitting with David. Previously, she had been sitting in the balcony.

June Miller, clerk of the court, read the docket number and the charge of murder for each indictment, then read the verdict for each one: guilty of murder. Leigh burst into tears. I sat numb, even though it was what I had expected. At this point, I was more worried about the sentence Susan would receive.

Judge Howard explained that under South Carolina law, they would have to wait twenty-four hours before resuming further proceedings. Since twenty-four hours would put them at eight o'clock Sunday night, he ruled that the proceedings would resume at 9:30 a.m. Monday morning. At that time, the sentencing phase of the trial would begin.

DAY 6

David's maternal grandmother, Sarah Singleton, had access to a fully-furnished home in Union; yet she chose to stay at the Holiday Inn in Spartanburg where the jurors were sequestered. On Sunday night, she went down to the motel laundry room. While waiting for a washing machine, she let one woman know she was in a big hurry, explaining that she was the grandmother of Michael and Alex. I guess she figured the woman would step aside and let her go ahead of her if she knew that.

Without saying a word, the woman left to report the contact to a SLED agent. Sarah had spoken to a juror.

When Sarah arrived at the courtroom Monday morning, the judge delayed the trial to call her back to chambers. He quizzed her carefully, with SLED agents present.

Shortly after talking with Judge Howard, Sarah left the courthouse. According to an eyewitness report from a friend, she told reporters, gathered out front, "Just leave me alone; everybody leave me alone." She didn't mind talking to reporters when it was about Susan; but when they turned on her, it was another matter. I never saw her at the trial again.

Judge Howard emerged from chambers to give a report in court. Out of the presence of the jury, he told what the hearing was about and stated that the contact with the juror was incidental and didn't affect the juror's fairness. He ruled that there was no basis for mistrial.

The sentencing phase of the trial finally began in late afternoon. Margaret Frierson of the Adam Walsh Society was the first witness called by the prosecution. She told about her group's involvement during the nine days of hoping to find the children alive.

Margaret Gregory was the prosecution's second witness. Like Frierson, she described her role during the nine days. When asked by Bruck about Susan's enthusiasm for being on TV, she stated that, on at least two occasions, she backed out completely and threatened to at other times. She acknowledged that Susan never was excited about being before the cameras and agreed to appear on TV only when she recommended it would keep Michael and Alex before the public.

She stated that Susan expressed less and less emotion day by day. By the Sunday after the children disappeared, she didn't see tears anymore. At one point, she felt Susan wanted to tell the truth but didn't know what to do.

Margaret admitted that she felt betrayed when the truth came out. In spite of that feeling, though, she still felt Susan should not be executed. She thought executing Susan "would take what has been a horrible tragedy and just make it that much worse." She did say she believed in the death penalty in certain cases, but this wasn't one of those cases.

Later, I reflected on the picture Margaret Gregory created. There we were, constantly pushing Susan to do something to help find the children: appeal to the abductor, answer question after question, think of something that would help. We unwittingly pushed her further and further into a web of deceit.

DAY 7

David Smith was called to the stand Tuesday morning by the prosecution team. While he testified, the book about his life with Susan was on display in book stores. It was scheduled for release the following Friday, but many stores jumped the gun.

He tearfully told about his love for Michael and Alex and the agony he had suffered since their deaths. It was such a show! I knew he had suffered because of the loss of his children, but all I could think was, *If you had been the husband and father you should have been, Michael and Alex would be alive today.*

He was still sitting in the witness box when it was time for a lunch break. As usual, the jury left first, then Susan. As she walked past him, she turned to him and said softly, "I'm so sorry, David." David didn't look at her; instead, he started crying harder and pounded the arm of the witness chair with his fist. Leigh and I turned to each other in disgust, then other family members did the same to those beside them.

When court reconvened at two o'clock, David Bruck said he had no questions for David. The expression on David's face was worth a million dollars. He looked upward with great relief as if to say, "Thank you, Lord." His nasty little life was going to go unexposed. As he stepped down from the witness box and walked by Bruck, he said, "Thank you. Thank you." I was disappointed and puzzled. I found out later that Susan begged Bruck not to question him.

DAY 8

On Wednesday, July 26, Scotty was called as the first witness for the defense in the sentencing phase. Scotty told about what a good mother Susan was to Michael and Alex, how their faces lit up when she entered a room.

At the request of Bruck, Scotty read a letter he wrote to Susan on January 12, 1995. It was a response to a letter from his sister. In her letter, Susan told him she remembered very little of her father and wanted him to tell her what he remembered. He told her about his feelings after Harry and I separated when Susan was two. Especially poignant was this paragraph:

"I know you missed Daddy when he wasn't there. I also know he missed you more than anybody. It breaks my heart, even as I write this letter, to think about and remember how your little brown eyes and Daddy's would light up whenever he came to visit. He loved us all, but you were his heart."

Scotty also told Susan about the time Harry came to our house with a shotgun, and I grabbed it and ran to a neighbor. He told her about the night Harry killed himself. He urged her not to give up:

"Just know, Susan, that there are so many people who love you and will stand by you; you can get through this. Please don't ever give up. Daddy, in his last moments, regretted having given up. I know he did. Don't you do it. We love you and God loves you. Don't ever forget that."

Scotty's expression of love and concern for his sister was heart-wrenching. I could feel the sorrow behind his words, sorrow for the fact that he didn't realize what was happening to her.

Bruck asked, "What would be the effect, do you think, if Susan were to be sentenced to death for the murder of these boys, on you and your family and the people that you love?"

Scotty replied, "Nobody really disputes what happened to Michael and Alex. It's the tragedy. But to strap Susan in a chair and send two thousand volts of electricity through her in the name of justice....I don't think my mother could take it....I just don't think her mind can handle any more sadness or tragedy."

Bruck asked Scotty if the Susan he knew and had known all her life would have made the decision to harm Michael and Alex intentionally?

Scotty replied, "Not the Susan that I know, never."

Arlene Andrews followed Scotty on the witness stand. To emphasize the fact that Susan was a good mother, she referred to Katie Couric's interview of David Smith on NBC, in which he talked about what a good mother Susan was. "Those were the same words that people I interviewed said about her over and over," she emphasized. "She loved those babies, and she lived for them."

Dr. Andrews described Susan as an extremely dependent person. She made this observation: "Lots of people handle tough situations. They live through hard times. Some people have to live through extraordinarily hard times. And through studies about humans, we know that some people are more re-silient than others. Some people seem to just be able to handle stress pretty well, and others don't handle it well at all."

After making those statements, Dr. Andrews stated: "Susan is not a resilient person. She's what we call a vulnerable per-son." She noted that Susan's mental condition began deteriorat-ing in August 1994 after failing to reconcile with David. She emphasized that the conflict with David on Friday before the drownings threw her into a downward spiral that ended with the deaths of Michael and Alex.

Viewing Susan's life from the perspective of Dr. Andrew's research, I saw sadness and suffering I never knew existed. It was an incredibly traumatic experience. I wondered how I could have missed so much. I had thought Susan would be okay if she could get David out of her life and find someone who would be good to her and the children. And that would have helped, but there was much more to it than that. She felt like a failure because the marriage didn't work. She felt like a bad wife, a bad mother. She heaped responsibility on herself that she never should have.

DAY 9

Kay Dillard was the first witness called by the defense on

The Trial

Friday morning. She was Susan's high school math teacher for three years, and Susan was her student assistant in her senior year. She stayed in touch with Susan after high school and had opportunities to observe her with the children. "Susan was great with them," Dillard testified.

Walt Garner followed Kay Dillard. He told how good Susan was with the kids. "And we know," he said, "in her right mind she never would hurt those kids."

One relative after another made similar statements. Tomi Vaughan, Harry's sister-in-law, testified that "the sweet, gentle girl with the smile from ear to ear for everybody was not the person who could commit such an act."

William Vaughan, Harry's brother, followed his wife on the stand. He testified that Susan was "just a loving mother, proud of her children." When asked how giving the death sentence to Susan would affect the family, he said, "I don't know how much more we can take with adding another death in this family."

Kevin Kingsmore, the friend who helped organize volunteers to distribute fliers, described Susan as a caring person. When asked what must have happened to her that night, he said, "She must have snapped. It wasn't Susan."

Dr. David Heatherly followed Kevin on the stand. He is the marriage and family therapist who counseled Bev, Susan, and me in 1987, after Susan reported the first incident of sexual abuse. He said Susan "stopped growing emotionally in terms of her sense of who she was" when Harry killed himself. He felt this loss left her very empty inside. He said she became confused when Bev abused her and didn't know whether he was her father or her lover. The last time Susan came to him for counseling was February 28, 1990. He felt that his services at that time had been effective, and she didn't need to come back. I had no reason to doubt his judgment. Looking back, I wonder: If professional people like this couldn't recognize how disturbed Susan was, how was I supposed to?

Felicia Mungo, a guard at the Women's Correctional Center in Columbia, testified that Susan was alone in a cell under twenty-four camera surveillance. She had observed Susan kneeling in prayer and crying. She described Susan as sad and depressed and always worrying about me because she has put me through so much. For eight months, Mungo had guarded Susan. She was under suicide watch the entire time. She said Susan had apologized to her and other black officers about her claim that a black man had taken her children.

Thomas Currie, pastor of First Presbyterian Church in Union, testified that he saw Susan for the last time when she asked him about reconciling with David in May of 1994. She told him the children were the only bright spot in her marriage.

When Currie first met Susan in the spring of 1988, she impressed him as "a young person whose life was out of control." He told Kay Dillard, who referred Susan to him, that she "needed counseling and a lot more than I could give." He emphasized: "What she did that night was completely out of character with the person I know."

Bev followed Dr. Currie. A hushed murmur emanated through the courtroom as he walked to the witness stand. It was the first time he had been in court since the trial began. During the questioning, Bruck had him acknowledge that he and I were separated.

Bruck asked Bev to read the following portion of a letter he wrote to Susan on Father's Day, June 17, 1995:

"I must tell you how sorry I am for letting you down as a father. I had responsibilities to you in which I utterly failed at. Many say this failure had nothing to do with October 25th. But I believe differently. Of course, had I known at the time what the result of my sin would be, I would have mustered the strength to behave according to my responsibilities. Looking back, I was the most important male figure in your life. Harry died when you were too young to have been established in relationship to him. When I came into the family, you leaned on me and looked to me for support and love. But when the line was crossed, I failed you, Linda, God, and the rest of my family. My remorse goes way past sorrow for getting caught and exposed, which is significant in itself. But to see unfolding before our eyes the principal of reaping and sowing; to lose Michael and Alex; to see you in prison; to see Linda crushed with extreme losses; for me to lose the whole family relationship, and the hurt to my children. And all you needed from me was the right kind of love. I had the capability to do the right thing and missed the mark. I don't pour this remorse out to ask for your forgiveness. You have already done that, and I have accepted your forgiveness. But I want you to know that you don't have all the guilt of this tragedy. Had I been true to you and my responsibilities, you would have been stronger in yourself; not needing to be constantly supported and reassured emotionally. I should have helped prepare you to meet the challenges of the world, to be more independent. But now I see that I had a negative impact. Instead, you left home always looking for love and acceptance. My heart breaks for what I have done to you, and for the pain and your loss.

"However, we must go on with life, learn to look forward and to serve Him who saves us and who holds Michael and Alex. We will get through this with God's grace and power."

Bruck asked Bev why he wrote the letter. He replied, "It was Father's Day. Those days are special to Susan, and I knew she needed a letter."

As I listened to Bev's testimony, I relived everything in the light of Dr. Halleck's insistence that he was totally responsible for the sexual abuse of Susan. He now admitted his responsibility in a way he never had before. How I wished he had realized his responsibility when it happened. He could have had a very positive role in Susan's life, but he blew it.

I do believe Bev's sexual abuse of Susan had much to do with what happened on October 25, 1994, and I have to fight my bitter feelings toward him for his part in taking two precious grandchildren away from me. He can enjoy all of his grandchildren, but I can't; he is partly responsible for denying me that complete joy. I deeply love Nick and Matt, but there will always be a longing to love and enjoy Michael and Alex.

My Daughter Susan Smith

On cross-examination by Pope, Bev admitted he had sexual contact with Susan as recently as August of 1994. Pope asked, "And you admitted them to Linda after you began to receive therapy?" He replied, "That's right." Pope followed up with, "And is that why you were separated from Linda?" He acknowledged, "That's the reason, yes."

Wendy was the last defense witness. As Bruck questioned her, he mentioned Scotty's letter to Susan and what he said about their father's suicide. "Is that something that's been talked about easily in y'all's family over the years?" he asked. Wendy replied, "It was never mentioned anywhere around in the family."

Bruck asked Wendy about her concerns for Susan over the years. She mentioned Susan's pregnancy and said, "I had told Scotty all during her pregnancy that I was real worried about Susan, what would happen for the most part after the baby was born. Women going through pregnancy have a tendency to have a hard time after birth. And with Susan's past, I was very worried that that would make her worse."

"And what happened when Michael came along?" Bruck asked.

"It didn't affect her like I thought it would," Wendy replied. "It seemed like...she was more stable with Michael. She didn't seem to have...what they call postpartum blues after the baby was born." She went on to say the children helped Susan, that they gave her "something that she was lacking."

About my relationship to David, Wendy said there had always been conflict between us. "David didn't like Susan to go see her mother a whole lot," Wendy explained; "so it kind of tore Susan in two directions because she didn't want to make David mad, but yet she wanted to see her mother."

Bruck asked Wendy how she would explain it to her children if Susan were sentenced to death? "I don't know," she replied. "I don't know what we would tell them. I don't know how to tell them. I don't know how you explain that."

And how another death would affect me? Like Scotty, she said she didn't think I could handle it. I never said that to

Wendy, but she was right. My children are what I live for right now—all of my children, including Susan. At that moment, I didn't know what I would do if she were sentenced to death. It was too horrible to contemplate. It is one thing to execute a vicious criminal; it is quite another matter to execute someone with a mental illness.

Bruck said, "Wendy, you are the last witness. What do you want for Susan?"

"I want Susan to live," she replied, choking back tears. "I want her to be there where I can at least touch her, talk to her, know that she's there. I mean, if it's got to be in prison, then we will make do, but at least she will be there."

DAY 10

After closing arguments by the prosecution and defense on Day 10 of the trial, the judge gave his charge to the jury. They began deliberations at 2:10 p.m., July 28, 1995. While they deliberated, all of our family and close friends met in the Grand Jury room. We prayed out loud in a group, and we prayed silently, asking that God spare Susan. At one point I wondered if David and his family were praying for the death penalty in another room of the courthouse.

I left the group to visit with Susan for a few minutes. She was nervous, concerned that they would sentence her to death. I tried to assure her that it wasn't going to happen. Too many people had said what a good mother she was. Dr. Andrews and Dr. Halleck had given powerful testimony about her state of mind. I told her about the crowd in the jury room praying for her. She seemed calmed down a bit when I left.

When I walked through the courtroom to return to the Grand Jury room, Bev was in there, seated on the front row. He was talking to Jenny Ward from DSS. *Of all people for him to be talking to*, I thought. It was one more example of how he could cover up his bad actions by being kind and friendly. It was also an example of how he could mask his guilt with a look of innocence.

My Daughter Susan Smith

I reminded Bev that everyone was in the Grand Jury room praying. He said, "Okay" and eventually came in there and joined in the praying. In his book, David described Bev as being "big on prayer." He said he went along with Bev's prayer circles but couldn't help being repelled by the hypocrisy of the man. That's one thing David got right.

The group was in a circle when I walked into the room, their heads bowed and holding hands. Stacy Lovelace, Susan's childhood friend, was praying. The content of her prayer was so mature and forceful and sincere. I thought to myself, *How many twenty-three--year-olds could pray like that?* Her prayer lifted my sagging spirits.

At 4:38 p.m., the jury returned to open court to report its verdict. Susan stood between David Bruck and Judy Clarke to hear June Miller, Clerk of the Court, read the sentence. As she began reading, a clap of thunder roared outside, followed by a sudden burst of rain pouring down on Union County Courthouse. It was as if God were saying this sentence was vengeance, not justice.

The decision, read twice, went as follows:

"We, the jury, in the above-entitled case decided that the defendant, Susan Smith, be imprisoned in the state penitentiary for the balance of her natural life."

When the judge made the sentence official, Susan whispered, "Thank you."

Tiffany was sitting beside David, just as she had for the guilty verdict. I'm sure she felt a great sense of satisfaction to know the woman she had stalked would spend the rest of her natural life in prison.

I guess I was relieved that Susan wasn't sentenced to death, although I never expected that to happen. Walt told me a friend of his on the jury said they never seriously considered a death sentence. The newspaper reported that there was only one juror who felt the death penalty should be imposed. The others convinced him Susan was a sick young woman who needed help,

The Trial

not a death sentence.

We all hugged one another and cried, not because we were happy about the sentence but because she wouldn't die. Then came reality. True, she wouldn't die, but she wouldn't be eligible for parole for thirty years.

Outside the courtroom, David Smith told the press he and his family were disappointed that Susan didn't get the death penalty. "I'll see that she stays in prison as long as possible," he vowed. "I want to see that life means life for Susan." He said he would be at the parole board hearings every time she came up for possible release.

David's father said he was extremely saddened by the jury's verdict. His Uncle Doug said "the possibility of Susan Smith getting parole in thirty years is not sufficient for the crimes."

One juror said Susan needed help and this was a good opportunity to give it. Solicitor Tommy Pope said he respected the jury's verdict: "I think justice was done by this jury. No matter what penalty we have or don't have in South Carolina, there is nothing that can do justice for the situation that happened to Michael and Alex, but again, I respect the jury's verdict."

"Are you happy with the verdict?" one reporter called to me, as we were leaving the courtroom

"Do I look happy?" I snapped, then hurried out the door. I couldn't be happy about the fact that the prosecution should have accepted a plea bargain in the case of a mentally ill young woman and refused to do so. I couldn't be happy we were put through a trial that never should have happened. And I couldn't be happy that the world knew about every bad thing that had ever happened to our family.

****

Friday evening, when they took Susan back to Columbia, our family and many friends gathered at my house. Sadness hung like a black cloud over us.

Susan was allowed two telephone calls each week. She used one that Friday night. "Mama, this is awful," she sighed.

"They've put me back in solitary confinement." She was on suicide watch. She could have no rubber bands to hold back her hair. She was stripped of everything and handed a blanket and a paper sheet. She went from having all of us around her to being totally alone "for her own good."

I tried to console her, saying, "Susan, Honey, just try to remember that some stupid bureaucrat thinks you need this for your own good. Try to focus on something other than the little cell with a paper sheet, paper gown, and Bible."

I know Susan couldn't have sat in the courtroom and appeared normal, if she hadn't been on medication. I wish now that there had been some way for her to be left to her own resources, as she was that fateful night. Then everyone could have seen how mentally ill she was at the time of the trial and before. Medication made her appear to be in much better shape than she was. But it was doctors, employed by the state, who said she had to have some kind of medication. They prescribed it, and it was administered through the prison.

23

Birthdays

Michael and Alex loved my flowers. Flowers are part of me and were part of them. They especially loved my backyard island arrangement of flowers and plants and enjoyed sitting at the picnic table nearby. Michael called it the knickknack table. He never could remember *picnic.*

Often when they came to visit, Michael grabbed me by the hand and said, "Grandma, let's go down and look at the flowers." I had shown him how to pop off the dead blooms. One day when the zinnias were over his head, he reached up as far as he could to a dead bloom. "This ugly one, isn't it, Grandma," he said and popped it off. He did that until he thought he had found every wilted bloom.

One day when I went by to see the children at their home on Toney Road, Michael greeted me excitedly, saying, "Come on, Grandma, I want to show you *my* flowers." He led me to the yellow dandelions in the backyard. "That's pretty," he said, his eyes sparkling. "Smell, Grandma." He tried to find every stem with a blossom and have me smell it.

Anyone can order flowers from a florist. Flowers from one's own garden have a meaning no florist can supply. On the children's birthdays, I always cut flowers to place on their grave. August 5, 1996, a little more than a year after the trial, Alex would have been three. That morning, I cut flowers from my garden, put them in a jar with water, and drove to the cemetery.

Approaching the grave site, I saw two little stuffed animals. Each one had a zip-lock bag positioned under its arms with a note in it. One was a poem that began "Someone in New Jersey loves you." The other was a birthday card with a note in Tiffany's handwriting, signed "Daddy and Tiffany." She said something about how much she loved him and Michael, how much she missed them, and that "we" would have a big celebration for their birthdays if they could still be here. She said she hoped they would have fun playing on the truck and told them to enjoy the balloons and flowers. The note made me sick at my stomach.

I placed the jar of flowers next to the headstone and stood there for a few minutes, musing about how precious they were. I could picture Alex on his first birthday, sticking his finger in his cake while posing for the camcorder. In my mind's eye, I saw him opening his presents with a lot of help from Susan and Michael and relatives and friends cheering them on. I saw him outside after the party running up and down the driveway, laughing all the way. The video of that party was the one seen around the world during the nine days of waiting and searching and hoping.

I visualized Michael in my mind, too, with those beautiful, dark brown eyes and his infectious smile radiating happiness. I thought about his second birthday party in our backyard. Alex was just two months old. Susan and David were separated then. He was invited and Susan kept looking for him; but he never showed up, even though he was off work. Tracy Loveless came, and Donna, Barbara, Mama, Scotty, Wendy, Nick, Matt, Michael, Bev, and I.

Susan brought all the stuff for the party. She blew up balloons and tied them around the trees. Her birthday gift to Michael was a tricycle. His little legs weren't long enough to reach the pedals, and we almost broke our backs bending over to push him.

When he got big enough to reach the pedals, I would bend over him and push one leg and then the other, until I taught him how to pedal. And pedal he did! For a long time, Susan brought the tricycle with her when she visited; eventually, she left it. Michael rode it everywhere at our house—on the screened-in porch, through the den, around the dining-room table, in the kitchen, outside on the driveway. The little tricycle sat in a corner of my bedroom for two years after his death, along with the yellow Tonka dump truck that Alex so delighted in riding as we pushed him back and forth on the porch.

I remembered when Susan came by with the children on Oc-

tober 23, 1994, two days before they were gone. They ran all
over the place. Alex was especially lively. He played his own
little game with me—running to the bedroom door, turning
around, and running back into the den to the rocking chair
where I was sitting and climbing up in my lap. After I hugged
him and rocked him back and forth a few times, he jumped
down and repeated the same routine, giggling all the while. After a number of runs to me, he did the same with Bev, until he
decided to play with his toys.

One of Bev's grandchildren was here that day. He and Michael had a great time playing with the toys I kept in the plastic
swimming pool behind the sofa. After a while, Alex joined
them; and in the midst of all their chatter, we heard him say,
"Ikel."

"Did you hear him, Mama!" Susan exclaimed. "Did you hear
him? He said *Michael*! That's how he says *Michael*." It was the
only word I ever heard Alex say.

A car driving through the cemetery interrupted my thoughts.
I straightened up the arrangements on the grave, picked up
flowers that had fallen, and went to my car. Slowly, I drove out
of the cemetery, tears streaming down my face.

I wondered how Susan was doing, as I always do on the children's birthdays. When she called in the evening, she said she
had been with the counselor during the day.

"Mama, I miss them so much," she sighed. There was pathos
in her voice.

"I miss them, too," I said, then told her about placing the
flowers at the headstone.

"Did you take a picture?" she asked. "I wish you could send
me one."

"No," I said softly.

We talked about family and what was going on at the prison
and even managed to laugh about little things. But the pathos in
her voice would not go away. When our time was almost up, I
asked her to call me later if she could. I had to talk to her again
for my own peace of mind. She called again at 11:00 p.m. Her
mood hadn't improved much.

Shortly after my visit to the cemetery, I saw Tiffany at

Winn-Dixie, where I've always done my grocery shopping. For a long time after the trial, she ran to the back of the store when I came through the front door. This time, though, I spotted her before she saw me and met her in the aisle as she was scurrying to make her exit.

"Hello, Tiffany," I said, my voice filled with sarcasm, "have you been following anyone lately?"

"What?" she snapped.

I repeated the question.

"No, I haven't," she said dryly.

"Good," I said, then turned around and walked down the aisle in the opposite direction.

She angrily called after me, "And I haven't been out killing anybody, either."

I stopped, turned around, and marched toward her. "What did you say?" I asked curtly.

"And I haven't been screwing everybody's husband," she said, defiantly glaring at me.

"Well, whose husband were you screwing?" I asked, contempt dripping from every word.

"I know what David and I did wasn't right, but what your daughter did wasn't right, either. At least I was only screwing one man. You even stood by while she screwed your own husband."

"You don't know what you're talking about," I shot back.

"We did the right thing for Michael and Alex," she said, abruptly changing the subject. "And I'm proud of it. All you were doing was defending your daughter."

Her words must have sounded so noble to her, but all she did was echo the solicitor's line that went something like this: "Linda Russell is going to defend her daughter. You need to defend Michael and Alex."

"What right do you have putting your silly notes at the cemetery?" I questioned angrily. "What right would you have to celebrate with them?"

"Well, you didn't love them."

Her words stung like a dagger. I moved closer, took her by the arm, and glared straight in her face. "If you were so proud

Birthdays

of what you were doing, why didn't you get out of that balcony and sit by David the whole time at the trial?"

She was speechless.

"What would have been best for Michael and Alex," I continued, "was for their daddy to be at home with his children."

Without another word, I moved past her and went to get a grocery cart.

A few days after that heated exchange, Tiffany wrote a letter to the editor of the *Union Daily Times,* complaining that I had accosted her. She said Susan had been tried and found guilty of murder and it was time for some people to wake up and start blaming her for what she had done. She also accused me of telling her not to put things on Michael and Alex's grave. The paper printed the letter without hearing one word from me. The headline just below Tiffany's letter read, "Reasons why nobody trusts the media."

****

For two years, I grieved constantly for Michael and Alex and agonized about what had happened to Susan. I was literally stuck in sadness. In the summer of 1996, I made a conscious decision to get on with my life. I decided that I had to tell my story. It was something Dr. Arlene Andrews had suggested I do right after the trial. She even gave me the phone number of an author in Nashville, Tennessee, that was recommended by a close friend of hers. I filed the number and decided I would tackle the project alone.

I borrowed a computer and started writing. I found this undertaking to be exhausting physically, emotionally, and every other way. I needed help. On July 29, 1996, I dialed the number in Nashville. After introductions, Shirley Stephens asked, "Are you ready to tell your story?" I replied, "Yes. It's the only way to get on with my life." She was in Union a week later, arriving the day after Alex's birthday.

October 7, 1996, while the book was in progress, I took a second step in getting on with my life. I woke up that morning thinking about the boxes of letters, Bibles, and other items in

My Daughter Susan Smith

the bedroom that was Susan's before she married. A year before, I had finally gotten Susan's possessions stored in my house in the attic, basement, and her bedroom. I had shut the door to the bedroom and never went in there. But now, I was going to get rid of things that needed to go, beginning with her bedroom. I was determined to get my mind uncluttered and my house uncluttered.

After drinking my morning cup of coffee, I walked down the hall and opened the bedroom door. I stood there for a few minutes, staring at the boxes. They were stacked to the ceiling, filling three-fourths of the room. Susan's clothes hung in the closet. I could smell the fabric softener. I couldn't bring myself to dive into the task. I needed a little more time.

The following day I opened the bedroom door again. This time I moved on in and opened one of the boxes. It was filled with Bibles, religious tapes, and tracts that people had sent to Susan from all over the world. I marked the box to go to the Salvation Army. Next, I went through Susan's clothes and set aside a few items for one of Susan's cousins.

Day by day I went through the boxes, putting into an antique cedar chest special things I thought Susan would want to keep—a pair of childhood ballet slippers, a scrap book, a baby book, some toys. I wanted it to be a "chest of remembrances" of three lives.

Although I set January 1, 1997, as the completion date for sorting the items in Susan's room, it was another year before I got it cleaned out completely and had decided what to keep for her in the cedar chest. I could only do a little at a time before I got overwhelmed and had to stop.

After starting on Susan's room, I moved to the den. I had to do something about the toys I kept in the plastic wading pool. I brooded over them for more than a week. My niece's children are enjoying them now. The wading pool went to the dump. I couldn't part with the tricycle and truck in my bedroom, but I did put them in my closet.

In early December of 1996, I asked Michael and Scotty to help me dispose of the boxes filled with letters that were in Susan's room and on the carport. They hauled them to a vacant lot near our home and burned them. I saved only a few.

For so long, Bev and I were in some type of comfort zone. If I needed anything, I could call on him and he would be there. I knew I had to step out of that comfort zone. There was no other way to get on with whatever was to be. So, in January of 1997, I took the third step in getting on with my life. I finally started the process to divorce Bev, something I should have done right after the trial. We had lived apart for almost three years.

Actually, moving forward with the divorce was Bev's idea. He was involved with someone and was anxious to get things resolved. About a month later, he told me the relationship didn't work out and would I wait until the tax season was over? I agreed to hold off.

May 1997, I finally filed for divorce. Nine months later, we were still working out a divorce settlement. Then another tax season came, and it was delayed again. But there was no turning back.

In early September 1998, when the time came to make everything final with the divorce, Susan knew I was having a hard time. She used one of the cards they recycle in the prison and sent me a note:

"Just a little note to let you know I love you. You know things aren't so great right now, but God is beside you all the way. And I've lifted you up in prayer often. You are my heart and my very best friend. Be strong and feel the love that surrounds you daily. God bless you, my dear Mama.

"Love, Susan—and give Michael a hug."

On September 22, 1998, the divorce became final. And my third step was complete.

With my divorce behind me, I took a fourth step in getting on with my life and in helping me understand what has happened to Susan. I began to attend meetings of the National Alliance for the Mentally Ill. This is an organization that helps families deal with mental illness.

I grieve for Susan and with her. I pray every day for her to

My Daughter Susan Smith

find some peace. I still think her punishment is too severe for a mentally disturbed person. She should be where she can get the help she needs. I find it ironic that, under South Carolina law, a person can be found guilty but mentally ill and the punishment be the same as if the illness did not exist.

Had Susan's illness been diagnosed by the professionals, this terrible tragedy could have been prevented. I do have to share part of the blame. Maybe I should have been more insistence that treatment be continued. Maybe I was afraid she would be stigmatized. I don't know. At the same time, I have to ask, If the professionals couldn't recognize what was wrong with her, how could I be expected to?

Susan told Dr. Morgan, the prosecution psychiatrist, that the only good that could possibly come out of the trial was that other people would seek help sooner. I hope mental illness can be brought out of the closet. It needs to be addressed and understood that our minds can become sick just as any other part of our body.

As for those who share in Susan's guilt, I think Tom Findlay, Cary Findlay, David Smith, and Bev all had a part in the tragedy. I don't see an honorable man among them. I do think Bev has done everything in his power to right the wrong. That is more than I can say for the rest of them.

****

Our family lives daily with the notoriety of that tragic event. When Scotty announced that he was running for political office in Union in 1996, a reporter from *The Union Daily Times* noted that he was the brother of Susan Smith, convicted murderer.

When Holly Abee, Susan's stepsister, joined sixteen other paramedics in a class-action lawsuit against a hospital in Spartanburg, the reporter identified her as the stepsister of Susan Smith who was "convicted in 1995 of killing her two young sons." He said nothing specific about the other sixteen plaintiffs.

Susan's cousin Leigh had an immediate setback when everything was revealed. She stayed at our home day and night for the full nine days and for a few days after Susan's confession. She simply had to be with her family during such a difficult time. When she went back to college, she was so behind in one class that she asked the teacher to let her take an incomplete and make it up later. The teacher wouldn't grant that permission, using the example of her wayward son to justify her decision. She told Leigh, "We all have our problems." She then said she even had to put her own son out of her house because he was acting up, and that was very painful to her.

Leigh was shocked to think anyone would make that kind of comparison. She got an "F" in the class, but she wouldn't change a thing if she had it to do all over again. She could make up an "F"; but she couldn't relive the time with her family.

Leigh went to USC, Spartanburg, on a softball scholarship. The Spring following the tragedy, she had a new coach in softball. By that time, the whole world knew about Susan and Bev and everything else. She was still strung out, but she didn't do anything to violate her scholarship. Instead of helping her through a tough time, the coach cut her scholarship. He said he had to find more funds somewhere. She could have appealed because she had a signed contract for four years. She chose not to do that; she had been through enough. She overcame the "F" and the scholarship cut, went on to graduate, and now has a good job.

When Leigh tells a new acquaintance she is from Union, South Carolina, the immediate response often is, "Oh, you had a lot of things happen there." Right up front, she tells people she is Susan Smith's cousin—before they have a chance to say anything one way or another. Most don't hold it against her. None should.

The tabloids are still busy making up stories. Before the trial, Susan sat in a cell for twenty-three hours a day. They took her outside for only one hour and then in leg chains. She gained a lot of weight. After the trial she was determined to lose the weight. But she went too far, eating almost nothing. She's skin and bones now. She looks bad, and I worry about her.

In a recent interview I told a reporter that Susan looked bad. Another reporter was on my doorstep the minute the article came out in the newspaper. He said he was a free-lance journalist. He wanted to know if Susan had aids.

"All I'm going to tell you is absolutely not!" I replied. "Before her trial she had all kinds of tests, and she definitely does not have aids."

"Maybe she contracted it after that," he suggested. "I've got some good contacts inside the prison, and I know she has lost a lot of weight. Why has this happened?"

"Well look, I can't stomp out every rumor." I snapped back. "But if you have such good contacts, you should know that South Carolina tested all the inmates and segregated those with aids."

"Maybe not all," he insisted.

"Do you think they're going to segregate all but one?" I questioned impatiently.

He went on his way. I wanted to tell him that she had been struggling with an eating disorder, but I knew what he would do with that. I couldn't believe he had the nerve to come to my home, unannounced, and ask something like that. But, in a way, I've come to expect such assaults on me and my family by the media.

As it turned out, the man was from the *Star* tabloid. He wrote a scandalous article saying Susan was wasting away in prison and suggested that she had aids.

I don't know that anyone realizes how my family has grieved over all of this. I still resent the media for treating us like bugs under a microscope during the July 1995 trial. And it continues. Recently, a black man in a wheelchair was pushing drugs. When the police proceeded to arrest him, he swallowed some of the drugs. He had trouble breathing and died. A black preacher from Atlanta hurried to Union, got everything stirred up, and organized a march down main street. Susan's name came up because she had accused a black man of abducting her children, and the incident was cited as another indication that Union is a racist town.

A few days after that incident, a black man stopped me as I was coming out of a convenience store. "Excuse me," he said. "Are you Ms. Smith?"

Birthdays

"No," I replied. "I'm Ms. Russell, Susan Smith's mother.

"I just want to tell you," he continued. "I didn't like all this stuff and bringing up Susan's name. I've prayed for your daughter and all of your family. Don't you give up on the power of prayer. I just want you to know I don't think she's a bad person. Maybe the lord meant for me to run into you."

Maybe He did.

So many people in Union have said in various ways, "I'll help you through this." Everywhere I go, they ask about Susan. They want me to know they care about Susan, and they care about my struggles.

A pastor from Union who counseled Susan, has written to her every week since she went to prison. She called after receiving a letter the first of October. "Oh, Mama," she said. "This was the sweetest letter. It was filled with encouragement. He knew it was Michael's birthday and that it would be an especially hard time."

And the concern extends beyond Union. Mama and Michael were at a mall in Spartanburg, thirty miles from Union. Mama struck up a conversation with a woman who was visiting her son. The woman asked where Mama was from. When she said "Union," the woman asked, "Did you know that little Smith girl?"

"Yes," Mama replied. "What do you want to know about her? I'm her grandmother."

"I felt so sorry for her," the woman said. "And I've prayed for her. I know something just happened to her."

"When I see her," Mama promised, "I'm going to tell her."

"I wish you would," the woman urged.

For myself, I am doing my best to get on with my life—one step at a time. But even as I get on with my life, I will never forget Michael and Alex. I rocked them, fed them, bathed them, and played with them for hours on end. I loved them; I miss them; I still love them. They will always be in my heart. But, when I ache to hold them, I know the longing couldn't be anything compared to how Susan feels.

I know Michael and Alex aren't in the grave. They're in heaven, and they are fine. I lean on that assurance. The only thing worse than losing Michael and Alex would be to have never known them. I cherish the memories of our happy times together those three short years.